Cybèle Varela

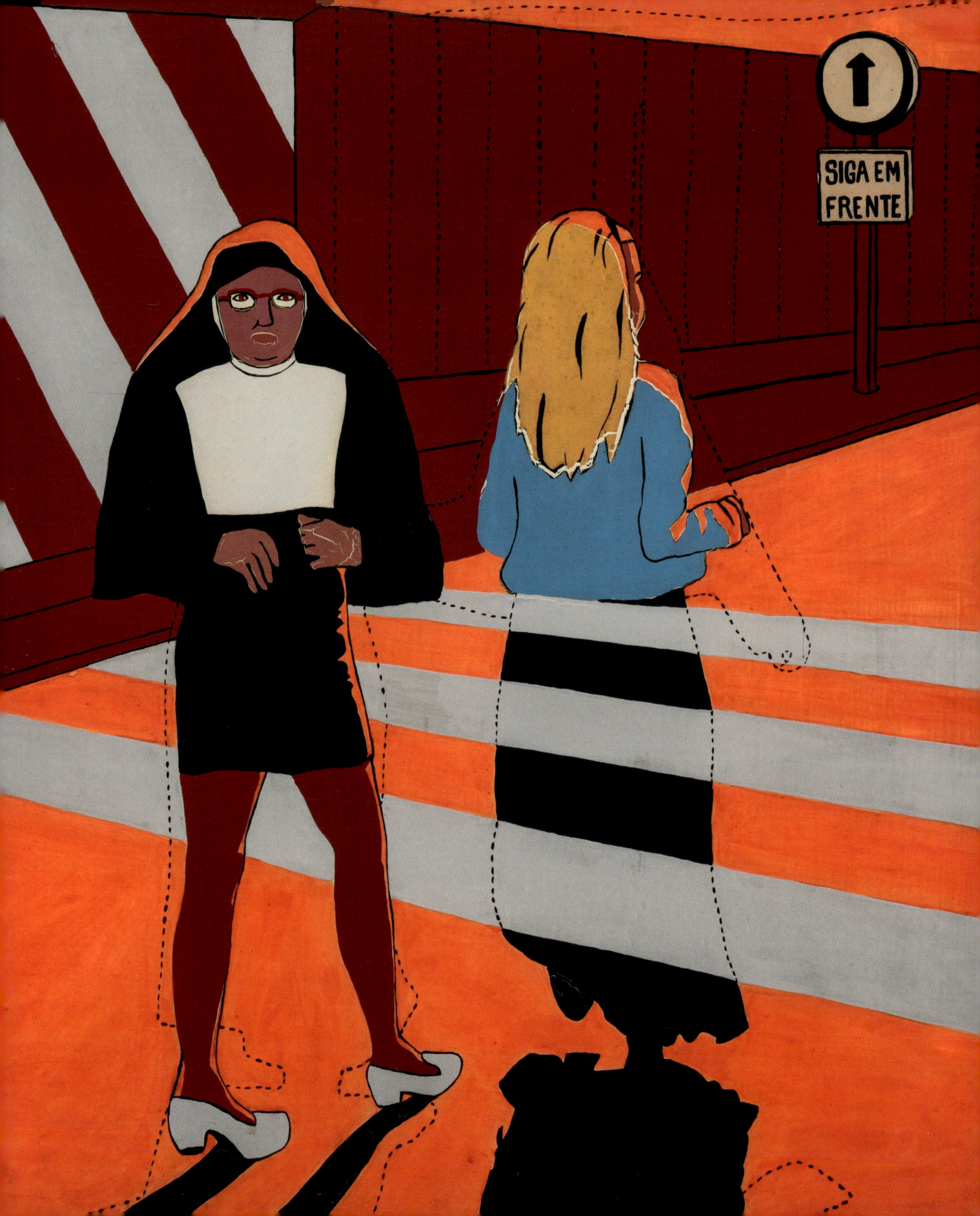
SIGA EM
FRENTE

Cybèle Varela

Tropicalismo Remixed

edited by / herausgegeben von / organizado por

Valentina Locatelli
Ariane Varela Braga

for the / für die / para a

Stiftung Brasilea

SilvanaEditoriale

Contents

Inhalt
Índice

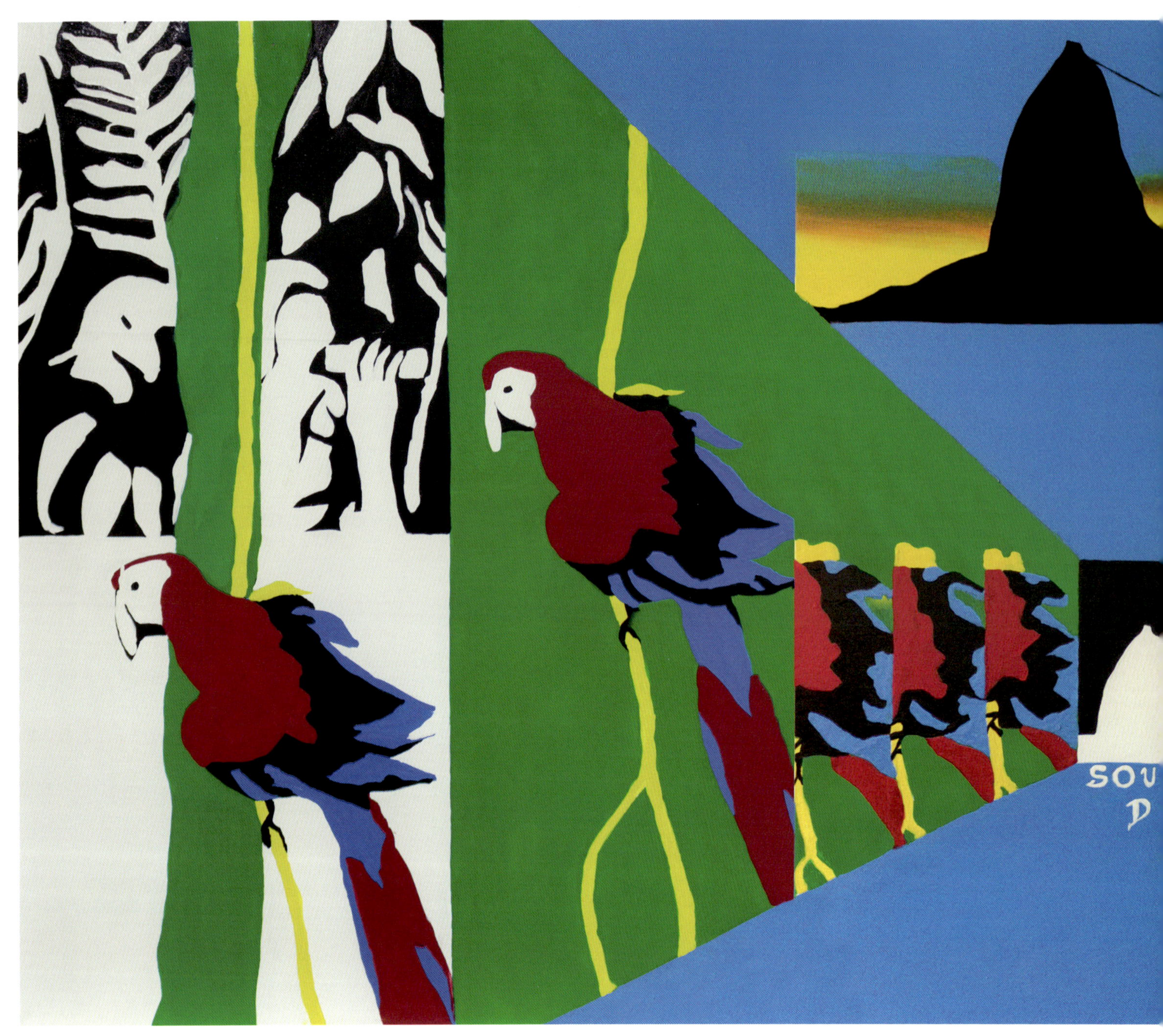

Souvenir de Rio 2
2016

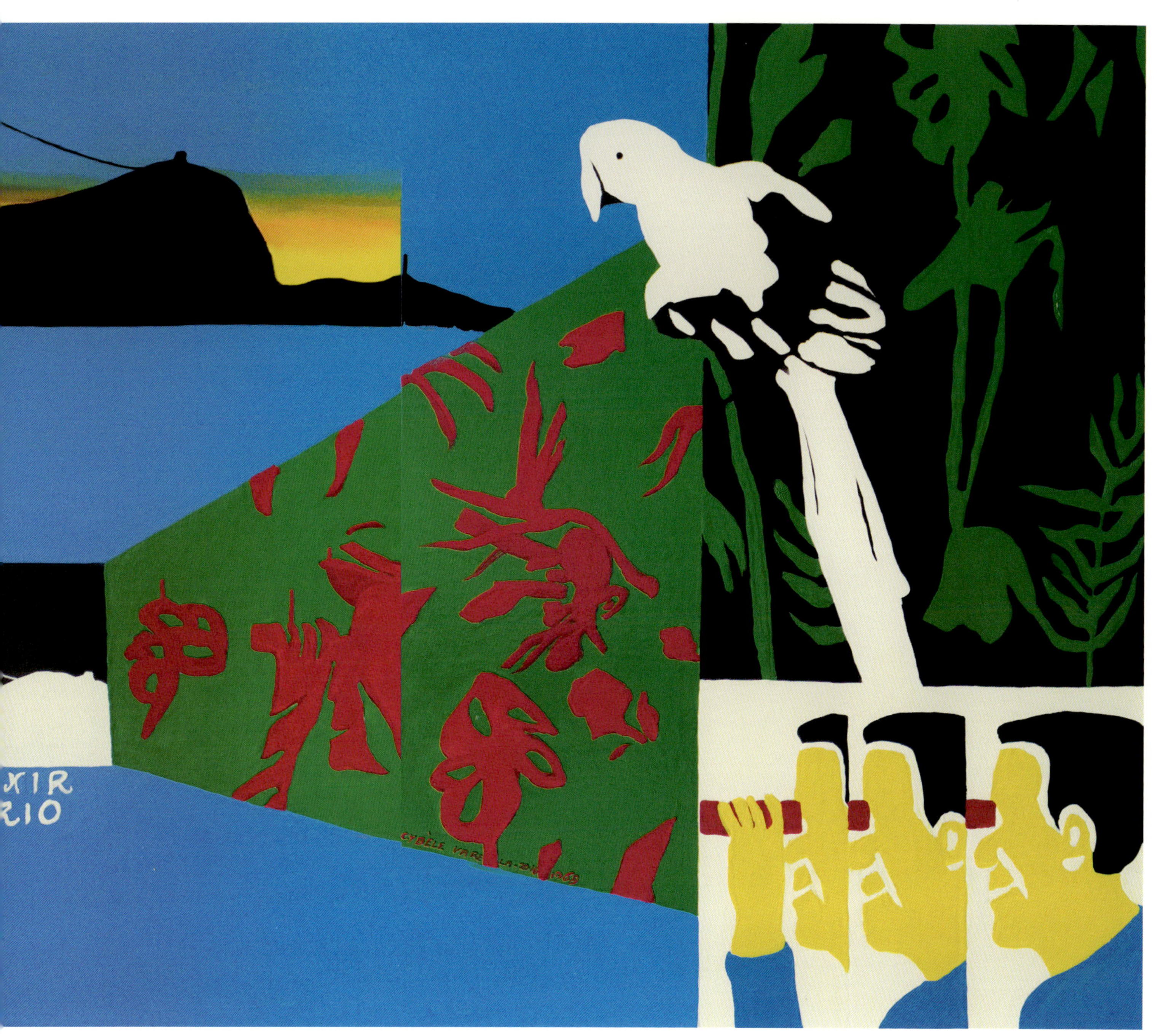

Daniel Faust

Preface

Cybèle Varela's first retrospective in Switzerland encompasses almost entirely what the Brasilea Foundation in Basel stands for: emigration and putting down roots far away from home. Portraying memories of Brazil which convey its culture, colour and joie de vivre. Images of Brazil's strikingly beautiful natural world and of its diverse population, socio-cultural trends and social ills.
Cybèle Varela's work looks at Brazil from the distant perspective of Europe where she has spent most of her life. But at the same time, it also represents an on-the-spot observation in Europe seen through Brazilian eyes. Varela's *Tropicalismo Remixed* is Latin American Pop Art passing through Surrealism and always has European cultural developments of the second half of the 20th century running through it.
Key works for *Cybèle Varela: Tropicalismo Remixed* in Basel are two sliding puzzles specially created by the artist for the exhibition (figs. pp. 10 and 12–13), whose source of inspiration is several works from the 1960s and 1970s, such as, for example, *Um passeo feliz* (fig. p. 23). As one piece of the puzzle is missing, its depicted representation, its *reality*, can be shifted and displayed differently again and again. The viewer is tempted and virtually called upon to unravel the individual squares and to re-create its *true representation* in his imagination. Surrealist Pop Art that seeks interaction with the viewer.
Over 30 works in different media are on display in Basel. The exhibition is divided into chronological sections which also arrange Varela's work according to subject matter and demonstrate the most important creative periods of her art. Tropicalismo and Pop Art of her early work in the 1960s and 1970s; Narrative Figuration and the conceptual investigation of the representation of realities in her images, photographs and videos of the 1970s and 1980s. This is followed by self-portraits from the 1970s until the present day contributing to the discussion on self-representation in contemporary art. A further section (1960s

Vorwort

Cybèle Varelas erste Retrospektive in der Schweiz umfasst beinahe ganzheitlich, wofür die Stiftung Brasilea in Basel steht: auswandern und Wurzeln schlagen fernab der Heimat. Darstellen von Erinnerungen Brasiliens, die die Kultur, die Farbenpracht und Lebensfreude transportieren. Abbildungen der beeindruckend schönen Natur Brasiliens und der vielfältigen Bevölkerungsschichten, unter Einbezug von sozio-kulturellen Strömungen und gesellschaftlichen Missständen.
Cybèle Varelas Werk ist eine Betrachtung Brasiliens aus der europäischen Distanz, wo sie den Grossteil ihres Lebens verbrachte. Es ist aber auch gleichzeitig eine Vor-Ort-Betrachtung innerhalb Europas mit brasilianischen Augen. Varelas *Tropicalismo Remixed* ist lateinamerikanische Pop-Art, durchwandert den Surrealismus und bleibt immer durchzogen von europäischen Kulturentwicklungen der zweiten Hälfte des 20. Jahrhunderts.
Schlüsselwerke für *Tropicalismo Remixed* in Basel sind zwei eigens für die Ausstellung realisierte Schiebe-Spiele (Abb. S. 10 und 12–13), deren Inspirationsquelle mehrere Werke aus den 1960er und 1970er Jahren sind, wie zum Beispiel *Um passeo feliz* (1970; Abb. S. 23). Durch das Fehlen eines Puzzleteils lässt sich die abgebildete Darstellung, die *Realität*, verschieben und immer wieder anders darstellen.
Der Betrachter ist versucht und geradezu aufgerufen, die einzelnen Quadrate zu entwirren und die *wahre Abbildung* imaginär wieder herzustellen. Surrealistische Pop-Art, die mit dem Betrachtenden Interaktion sucht.
Über 30 Werke verschiedener Mediengattungen werden in Basel präsentiert. Die Ausstellung gliedert sich in chronologische Kapitel, die Varelas Werk auch thematisch strukturieren und für die wichtigsten Schaffensphasen ihrer Kunst exemplarisch stehen. Tropicalismo und Pop-Art ihres frühen Schaffens in den 1960er und 1970er Jahren; Narrative Figuration und die konzeptuelle Untersuchung dargestellter Wirklichkeiten in den Bildern, Fotografien und Videos der 1970er und 1980er Jahre. Es folgen Selbstportraits der 1970er Jahre bis heute zum Diskurs der Selbstdarstellung in der zeitgenössischen Kunst. Ein weiteres Kapitel widmet sich den sagenhaften brasilianischen »Cangaceiros« – die »Gesetzlosen«, durch Armut gewordene Banditen, deren berühmteste Vertreter Lampião und Maria Bonita mit ihrer Ganovenbande sind

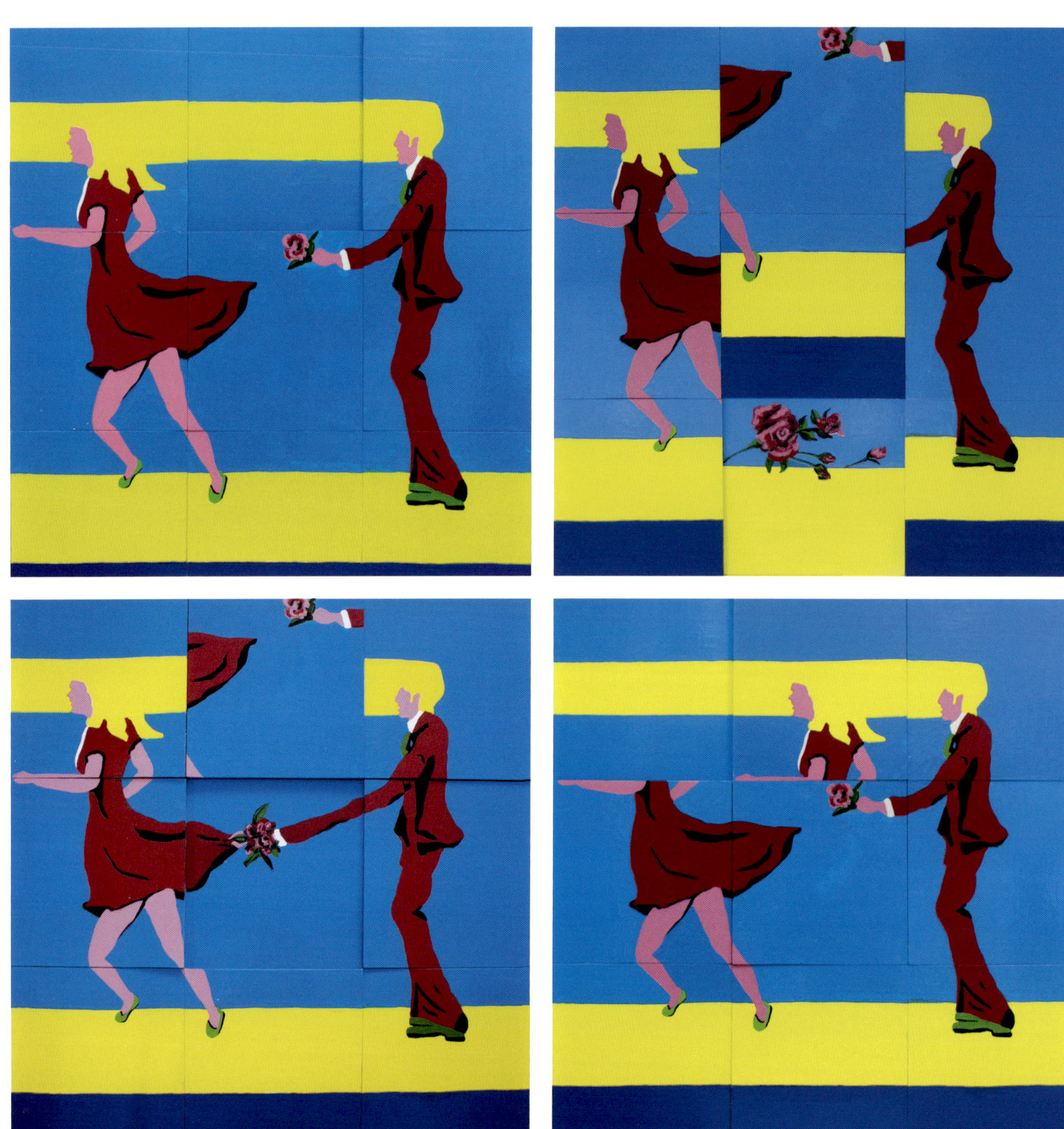

Uma rosa para Rosa
2016

to 2000s) is devoted to the legendary Brazilian "cangaceiros" – the "lawless" who became bandits as a result of poverty, whose most famous representatives were Lampião and Maria Bonita with their band of thieves. The series *Unknown* (2015–16) concludes the exhibition with the artist's reflection on social and personal fragmentation and alienation.
Showing these works in Switzerland – where the artist herself spent fifteen years of her life and had many solo exhibitions – in our Brasilea Foundation, dedicated to Brazilian artists, seems logical if you have explored the work of Cybèle Varela.
Both curators, Ariane Varela Braga and Valentina Locatelli, working closely with the artist Cybèle Varela, have succeeded brilliantly in making this comprehensive retrospective of her work possible in a way which has never happened before. We owe them our great appreciation and thanks. In addition, we would like to thank Giulia Lamoni for her scholarly text on the artist. We also thank the Silvana Editoriale publishing team in Milan for putting this catalogue together creatively and managing to translate the texts into three languages. We extend our very special thanks to the artEDU Foundation and the Brazilian Embassy in Bern who made the exhibition *Cybèle Varela: Tropicalismo Remixed* and this accompanying publication possible through their financial support.

Cybèle Varela's first retrospective in Switzerland encompasses almost entirely what the Brasilea Foundation in Basel stands for: emigration and putting down roots far away from home

Cybèle Varelas erste Retrospektive in der Schweiz umfasst beinahe ganzheitlich, wofür die Stiftung Brasilea in Basel steht: auswandern und Wurzeln schlagen fernab der Heimat

(1960er–2000er). Die Serie *Unknown* (2015–16) schliesst die Ausstellung – eine Reflektion der Künstlerin zu sozialer und persönlicher Fragmentierung und Entfremdung.
Diese Ausstellung in der Schweiz zu präsentieren – wo die Künstlerin selbst fünfzehn Jahre ihres Lebens verbrachte und viele Einzelausstellungen hatte – in unserem, brasilianischen KünstlerInnen gewidmeten, Ausstellungshaus Brasilea, scheint folgerichtig zu sein, wenn man das Werk Cybèle Varelas durchwandert hat.
Es ist den beiden Kuratorinnen Ariane Varela Braga und Valentina Locatelli bravourös gelungen, in enger Zusammenarbeit mit Cybèle Varela, einen umfassenden Blick auf ihr Werk zu ermöglichen, wie es bisher noch nicht geschah. Ihnen gebührt grosse Anerkennung und Dank. Ferner bedanken wir uns bei Giulia Lamoni für ihren wissenschaftlichen Text zum Werk der Künstlerin.
Wir bedanken uns auch bei dem Verlagsteam von Silvana Editoriale in Mailand, welches diesen Katalog kreativ gestaltete und die Übersetzung der Texte in drei Sprachen meisterte. Ein ganz besonderer Dank gilt der artEDU Stiftung und der brasilianischen Botschaft in Bern, welche die Ausstellung *Cybèle Varela: Tropicalismo Remixed* und diese begleitende Publikation durch ihre finanzielle Unterstützung realisierbar machten.

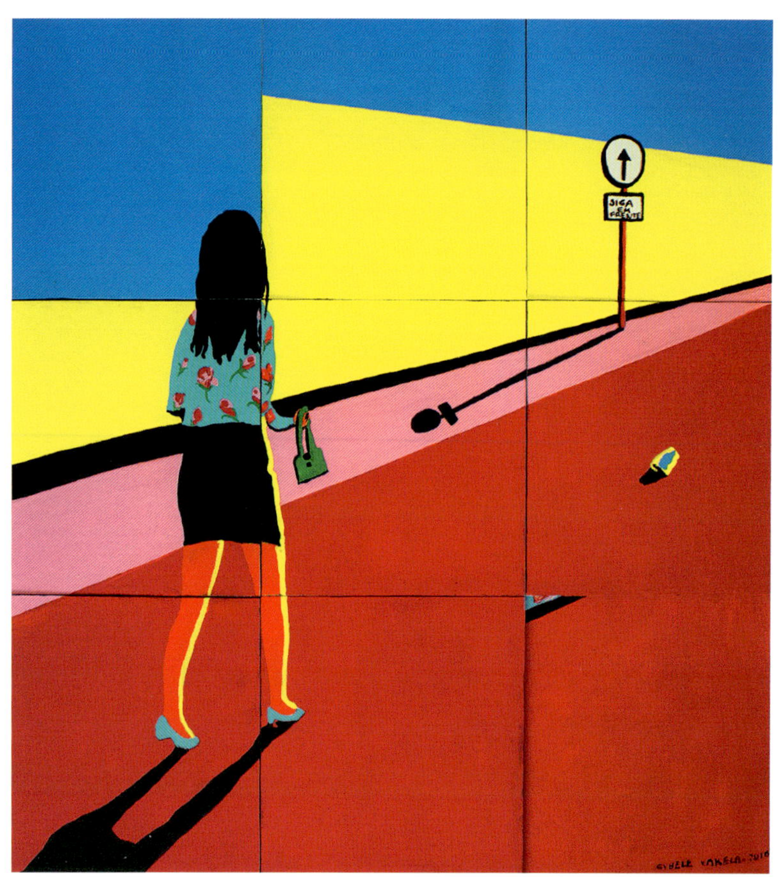

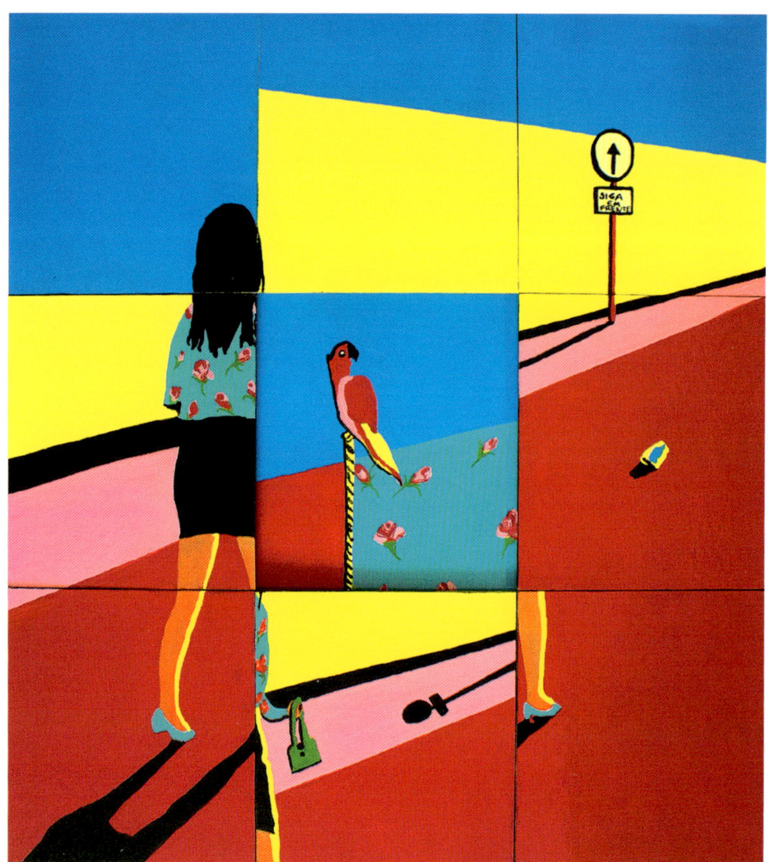

Siga em frente
2016

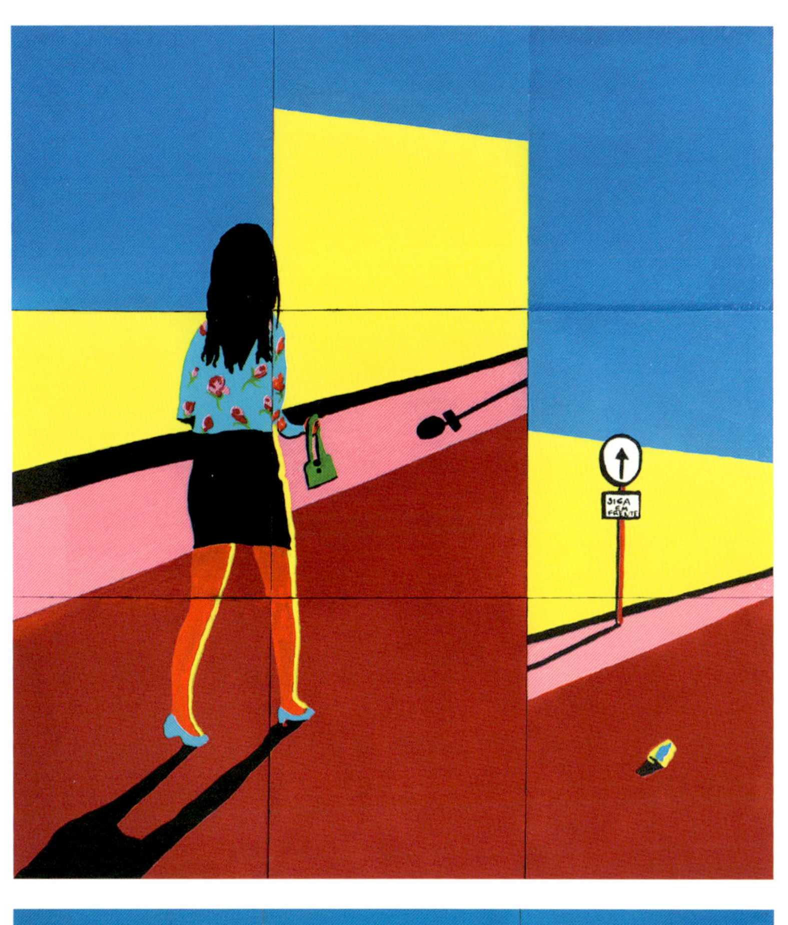
SIGA
EM
FRENTE

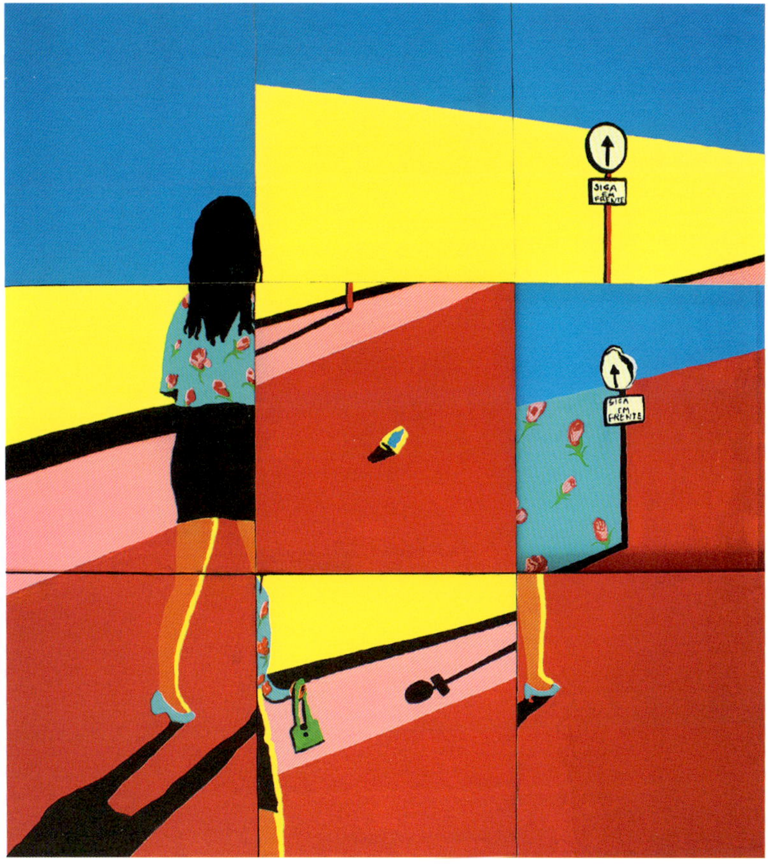
SIGA
EM
FRENTE

Valentina Locatelli
Ariane Varela Braga

Cybèle Varela: Tropicalismo Remixed. An Introduction

"Tropicalismo" (or "Tropicália") was a short-lived artistic movement which emerged in Brazil towards the end of the 1960s. By 1972, it was already over. The term is directly derived from an environmental installation created in 1967 by Hélio Oiticica (1937–1980), at the time one of the main protagonists of the Brazilian visual arts scene. Tropicalismo, however, was an all-encompassing cultural phenomenon which reverberated within every creative sector, from art to music, from theater to fashion, united by a common sense of experimentation and social critique. It was grounded in the idea of "antropofagia", literally a cultural cannibalism that had emerged in Brazil in the late 1920s as a reaction to cultural colonialism,[1] and envisioned the blending of traditional Brazilian culture and art with international Optic and Pop Art.
It is this vibrant artistic context in which Cybèle Varela (b. 1943, Petrópolis) kicked off her career in Brazil. The artist participated in the most relevant exhibitions and biennials of the time, soon becoming one of the key figures of Tropicalismo and Brazilian Pop Art,[2] before moving to Paris in the early 1970s. Engaging in a prolific artistic exchange with many colleagues and peers both in Brazil and abroad, over the years Varela has developed a critical, but never ideological language of her own tinged with occasional irony. Among her preferred subjects are the common people and their relation to the urban environment, the anonymity of life in the big city and the roles imposed by gender restrictions and social expectations. First and foremost a painter, with her box-form objects and puzzle-paintings on wood she engages in the same cheerful and interactive approach which has made Brazilian artists internationally respected. At the same time, experimentations with video and photography have been fundamental for her research on the interaction of light, shadow and movement.[3]
The title of the present exhibition *Tropicalismo Remixed* is a playful reference to music and seeks to recall the fresh and youthful atmosphere of optimism which characterized the beginnings of Varela's long artistic journey, leaving a

Cybèle Varela: Tropicalismo Remixed. Eine Einführung

Der »Tropicalismo« (oder »Tropicália«) ist eine kurzlebige künstlerische Bewegung, die sich gegen Ende der 1960er Jahre in Brasilien formierte und im Jahr 1972 bereits zu ihrem Abschluss gekommen war. Der Begriff leitet sich direkt von einer Rauminstallation ab, die Hélio Oiticica (1937–1980) 1967 realisierte, der als einer der Hauptprotagonisten der damaligen brasilianischen Kunstszene gilt. Der Tropicalismo war jedoch ein umfangreiches kulturelles Phänomen, das sich in allen kreativen Bereichen von der Kunst bis zur Musik und vom Theater bis zur Mode niederschlug und durch ein gemeinsames Interesse am Experimentieren und an der Gesellschaftskritik verbunden war. Dem Tropicalismo liegt die Vorstellung der »Antropofagia« zugrunde.[1] Hierbei handelt es sich um einen kulturellen Kannibalismus, der gegen Ende der 1920er Jahre in Brasilien als Reaktion auf den kulturellen Kolonialismus auftrat und auf die Vermischung der traditionellen brasilianischen Kultur mit internationalen Kunstströmungen wie der Op-Art und der Pop-Art abzielte.
In diesem lebendigen künstlerischen Kontext begann Cybèle Varela (geb. 1943, Petrópolis) ihre Laufbahn in Brasilien. Die Künstlerin nahm an den damals wichtigsten Ausstellungen und Biennalen teil und avancierte schon bald zu einer der Schlüsselfiguren des Tropicalismo und der brasilianischen Pop-Art,[2] bevor sie in den frühen 1970er Jahren nach Paris aufbrach. Dank eines produktiven künstlerischen Austauschs mit zahlreichen Kolleginnen und Kollegen aus Brasilien und dem Ausland ist es Varela im Lauf der Jahre gelungen, eine persönliche Formensprache zu entwickeln, die kritisch ist, ohne ideologisch zu wirken, und nicht einer gewissen Ironie entbehrt. Zu ihren bevorzugten Sujets zählen die einfachen Menschen und ihr Verhältnis zu ihrem urbanen Umfeld, die Anonymität ihres Grossstadtlebens und die Rollen, die ihnen Geschlechterbeschränkungen und soziale Erwartungen auferlegen. Als Malerin verfolgt sie mit ihren schachtelförmigen Objekten und Puzzle-Arbeiten auf Holz den unbeschwerten und interaktiven Ansatz, der den brasilianischen Künstlerinnen und Künstlern zu internationalem Renommee verholfen hat. Im Rahmen ihrer Recherche zur Interaktion von Licht, Schatten und Bewegung war aber auch das Experimentieren mit den Medien Video und Fotografie fundamental.[3]

clear trace also on her subsequent production. A "remixed" Tropicalismo is a Tropicalismo which has been altered, modified from its original state in order to create something new and audacious. This well-balanced sense of continuity and renewal is precisely what characterizes Varela's oeuvre.
Cybèle Varela: Tropicalismo Remixed presents a selection of the artist's most emblematic paintings, objects and videos from the 1960s to the present day. The exhibition at the Brasilea Foundation in Basel is Varela's first retrospective in Europe. It is also the occasion to reassess the artist's relationship to Switzerland, where she lived between 1978 and 1993, and to examine how the encounter with and appropriation of European culture impacted her work. By exploring the main stages of Varela's artistic development and by presenting them in chapters organized in chronological order, the exhibition aims to shed new light on the artist's many achievements. Furthermore, it investigates Varela's contribution to both Latin American and international artistic discourses, from Pop and Conceptual Art to Narrative Figuration and Video Art.
In the past 60 years, Varela's creative impulse has followed many paths, always deeply interrelated with each other, like different episodes of the same story: as the artist explains, after developing a concept for four to five years, she feels the urge to move on to the next one, in a natural continuation of her previous reflections. The exhibition builds on this idea of continuity and change. Beginning with Varela's early works in the 1960s, which are clearly under the influence of Tropicalismo and Pop Art, it brings together both objects and paintings from Varela's early production, combined with revisited versions of no longer existing works, such as *Souvenir de Rio 2* (fig. pp. 6–7) and two painting-puzzles (figs. pp. 10, 12–13). The second section of the show is devoted to the conceptual investigation of reality and its representation, declined through a series of paintings, photographs and videos from the 1970s and 1980s (figs. 64–69, 84–87). Works revolving around the image of the artist as a

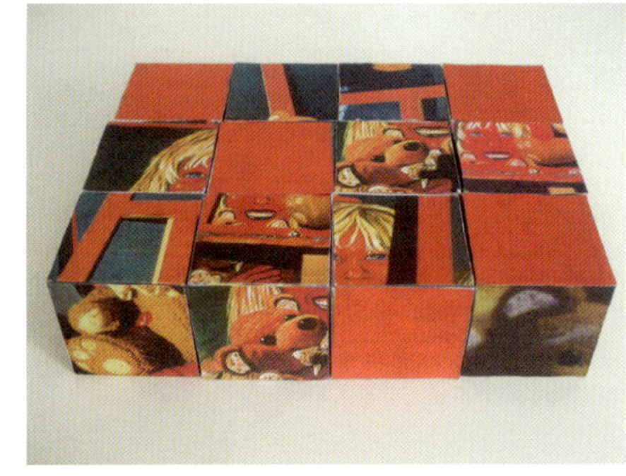

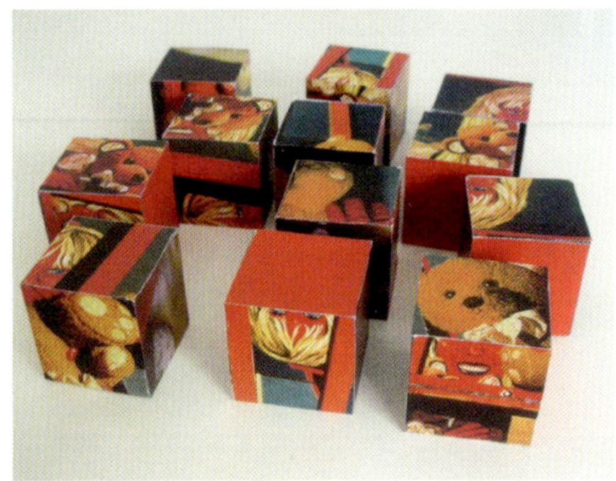

Once Upon a Time
1998

The title of the present exhibition *Tropicalismo Remixed* is a playful reference to music and seeks to recall the fresh and youthful atmosphere of optimism which characterized the beginnings of Varela's long artistic journey

Der Titel der aktuellen Ausstellung *Tropicalismo Remixed* nimmt spielerisch Bezug auf die Musik und versucht, die unbeschwerte und jugendlich-optimistische Atmosphäre in Erinnerung zu rufen, die den Beginn von Varelas langer künstlerischer Reise auszeichnete

Der Titel der aktuellen Ausstellung *Tropicalismo Remixed* nimmt spielerisch Bezug auf die Musik und versucht, die unbeschwerte und jugendlich-optimistische Atmosphäre in Erinnerung zu rufen, die den Beginn von Varelas langer künstlerischer Reise auszeichnete und auch ihre nachfolgende Produktion prägte. Ein neu »gemischter« Tropicalismo ist ein Tropikalismus, der im Hinblick auf seine ursprüngliche Form abgeändert wurde, um etwas Neues und Kühnes hervorzubringen. Es ist dieser wohl ausbalancierte Sinn für Kontinuität und Erneuerung, der Varelas Œuvre kennzeichnet.
Cybèle Varela: Tropicalismo Remixed präsentiert eine Auswahl ihrer relevantesten Bilder, Objekte und Videos von den 1960er Jahren bis heute. Die Ausstellung bei der Stiftung Brasilea in Basel ist Varelas erste Retrospektive in Europa. Sie bietet auch die Gelegenheit, das Verhältnis der Künstlerin zur Schweiz neu zu bewerten, wo sie zwischen 1978 und 1993 gelebt hat, und der Frage nachzugehen, inwieweit die Begegnung mit der europäischen Kultur und deren Aneignung ihre Arbeiten beeinflusst hat. Durch die Erkundung der wichtigsten Schaffensphasen von Varelas künstlerischer Entwicklung und ihrer Präsentation in chronologisch geordneten Kapiteln, möchte die Ausstellung ein neues Licht auf die zahlreichen Errungenschaften der Künstlerin werfen. Darüber hinaus erforscht sie Varelas Beitrag zu den lateinamerikanischen und internationalen Kunstdiskursen von der Pop-Art und der Konzeptkunst bis zur Narrativen Figuration und der Videokunst.
In den vergangenen 60 Jahren hat Varela aus einem kreativen Impuls heraus viele Richtungen eingeschlagen, die immer stark miteinander verbunden waren, gleich verschiedenen Episoden derselben Geschichte: Nachdem sie ein Konzept für vier oder fünf Jahre entwickelt hatte, verspürte sie nach eigenen Worten ein starkes Bedürfnis, zum nächsten überzugehen und ihre vorausgehenden Reflexionen in einer natürlichen Kontinuität weiterzuführen. Der Ausstellung liegt diese Idee von Kontinuität und Wandel zugrunde. Ausgehend von Varelas frühen Arbeiten aus den 1960er Jahren, die deutlich vom Tropicalismo und der Pop-Art beeinflusst sind, vereint sie Objekte und Gemälde aus Varelas früher Produktion und kombiniert diese mit überarbeiteten Versionen nicht mehr existierender Arbeiten, darunter *Souvenir de Rio 2* (Abb. S. 6–7) und zwei Puzzle-Arbeiten (Abb. S. 10 und 12–13).

woman (figs. pp. 71–75) and the "cangaceiros" (figs. pp. 93–99) are also represented in this retrospective. Finally, *Cybèle Varela: Tropicalismo Remixed* unveils for the first time Varela's most recent series *Unknown* (figs. pp. 100–05), which addresses questions of identity, memory and migration.

1 The origin of this concept can be traced back to Oswald de Andrade's *Manifesto Antropófago* (Cannibalist Manifesto, 1928).
2 In 2015 Varela's work was referenced in the ground-breaking exhibition *The World Goes Pop*, organized by the Tate Modern in London. See Giulia Lamoni, "Unfolding the 'Present': Some Notes on Brazilian 'Pop'", in Jessica Morgan and Flavia Frigeri (eds.), *The World Goes Pop*, exh. cat., Tate Modern (London, 2015), pp. 70-71.
3 See Camille Morineau (ed.), *elles@centrepompidou, artistes femmes dans la collection du Musée national d'art moderne*, exh. cat., Centre Pompidou (Paris, 2009), p. 222.

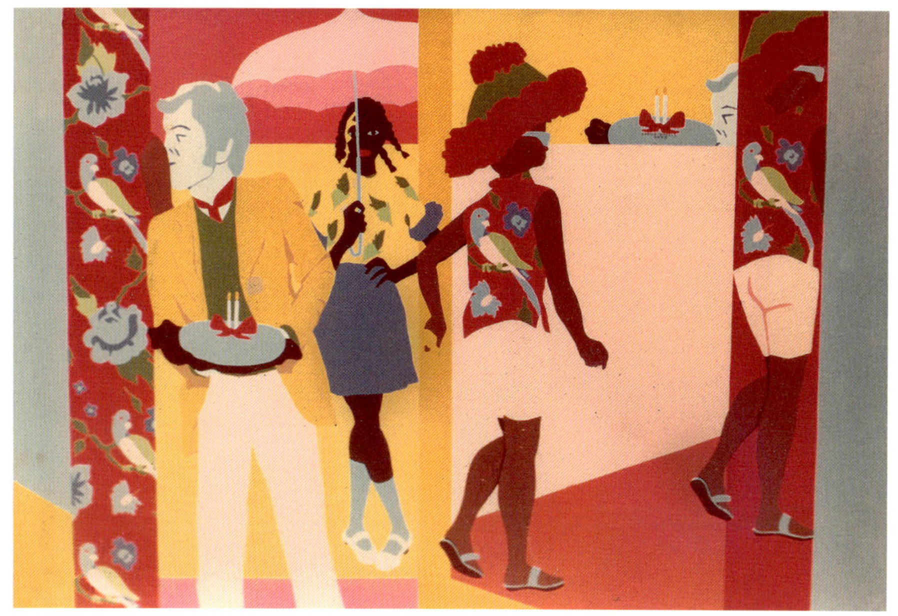

O bolo
1969

Der zweite Abschnitt der Ausstellung widmet sich der konzeptuellen Erkundung der Realität und ihrer Darstellung in einer Reihe von Bildern, Fotografien und Videos aus den 1970er und 1980er Jahren (Abb. S. 64–69, 84–87). Arbeiten, die das Bild der Künstlerin als Frau behandeln (Abb. S. 71–75) und die »Cangaceiros« (Abb. S. 93–99) sind gleichfalls in der Retrospektive vertreten. Abschliessend möchten wir darauf hinweisen, dass *Cybèle Varela: Tropicalismo Remixed* erstmals Varelas aktuelle Serie *Unknown* (Abb. S. 100–05) präsentiert, die sich mit Fragen nach Identität, Erinnerung und Migration auseinandersetzt.

1 Der Ursprung dieses Konzepts lässt sich bis zu Oswald de Andrades *Manifesto Antropófago* (Kannibalistisches Manifest, 1928) zurückführen.
2 2015 wurde auf Varelas Œuvre in der bahnbrechenden Ausstellung *The World Goes Pop* Bezug genommen, organisiert von der Tate Modern in London. Vgl. Giulia Lamoni: »Unfolding the ›Present‹: Some Notes on Brazilian ›Pop‹«, in Jessica Morgan und Flavia Frigeri (Hrsg.): *The World Goes Pop*, Ausst.-Kat., Tate Modern, London 2015, S. 70–71.
3 Vgl. Camille Morineau (Hrsg.): *elles@centrepompidou, artistes femmes dans la collection du Musée national d'art moderne*, Ausst.-Kat., Centre Pompidou, Paris 2009, S. 222.

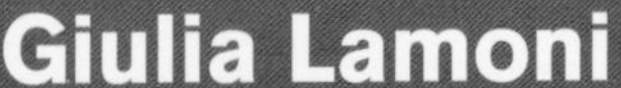

Shuffling Cards and Multiplying Images. Some Notes About the Work of Cybèle Varela

Created by Cybèle Varela in 1967, *Telefone Real* is a wooden object in the shape of a telephone (fig. p. 21). Although modest and inoffensive, almost a children's game, the telephone painted in garish colours has a hidden surprise inside. When you lift up the handset, you inadvertently open its dial, thus revealing an interior of mirrors multiplying the image of a playing card at the bottom: the king of diamonds. It may seem contradictory that this object, apparently banal and unsophisticated, could be a particularly challenging starting point for exploring the artistic path of Cybèle Varela – her geographic, cultural and formal migrations between sculpture, photography, video and, above all, painting. However, *Telefone Real* – whose aesthetic coordinates are part of the ramifications of the Brazilian "critical realism" of the late 1960s, with its focus on transforming painting into an object and contemplation through active participation by the spectator[1] – shows a set of formal and conceptual options that marks the work of the artist throughout her entire career, albeit in different ways.

If 1967, when this piece was created, was a significant moment for Cybèle Varela – the Museu de Arte Contemporânea in São Paulo honoured her with the important "Jovem Arte Contemporânea" (Young Contemporary Art) exhibition award, aimed at artists aged under 35 – it was also the year when a set of American Pop Art objects were exhibited in Brazil, at the São Paulo Biennial, triggering a very lively debate on local art criticism. On the one hand, the selection of Brazilian artists was considered to be too wide and technically poor. On the other hand, such selection was advocated for its fierce, diverse youth, its attempt to involve spectators, making them participants, even if that resulted in the destruction of the works themselves.[2] In contrast, the pop representation from the United States was praised as being very sophisticated and well put together. At the same event, the police ordered the removal from the exhibition of the box-shaped object by Cybèle Varela, *O Presente* (1967, fig. p. 22),[3] for political reasons.

Die Karten mischen, die Bilder vervielfältigen. Aufzeichnungen zum Werk von Cybèle Varela

Telefone Real, ein Werk Cybèle Varelas von 1967, ist ein hölzernes Objekt in Form eines Telefons (Abb. S. 21). Das in grellen Farben bemalte Telefon, das bescheiden und harmlos daherkommt und fast wie ein Kinderspielzeug wirkt, birgt ein überraschendes Innenleben. Hebt man den Hörer ab, öffnet sich unvermittelt die runde Wählscheibe und gibt den Blick frei auf Spiegel im Inneren, die das Bild einer darunterliegenden Spielkarte vervielfältigen: ein König der Münzen. Dass dieses augenscheinlich banale, wenig durchdachte Objekt einen besonders anspruchsvollen Ausgangspunkt für die Entdeckung des künstlerischen Schaffens von Cybèle Varela darstellen kann – von ihren geografischen, kulturellen und formalen Wanderungen zwischen Bildhauerei, Fotografie, Video und vor allem Malerei –, mag vielleicht widersprüchlich erscheinen. Jedoch verkörpert *Telefone Real* – dessen ästhetische Koordinaten zu den Entwicklungen des brasilianischen »kritischen Realismus« der späten 1960er Jahre gehören, mit seinem Fokus auf der Verwandlung der Malerei in Gegenständliches und der Betrachtung in aktive Teilnahme des Zuschauers[1] – eine Vielzahl formaler und konzeptueller Möglichkeiten, die, wenn auch auf unterschiedliche Arten, die Arbeit der Künstlerin während ihrer gesamten Schaffensperiode prägen.

Wenn 1967, das Jahr in dem dieses Werk entstand, ein bedeutender Moment für Cybèle Varela ist – das Museu de Arte Contemporânea in São Paulo zeichnet sie mit dem wichtigen Preis der Ausstellung »Jovem Arte Contemporânea« (Junge zeitgenössische Kunst) für Künstler unter 35 Jahren aus –, so ist es auch das Jahr, in dem eine Reihe von Pop Art-Werken aus Nordamerika in Brasilien, bei der Biennale von São Paulo ausgestellt werden, was eine heftige Debatte in der Kunstkritikerszene der Stadt auslöst. So werden zum Einen die Auswahl der brasilianischen Künstler als zu breit und die Techniken als zu durchschnittlich angesehen. Zum Anderen verteidigen Befürworter sie für ihr jugendliches Ungestüm und ihre Vielfalt, ihren Versuch, den Betrachter mit einzubeziehen, ihn zum Teilnehmer zu machen, auch wenn der Preis dafür die Zerstörung der eigenen Kunstwerke ist.[2] Im Gegensatz dazu wird die amerikanische Pop Art als sehr elaboriert und hervorragend präsentiert gelobt. Auf ebendieser Veranstaltung

O Presente, like *Telefone Real*, affirms the artist's commitment to wider spectator involvement above all else. At the same time, resistance to the military regime in the country since 1964 is seen through irony and caricature, just like in the work of other artists of her generation. *O Presente* alludes both to the present as a gift – the box does in fact seem to be a gift-wrapped present – and to the present time, marked by political oppression that was doomed to worsen. Thus, on opening the box, the participant discovers a caricature of a soldier and the lyrics of a nationalist anthem. Similarly the title *Telefone Real* refers to both the "royal" figure of power, hidden inside the telephone – the king of diamonds – and the way this power was trying to dominate the Brazilian reality at that time. The coexistence of formal concerns, involving questioning the work of art itself and its materiality, and paying attention to the social and political world has thus been one of the strong threads running through the artist's work since the mid-1960s. In 1970, on the occasion of her individual exhibition at the Galeria Copacabana Palace in Rio de Janeiro, the artist herself suggested this dual orientation: "I look for the openness of new spaces, maybe with a sense of total freedom. But I am also very interested in time in relation to form".[4]
Regarding the artist's tropicalist production in the late 1960s and early 1970s[5] – which includes *Telefone Real* – focused on exploring the urban and suburban environment and popular taste and culture, in 1968, critic Frederico Morais spoke of a "[…] nostalgia for telluric, rural, tropical Brazil, nostalgia that those living in the suburbs still sentimentally experience in the countryside and in the past."[6] If this focus creates a particularly strong dialogue with artists whose work explores the meanderings of the city, such as Rubens Gerchman (Rio de Janeiro, 1942–2008), the interest in the relationships between movement and form – perhaps some vestige of a neo-concrete legacy appropriated and anthropophagously transformed – and figuration and geometric abstraction, to some extent, it brings Cybèle Varela's practices closer to those of the artist from the same generation,

veranlasst die Polizei die Entfernung von Cybèle Varelas kastenförmigen Kunstwerks *O Presente* (1967, Abb. S. 22)[3] aus politischen Gründen.
O Presente bekräftigt – ebenso wie *Telefone Real* – vor allem das Engagement der Künstlerin, den Zuschauer stärker mit einzubeziehen. Zugleich manifestiert sich bei Varela der Widerstand gegen das seit 1964 in Brasilien herrschende Militärregime durch die Ironie und die Karikatur, was auch in den Arbeiten anderer Künstler ihrer Generation deutlich wird.
O Presente spielt sowohl auf das Geschenk als Gabe hin – die Kiste sieht tatsächlich wie ein eingepacktes Geschenk aus – als auch auf die Zeit, die Gegenwart, die von einer immer bedrohlicher werdenden politischen Unterdrückung geprägt ist. Öffnet der Betrachter die Kiste, entdeckt er die Karikatur eines Soldaten und den Text einer nationalistischen Hymne. Auf ähnliche Weise deutet der Titel *Telefone Real* sowohl auf die »royale« Figur der Macht, die sich im Telefon verbirgt – den König der Münzen – als auch auf die Art, wie diese Macht die brasilianische Realität dieser Jahre zu beherrschen versucht. Eine der Hauptlinien, die sich seit Mitte der 1960er Jahre durch die Arbeit der Künstlerin ziehen, ist die Koexistenz von formalen Interessen, die das eigentliche Kunstwerk und seine Materialität in Frage stellen, und der Sorge um die sozialpolitische Welt. Im Rahmen ihrer Einzelausstellung in der Galerie Copacabana Palace in Rio de Janeiro sprach 1970 die Künstlerin selbst von dieser Doppelgleisigkeit: »Ich strebe danach, neue Räume zu eröffnen, vielleicht mit einem absoluten Freiheitsgefühl. Ich interessiere mich auch sehr für die Zeit im Verhältnis zur Form.«[4]
In ihrem vom Tropicalismo beeinflussten Schaffen der späten 1960er und frühen 1970er Jahre[5] – zu dem auch *Telefone Real* gehört –, das sich auf die Erkundung der Stadt- und Vorstadtlandschaft und des Geschmacks und der Kultur des Volkes konzentriert, sah der Kritiker Frederico Morais 1968 eine »[…] Sehnsucht nach einem ländlichen, tropischen Brasilien, Sehnsucht nach denen, die in den Vorstädten und damit gefühlt noch immer auf dem Land, in der Vergangenheit leben.«[6] Dieser Fokus stellt einen besonders starken Dialog her mit Künstlern, deren Arbeit sich mit den Mäandern der Stadt befasst, wie der Künstler Rubens Gerchman (1942–2008) aus Rio de

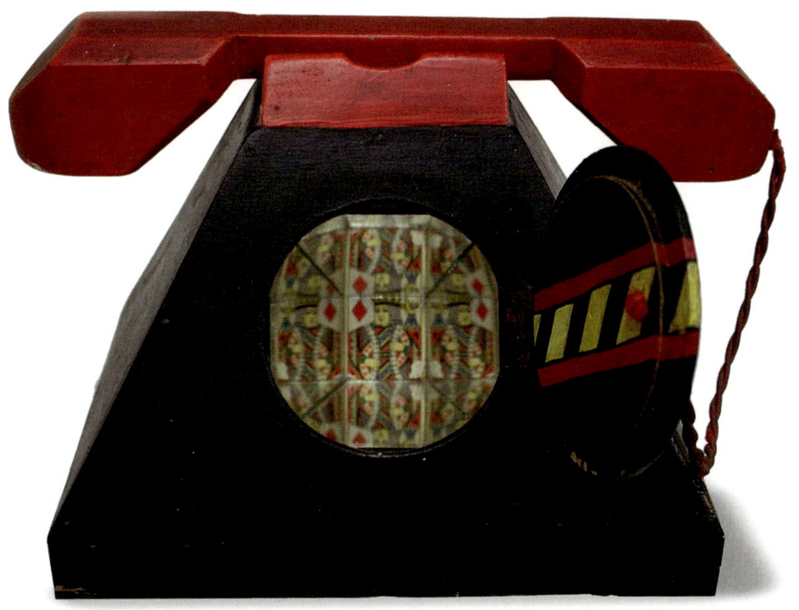

Telefone Real refers to both the "royal" figure of power and the way this power was trying to dominate the Brazilian reality at that time

Telefone Real deutet sowohl auf die »royale« Figur der Macht als auch auf die Art, wie diese Macht die brasilianische Realität dieser Jahre zu beherrschen versucht

Janeiro; das Interesse an den Beziehungen zwischen Bewegung und Kraft – vielleicht ein Überbleibsel eines angeeigneten neokonkreten Vermächtnisses, das kannibalistisch verwandelt wurde – sowie zwischen geometrischer Darstellung und Abstraktion bringt auf gewisse Weise ihre Praxis der eines befreundeten Künstlers ihrer Generation, Raymundo Colares (1944–1986), näher. So prägen in Gemälden auf Holz wie *Cinco moças passeando* (1967, Abb. S. 30) oder *Cenas de rua* (1968, Abb. S. 58–59) sich wiederholende Linien die Darstellung der Stadtlandschaft – Zebrastreifen oder abstrakte Linien –, die zugleich den Raum bilden und die Illusion einer bildlichen Darstellung zunichte machen. Bei Werken, die wie *Um passeio feliz* (1970, Abb. S. 23) aus Bodenstücken bestehen, kann der Besucher selbst wie bei einem Puzzle die einzelnen Teile des Bildes bewegen, an der Entstehung und Zerstörung einer Komposition teilhaben, die niemals einer mimetischen Logik folgt.

Diese Zweideutigkeit, die den Übergang von Cybèle Varela zum »kritischen Realismus« Brasiliens charakterisiert – der ursprüngliche und internationale Ausdrucksweisen verschlingt und ein kritisches Nachdenken über »den sozio-politisch-kulturellen Kontext« Brasiliens[7] anstösst –, drückt sich in einer gewollt vereinfachten bildlichen Ausdruckweise aus, von wenig raffiniertem Anschein, in der industrielle Materialien zum Einsatz kommen und durch die die Künstlerin ironischerweise die Rolle der »Pop-Künstlerin der Unterentwicklung«[8] annimmt, um eine bekannte Formulierung von Mário Pedrosa zu verwenden. Jedoch lassen sowohl der Einsatz von Spiegeln und das Interesse für die Entwicklungen des Bildes und des Lichts bei *Telefone Real* als auch die Wiederholung der Figur und der Linien in den Stadt- und Vorstadtlandschaften der 1960er Jahre eine Nachforschung über Lichteffekte im Raum und die Macht der Darstellung erahnen, die in den 1970er Jahren vollends aufblühen wird.

In diesem Sinne scheint es sinnvoll, den Dialog mit dem argentinischen Künstler Julio Le Parc (geb. 1928) in Paris zu erwähnen, wohin Cybèle Varela in den Jahren 1968–69 dank eines Stipendiums der französischen Regierung reist. Bei ihrer Ankunft in der französischen Hauptstadt im Herbst 1968 – zur Zeit der Auflösung der Groupe de Recherche d'Art Visuel (GRAV), in der Le Parc aktives Mitglied

and friend, Raymundo Colares (1944–1986). Thus, in paintings on wood, like *Cinco moças passeando* (1967, fig. p. 30) or *Cenas de rua* (1968, fig. pp. 58–59) the representation of the urban environment is marked by lines that are repeated – pedestrian crossings or abstract lines – and at the same time build the space and reveal the illusion of the pictorial representation. With floor pieces in the form of a sliding puzzle, like *Um passeio feliz* (1970, fig. p. 23) by moving the pieces that make up the image, the actual spectator is taking part in the creation and destruction of a composition that is never caught up in a mimetic logic.

This ambiguity, which characterises Cybèle Varela's journey through Brazilian "critical realism" – devouring vernacular and international languages to develop a critical reflection on the Brazilian "social, political and cultural context"[7] – is shown in a pictorial language that is simplified in a calculated manner, with a somewhat unrefined appearance, that uses industrial materials and through which the artist ironically takes on the role of "underdevelopment popist",[8] to paraphrase Mário Pedrosa's famous words. However, both the use of mirrors and the attention on the ramifications of the image and the light in *Telefone Real*, in the repetition of the figure and the lines in the urban and suburban landscapes of the 1960s, herald research into the effects of light on space and the powers of representation that would blossom in the 1970s.

In this sense, it is worth calling up the dialogue with Argentinian artist Julio Le Parc (b. 1928) in Paris, where Cybèle Varela travelled in 1968–69 thanks to a scholarship from the French government. When she arrived in Paris in the autumn of 1968 – when the Groupe de Recherche d'Art Visuel (Visual Art Research Group - G.R.A.V.) was dissolved, of which Le Parc was an active member – the artist discovered a city steeped in turmoil. Her meeting with the kinetic experience of the Argentinian and the broader Parisian artistic environment seemed to work, at first, as a radicalisation of her research into the relationship between form and movement and the involvement of the spectator through the use of games.

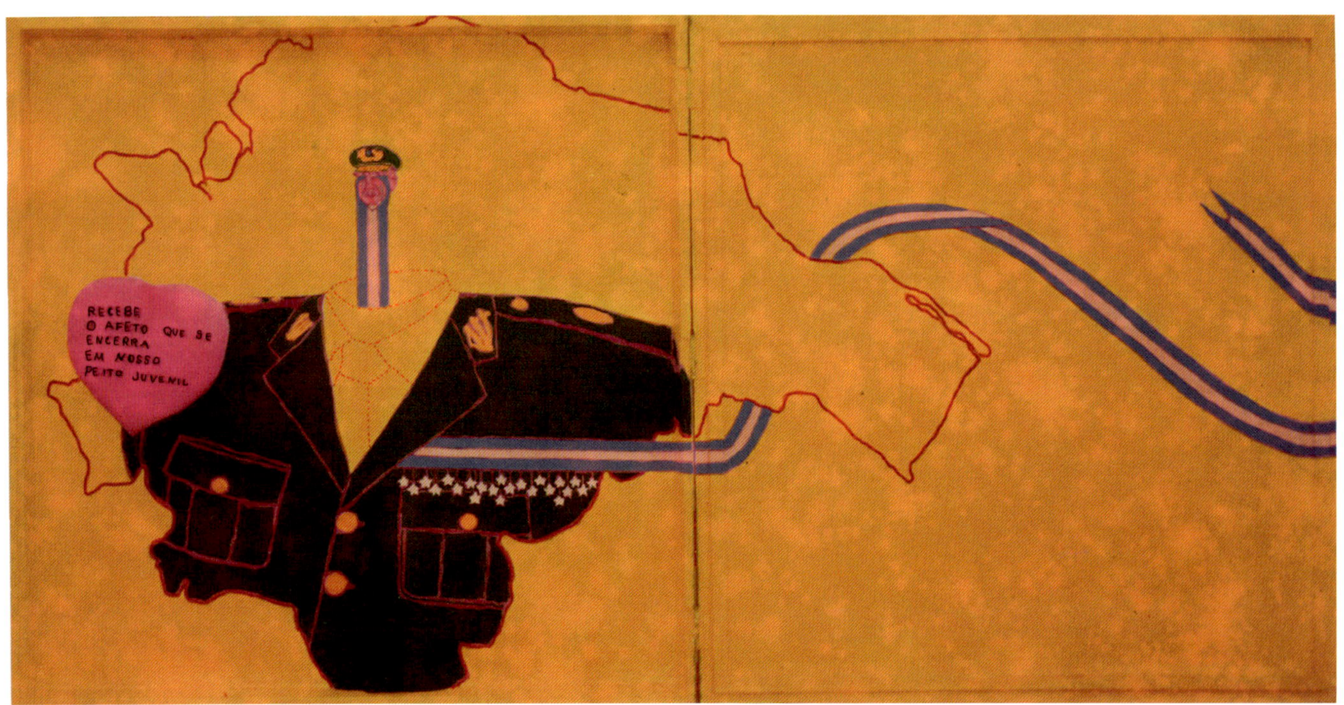

Thus, when she had her exhibition at the Galerie Debret in Paris in 1972, after going back to the city thanks to a second scholarship, the artist created a playful environment inhabited by object-games that could be manipulated, marked with inscriptions that were sometimes poetic, sometimes ironic, certainly reminiscent in some aspects of the "games rooms" G.R.A.V. began creating in 1963. But this proposal from Cybèle Varela slips from the perceptive perspective into the poetic perspective which, once again, recalls a process of appropriation, digestion and transformation of the impulses that come from a set of new meetings and situations. Ironically, a work in bread is served and eaten during the inauguration: it is the actual word "manger" (to eat) that is transformed into an edible object, to be shared collectively (fig. p. 35).
Her stay in Paris, which continued and ended up resulting in a long-term migratory process, also fuelled the artist's commitment to light and shadow and deepened her questioning of the illusion within the actual pictorial

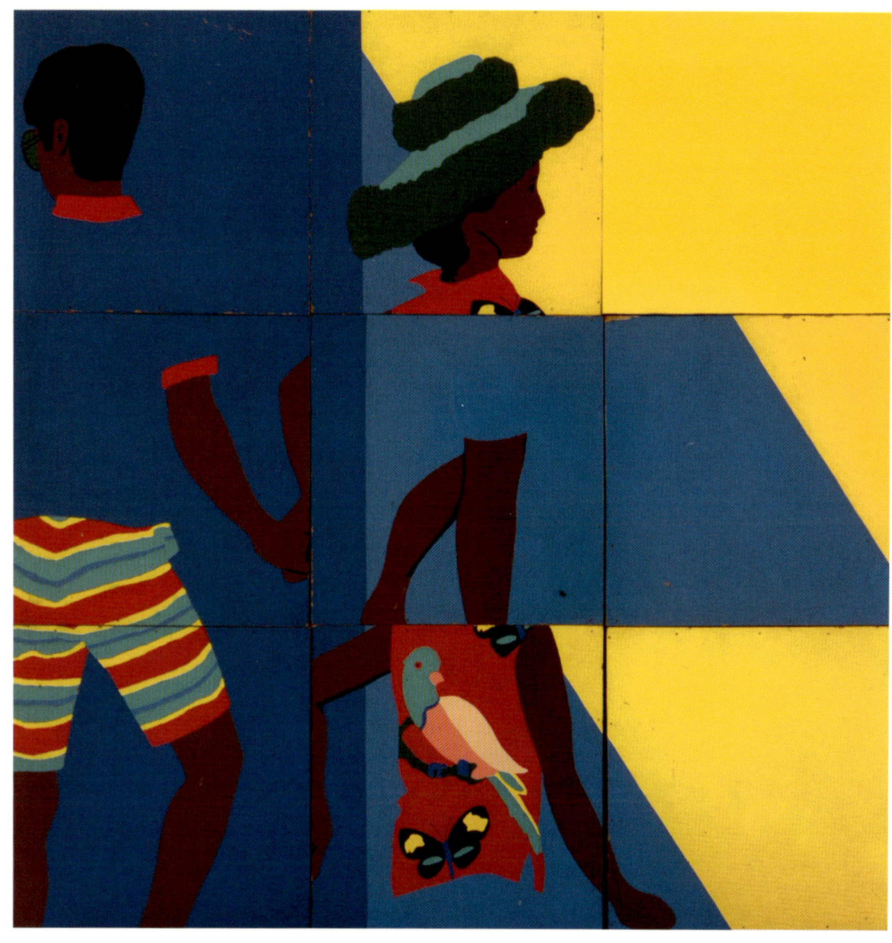

O Presente
1967

Um passeio feliz
1970

ist – findet die Künstlerin eine Stadt in Aufruhr vor. Das Aufeinandertreffen mit den kinetischen Erfahrungen des Argentiniers und der erweiterten Pariser Kunstszene scheint sich zunächst in einer Radikalisierung ihrer Nachforschungen über die Beziehung Form/Bewegung und die Beteiligung des Betrachters durch den Einsatz des Spiels zu äussern. 1972 kehrt sie dank eines weiteren Stipendiums in die Stadt zurück und kreiert für eine Ausstellung in der Galerie Debret ein spielerisches Ambiente voller bespielbarer Objekte mit teils poetischen, teils ironischen Inschriften, das in einigen Aspekten an die »Spielzimmer« der GRAV ab 1963 erinnert.
Allerdings ist in diesem Vorschlag von Cybèle Varela ein Abrutschen von der Wahrnehmungs- hin zur poetischen Ebene erkennbar, das erneut auf einen Prozess der Aneignung, Verdauung und Verwandlung der Impulse, die von einer Vielzahl neuer Kontakte und Situationen kommt, hindeutet. Ironischerweise wird während der Ausstellungseröffnung ein Kunstwerk im Brot serviert und verspeist: das eigentliche Wort »manger« (essen), das in ein essbares, gemeinsam geteiltes Objekt verwandelt wird (Abb. S. 35).

Doch der Aufenthalt in Paris, der sich in die Länge zieht und schliesslich zu einem lang andauernden Umzugsprozess wird, nährt gleichsam die Hingabe der Künstlerin zum Licht und zum Schatten und führt dazu, dass sie die Illusion in ihrer eigenen bildlichen Darstellung in früheren Werken noch stärker hinterfragt. Ihre eigenen Erfahrungen aufgrund der Distanzierung von Brasilien regen die Darstellung von Innenräumen, möglicherweise Wohnräumen an, in denen brasilianische Landschaften zu zweideutigen, irrealen Anwesenden werden, wie in einem Poster. So nimmt die Projektion des Schattens in Gemälden wie *O tucano* und *Pantanal* (beide 1973, Abb. S. 25) die Funktion eines Elements der Konstruktion und der räumlichen Entwicklung ein. Obwohl die Künstlerin Mitte der 1970er Jahre an bedeutenden Sammelausstellungen in Paris, wie dem Salon de Mai und dem Salon Comparaisons, sowie an Gruppenausstellungen, u.a. mit Künstlern, die der erzählenden Darstellung zugeschrieben werden, wie Jacques Monory (geb. 1924) und Antonio Recalcati (geb. 1938), teilnimmt, ist ihr Werdegang innerhalb der »Realismo«-Landschaft in den 1970er Jahren überaus

representation that previous works had already suggested. It was her experience of being away from Brazil that drove the representation of interior spaces, probably domestic, where Brazilian landscapes became ambiguous presences, unreal, like a representation on a poster. Thus, in paintings like *O tucano* and *Pantanal* (both 1973, figs. p. 25), the projection of shadow begins to act as an element of construction and spatial revelation. Therefore, although the artist took part in important collective events in Paris in the mid-1970s, such as Salon de Mai and Salon Comparaisons, and in group exhibitions with artists associated with Narrative Figuration, including Jacques Monory (b. 1924) and Antonio Recalcati (b. 1938), her journey through the panorama of realism in the 1970s is very unique and focused, as Pierre Restany noted in 1975, on a "linguistic method"[9] – "Cybèle Varela's reality exists only at the language level"[10] asserts the critic. In fact, the series of works entitled *Image* (figs. pp. 36–37, 64–69 and 85–87), in the late 1970s and early 1980s reveals a deepening of this linguistic questioning, not only in the scope of her paintings, but also in her videos and photographs. How do you build the space of an image? Where is the line between figuration and geometric abstraction? The limitation of the research field – the representation of a landscape in an interior space where light shines through, a tree and the sky with its clouds, the red benches in the gardens of the Museu Imperial in Petrópolis – allows the artist to rehearse possible answers to this and other questions.
Although this research gained space in Cybèle Varela's work in the 1980s and 1990s the political line of *Telefone Real* continues to run through her production, sometimes subtly, sometimes, on the contrary, more openly. In the Brazil of the late 1960s, the extremely ironic perspective of the artist shows clear signs of change in the relationships between the sexes and milestones in female emancipation and freedom of the body – for example in the staging of a meeting between nuns and young women wearing miniskirts in *De tudo aquilo que*

It was her experience of being away from Brazil that drove the representation of interior spaces, probably domestic, where Brazilian landscapes became ambiguous presences, unreal, like a representation on a poster

Ihre eigenen Erfahrungen aufgrund der Distanzierung von Brasilien regen die Darstellung von Innenräumen, möglicherweise Wohnräumen an, in denen brasilianische Landschaften zu zweideutigen, irrealen Anwesenden werden, wie in einem Poster

einzigartig und auf eine, wie Pierre Restany 1975 bemerkt, »linguistische Methode«[9] fokussiert – »Das Reale existiert bei Cybèle Varela lediglich auf der sprachlichen Ebene«[10], so der Kritiker. In der Tat enthüllt ihre Serie von Arbeiten namens *Image* (Abb. S. 36–37, 64–69 und 85–87) am Ende der 1980er und zu Beginn der 1990er Jahre eine Vertiefung dieser sprachlichen Nachforschungen nicht nur auf dem Gebiet der Malerei, sondern auch in den Bereichen Video und Fotografie. Wie setzt sich der Raum eines Bildes zusammen? Wo liegt die Grenze zwischen geometrischer Darstellung und Abstraktion? Die Begrenzung des Forschungsgebiets – die Darstellung einer Landschaft in einem lichtdurchfluteten Innenraum, ein Baum und der Himmel mit seinen Wolken, die roten Sitzbänke im Garten des Museu Imperial von Petrópolis – erlaubt es der Künstlerin, mögliche Antworten auf diese und andere Fragen einzustudieren.
Obwohl diese Nachforschung in der Arbeit von Cybèle Varela in den 1980er und 1990er Jahren an Raum gewinnt, durchzieht die politische Linie von *Telefone Real* weiterhin ihr Schaffen, teils auf subtile Weise, teils weitaus offensichtlicher. Ihr stark ironischer Blick nimmt im Brasilien der späten 1960er Jahre eindeutige Anzeichen der Veränderung in den Beziehungen der Geschlechter sowie Errungenschaften der weiblichen Emanzipation und der Befreiung des Körpers wahr – zum Beispiel in der Inszenierung eines Treffens zwischen Nonnen und jungen Mädchen in Miniröcken im Werk *De tudo aquilo que poderia ter sido e que não foi* (1967, Abb. S. 60–61). Gleichzeitig stellt sich Varela durch die Machtvergabe an weibliche Figuren in jüngeren Werken, von der Künstlerin in der Serie *The Artist* (1999, Abb. S. 71–75) bis zur Öko-Kämpferin, die beinahe wie eine Comic-Heldin wirkt, in Arbeiten wie *O que é verdade é verdade* (2010, Abb. S. 81) und *Another Wonderful Summer* (2013, Abb. S. 26) den Herausforderungen der Gleichberechtigung und sozialen Gerechtigkeit, von einem gleichsam politischen wie symbolischen Standpunkt aus. Jedoch zeichnet sich in ihren Werken eine tiefere Kontinuität ab, vielleicht ihrem Bekenntnis zur brasilianischen Volkskultur und der politischen, sozialen und kulturellen Geschichte Lateinamerikas geschuldet – die von einer kolonialen Vergangenheit geprägt ist, deren Entwicklungen noch immer auf die Gegenwart einwirken. In der jüngeren Gemäldeserie

O tucano
1973

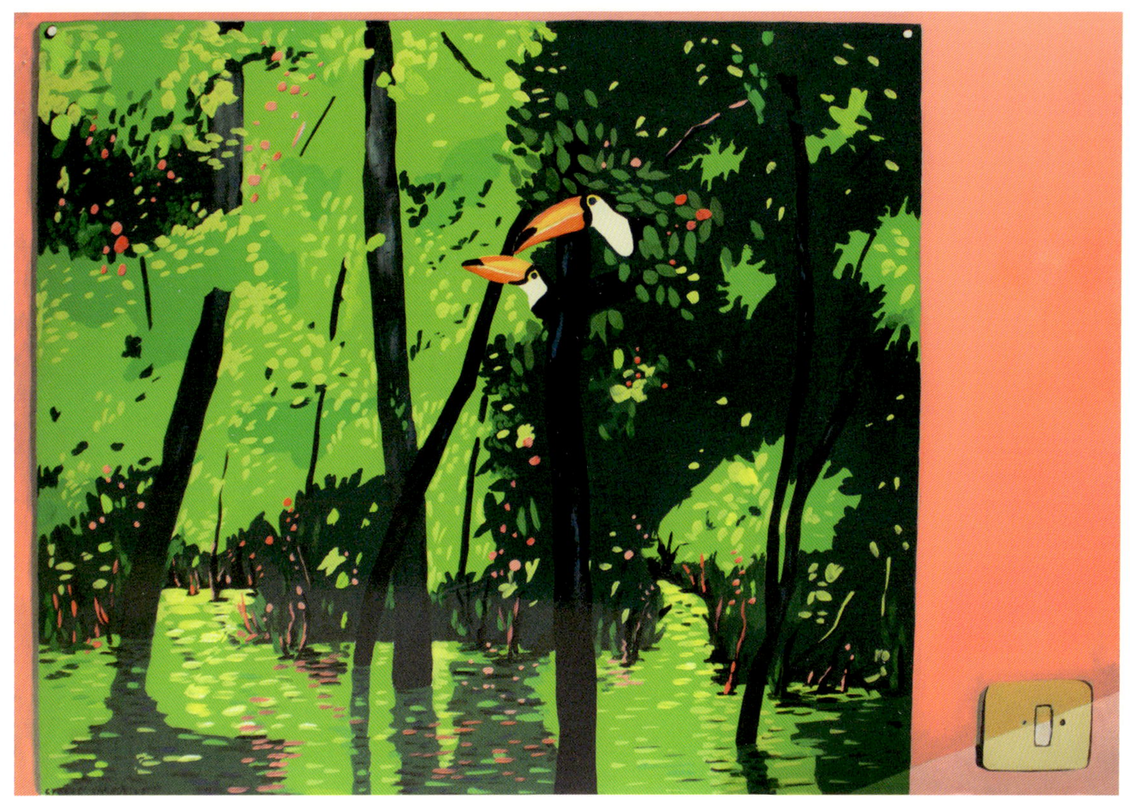

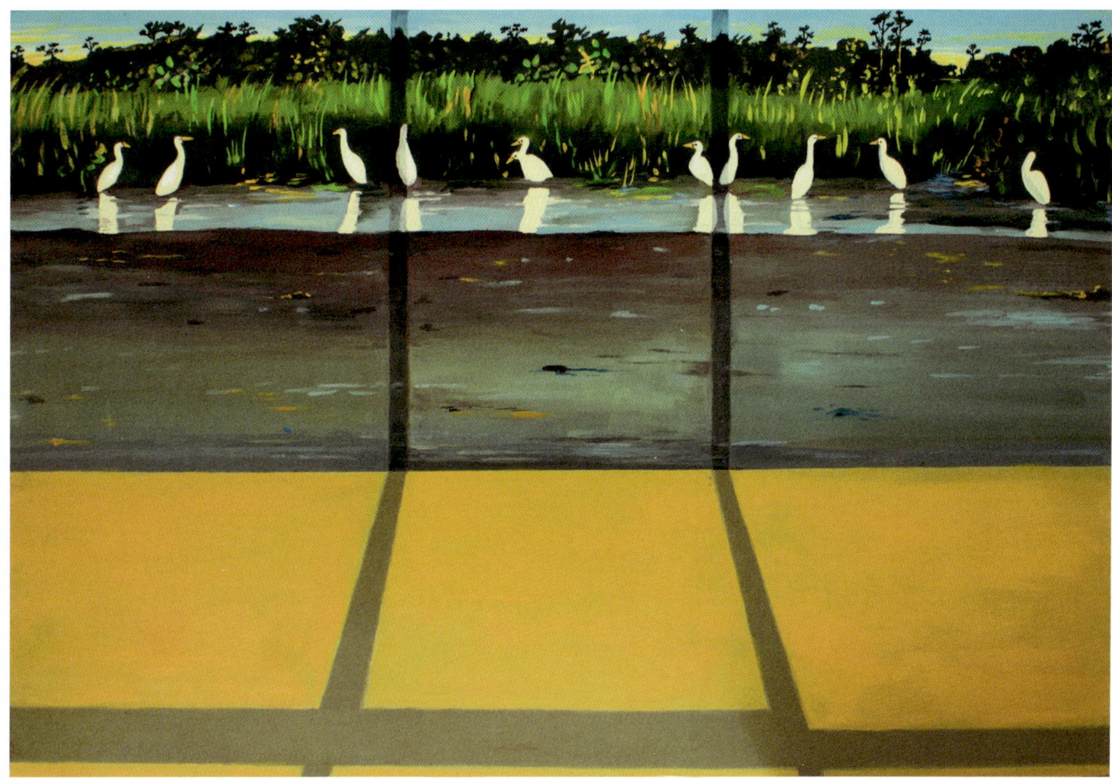

Pantanal
1973

poderia ter sido e que não foi (1967, fig. pp. 60–61). At the same time, giving female figures power in more recent works, from the artist in the series *The Artist* (1999, figs. pp. 71–75) to the eco-warrior, almost a comic strip heroine, in works like *O que é verdade é verdade* (2010, fig. p. 81) and *Another Wonderful Summer* (2013, fig. p. 26), responds to contemporary challenges of equality and social justice from a point of view that is both political and symbolic. However, it is perhaps in her commitment to popular Brazilian culture and the political, social and cultural history of Latin America – marked by a colonial past whose unfolding is still affecting the present – that a deeper line of continuity is drawn. In the series of recent paintings entitled *Unknown* (2015–16, figs. pp. 100–05), it is precisely these stories that are brought to life and intersect through portrayals of objects and anonymous characters. In some way, this positioning, which "[...] shows but also contests in a dialectic manner"[11] the myths of popular culture in all its forms – from the "cangaceiros" to the colourful rosary beads – never stopped being "tropicalist", even when it did.

It is perhaps in her commitment to popular Brazilian culture and the political, social and cultural history of Latin America that a deeper line of continuity is drawn

Jedoch zeichnet sich in ihren Werken eine tiefere Kontinuität ab, vielleicht ihrem Bekenntnis zur brasilianischen Volkskultur und der politischen, sozialen und kulturellen Geschichte Lateinamerikas geschuldet

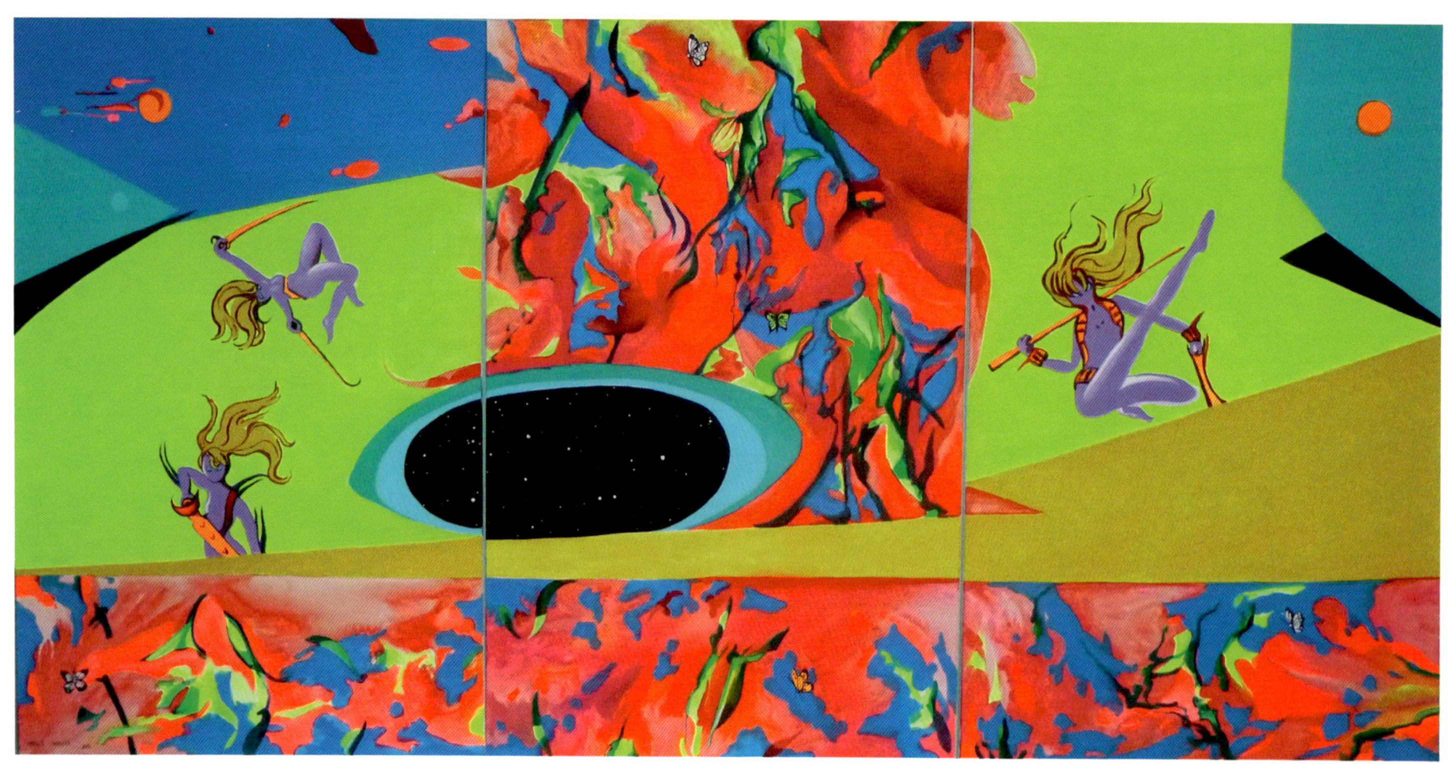

1 See, in particular, the catalogue for the *Nova Objectividade Brasileira* exhibition, at the Museu de Arte Moderna, Rio de Janeiro, April 1967.
2 See, in particular, Mário Schemberg, "A representação brasileira na IX Bienal de São Paulo", *Correio da Manhã*, section 4, Rio de Janeiro, 17 September 1967, p. 3 and Mário Pedrosa, "Bienal e participação... do povo", *Correio da Manhã*, section 4, Rio de Janeiro, 8 October 1967, p. 1. For a broader discussion, see: Giulia Lamoni, "Unfolding the 'Present': Some Notes on Brazilian 'Pop'", in Jessica Morgan, Flavia Frigeri (eds.), *The World Goes Pop*, exh. cat., Tate Modern (London, 2015), pp. 59–71.
3 Subsequently, the work was destroyed by the artist herself, but photographs still remain.
4 Antônio Bento, "Espaço com ritmo", *Última Hora*, Rio de Janeiro, 29 April, 1970.
5 To explore the broader context this practice is part of, see: Paulo Sérgio Duarte, *Anos 60, Transformações da arte no Brasil* (Rio de Janeiro, 1998); Daisy Peccinini, *Figurações, Brasil anos 60* (São Paulo, 1999); Paulo Reis, *Arte de vanguarda no Brasil, os anos 60* (Rio de Janeiro, 2006).
6 Frederico Morais in *Cybèle Varela, Pintura*, booklet for the artist's exhibition at the Goeldi gallery, Rio de Janeiro, June and July 1968.
7 Here, I am using the interpretation of Frederico Morais, particularly his use of the anthropophagic metaphor, spoken of in many writings, among them the text quoted in note 6.
8 Mário Pedrosa, "Do Pop americano ao sertanejo Dias", *Correio da Manhã*, section 4, Rio de Janeiro, 29 October 1967, p. 1.
9 "...sa méthode linguistique." Pierre Restany, "Le réel au niveau du langage", *Cybèle Varela, Pinturas*, exh. cat., Galeria Bonino (Rio de Janeiro, 1975), no page numbers. Author's translation.
10 "Le réel de Cybèle Varela n'existe qu'au niveau du langage." Author's translation, ibid.
11 Frederico Morais in *Cybèle Varela, Pintura*, as note 6.

namens *Unknown* (2015–16, Abb. S. 100–05) sind es genau diese Geschichten, die auftauchen und sich in Form von Darstellungen von Gegenständen und anonymen Persönlichkeiten kreuzen. In gewisser Weise war diese Positionierung, die die Mythen der Volkskultur in allen ihren Formen – von den »Gesetzlosen« bis hin zu den bunten Rosenkränzen – »[...] feststellt, aber auch dialektisch hinterfragt«[11], immer ein Teil des Tropicalismo, auch als sie es nicht mehr war.

1 Siehe insbesondere den Katalog zur Ausstellung *Nova Objectividade Brasileira*, Museu de Arte Moderna, Rio de Janeiro, April 1967.
2 Siehe insbesondere Mário Schemberg: »A representação brasileira na IX Bienal de São Paulo«, in *Correio da Manhã*, 4. Heft, Rio de Janeiro, 17. September 1967, S. 3, und Mário Pedrosa: »Bienal e participação... do povo«, in *Correio da Manhã*, 4. Heft, Rio de Janeiro, 8. Oktober 1967, S. 1. Für eine umfassendere Diskussion siehe: Giulia Lamoni: »Unfolding the ›Present‹: Some Notes on Brazilian ›Pop‹«, in Jessica Morgan und Flavia Frigeri (Hrsg.): *The World Goes Pop*, Ausst.-Kat., Tate Modern, London 2015, S. 59–71.
3 Das Kunstwerk wurde anschliessend von der Künstlerin selbst zerstört, allerdings existieren Fotografien davon.
4 Antônio Bento: »Espaço com ritmo«, in *Última Hora*, Rio de Janeiro, 29. April 1970.
5 Für eine umfassendere Kontextualisierung dieser Praxis siehe: Paulo Sérgio Duarte: *Anos 60, Transformações da arte no Brasil*, Rio de Janeiro 1998; Daisy Peccinini: *Figurações, Brasil anos 60*, São Paulo 1999; Paulo Reis: *Arte de vanguarda no Brasil, os anos 60*, Rio de Janeiro 2006.
6 Frederico Morais in *Cybèle Varela, Pintura*, Begleitblatt zur Ausstellung der Künstlerin in der Galerie Goeldi, Rio de Janeiro, Juni–Juli 1968.
7 Ich schliesse mich hier der Interpretation von Frederico Morais an, insbesondere was seine Verwendung der kannibalistischen Metapher angeht, die in mehreren seiner Schriften auftaucht, darunter im hier zitierten Text *Cybèle Varela, Pintura*, op. cit.
8 Mário Pedrosa: »Do Pop americano ao sertanejo Dias«, in *Correio da Manhã*, 4. Heft, Rio de Janeiro, 29. Oktober 1967, S. 1.
9 »... sa méthode linguistique.« Pierre Restany: »Le réel au niveau du langage«, in *Cybèle Varela, Pinturas*, Ausst.-Kat., Galerie Bonino, Rio de Janeiro 1975, o. S. Übers. d. Autorin.
10 »Le réel de Cybèle Varela n'existe qu'au niveau du langage.« Übers. d. Autorin. Ebd.
11 Frederico Morais in *Cybèle Varela, Pintura*, op. cit.

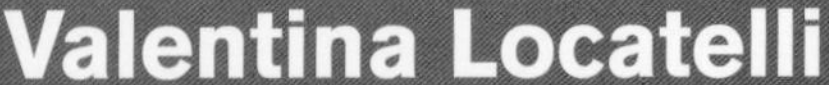

Valentina Locatelli

A Conversation with Cybèle Varela

VL Cybèle, you left Petrópolis for the first time in 1968 and have been living in Europe almost continuously ever since. Recently you moved from Rome to Madrid and before Rome you were a long time in Geneva and Paris. How did each one of these places impact your work?

CV: All these different places, with their many different cultures and mentalities, have left some traces on me and my work. In Brazil, when I was a child, I literally "breathed" the colors of the local landscape. I remember having an epiphany one day, as I was walking in my grandparents' garden. I saw the different colors of the earth, the different colored layers and started to collect some samples. The intense blue of the sky, the luxurious green of the trees, all this made a strong impression on me as a little girl. The diversity of the common people walking on the streets are also among the strongest memories of my childhood. Brazilian "folklore" is probably the right word to express what I was impressed by back then. Later on, when I went to Paris, I was especially interested by the city's intellectual atmosphere. The memories of Brazil started being filtered by the impressions of the French capital and, as a result, I engaged in a deeper reflection on art as cultural expression. My work became also more self-reflective.

Once I moved to Geneva in 1978, its natural setting with the lake turned my attention once more towards nature. Using the photograph of a tree against the blue sky, which I had taken in Paris, I worked on the idea of developing and changing forms and formats and on the repartition of space and images. As strange as it may sound, in Switzerland I found again the strong limpid skies that reminded me of Brazil (figs. pp. 68–69).

On the other hand, my experience in Rome, some forty years later, was quite different. It was the start of a new dialogue with the Old Masters, especially from the Renaissance. I actually think that Italy helped me develop an attention for the details. But the weight of its historical past is sometimes too strong and difficult for contemporary research.

Ein Gespräch mit Cybèle Varela

VL Cybèle, Sie haben Petrópolis 1968 das erste Mal verlassen und seitdem fast durchgehend in Europa gelebt. Vor Kurzem sind Sie von Rom nach Madrid gezogen. Vor Rom haben Sie lange Zeit in Genf und Paris gelebt. Auf welche Weise hat jeder dieser Orte Ihr Werk geprägt?

CV: All diese verschiedenen Orte, die sich durch verschiedene Kulturen und Mentalitäten charakterisieren, haben mich und meine Arbeiten beeinflusst. Während meiner Kindheit in Brasilien habe ich die Farben meiner heimatlichen Landschaft regelrecht »eingeatmet«. Eines Tages hatte ich ein Schlüsselerlebnis, als ich im Garten meiner Grosseltern herumspazierte. Ich nahm die verschiedenen Farben der Erde, ihre verschiedenfarbigen Schichten, wahr und begann, einige Proben zu sammeln. Das intensive Blau des Himmels, das üppige Grün der Bäume, all dies übte auf mich als kleines Mädchen eine starke Wirkung aus. Des Weiteren hat sich mir in meiner Kindheit die Diversität der ganz normalen Menschen auf der Strasse in mein Gedächtnis eingeprägt. Brasilianische »Folklore« ist wahrscheinlich der richtige Ausdruck für das, was mich damals so beeindruckte.

Als ich später nach Paris übersiedelte, interessierte ich mich insbesondere für das intellektuelle Klima der Stadt. Meine brasilianischen Erinnerungen wurden durch meine Eindrücke von der französischen Hauptstadt gefiltert. Das Ergebnis war, dass ich verstärkt über die Kunst als kulturellen Ausdruck zu reflektieren begann. Meine Arbeit wurde folglich selbstreflexiver.

Nachdem ich dann 1978 nach Genf weitergezogen bin, lenkte die dortige Naturkulisse mit dem See meine Aufmerksamkeit erneut auf die Natur. Indem ich die Fotografie eines Baumes vor blauem Himmel, die ich in Paris aufgenommen hatte, verwendete, arbeitete ich daran, Formen und Formate zu verändern sowie den Raum und die Bilder neu zu verteilen. So merkwürdig es auch klingen mag. In der Schweiz fand ich den klaren Himmel wieder, der mich an Brasilien erinnerte (Abb. S. 68–69).

Meine Rom-Erfahrung vierzig Jahre später war dagegen ganz anderer Art. Es war der Beginn eines neuen Dialogs mit den alten Meistern, insbesondere denen der Renaissance. Ich glaube, dass ich in Italien gelernt habe, auf Details zu achten. Das Gewicht der historischen

I have just moved to Madrid, so I cannot say yet how this place is going to impact my artistic practice, but even before knowing I would have lived here, I painted a series with prehistoric animals (figs. p. 76) inspired by Francisco de Goya's painting *El quitasol* (1777, Prado, Madrid). In some ways, it is as if I was led here.

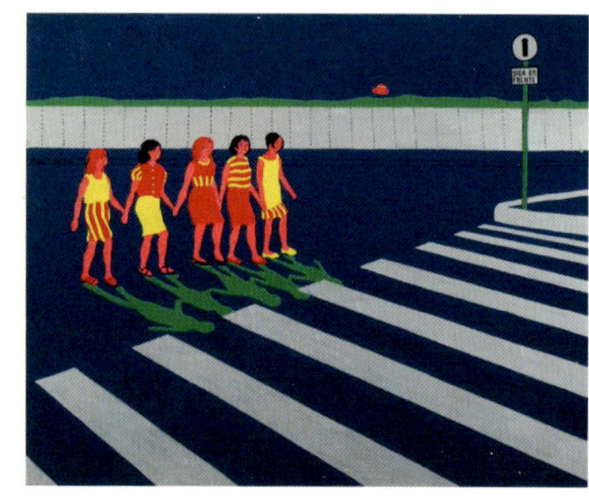

Cinco moças passeando
1967

VL: Could you recount how your career begun in Brazil? Early on, who were the Brazilian artists you most admired and found inspiring?
CV: I started painting when I was seven or eight years old, at first copying works by Jean-Honoré Fragonard and by the French Impressionists. But I would consider I started my career officially at sixteen, when I received my first prize, the "Mensão Honrosa" from the Brazilian Artists Association at the Museu Nacional de Belas Artes (MNBA) in Rio de Janeiro.
I was especially inspired by the work of a great painter, João Batista da Costa (1865–1926) who worked in my hometown Petrópolis. He painted wonderful landscapes using the same earthy colors I had been so impressed by as a child. Soon after, I started looking at North American Pop Art. The 1960s in Brazil, in spite of the complicated political situation, was a great moment for creativity. There was a lot of energy going around and debates of ideas. I think that the particular atmosphere of the time inspired me greatly. We were a group of artists all working together in Rio de Janeiro, using the same language. If I would have to mention two among many, I was very close with Rubens Gerchman (1942–2008), with whom I shared the predilection for some populistic topics such as football players and people on the streets, and also Raymundo Colares (1944–1986), whose work attracted me for its dynamism at the crossroad between Pop Art and Futurism.

VL: At that time, you like many of your peers faced restrictions of your civil liberties, including freedom of expression. At the São Paulo Biennial of 1967,

Vergangenheit ist jedoch manchmal zu schwer und komplex, um eine zeitgenössische Recherche durchzuführen.
In Madrid lebe ich erst seit Kurzem, sodass ich noch nicht sagen kann, welche Auswirkungen dieser Ort auf meine künstlerische Praxis haben wird. Bevor ich jedoch wusste, dass ich mich hier einmal niederlassen würde, habe ich eine Serie mit prähistorischen Tieren gemalt (Abb. S. 76), der Francisco de Goyas Gemälde *El quitasol* (1777, Prado, Madrid) als Vorbild diente. Es scheint ganz so, als ob ich hierher geführt wurde.

VL: Möchten Sie darüber sprechen, wie Ihre künstlerische Laufbahn in Brasilien begann? Welche brasilianischen Künstlerinnen und Künstler haben Sie schon früh bewundert und inspirierend gefunden?
CV: Im Alter von sieben oder acht Jahren entdeckte ich die Malerei, indem ich zuerst die Werke von Jean-Honoré Fragonard und der französischen Impressionisten kopierte. Meine offizielle künstlerische Laufbahn begann hingegen mit sechzehn Jahren, als ich den ersten Preis, den »Menção Honrosa« von der brasilianischen Künstlervereinigung im Museu Nacional de Belas Artes (MNBA) in Rio de Janeiro erhielt.
Insbesondere prägte mich das Werk des grossen Malers João Batista da Costa (1865–1926), der in meiner Heimatstadt Petrópolis arbeitete. Er malte wundervolle Landschaften, für die er immer dieselben Erdtöne verwendete, die mich als Kind so stark beeindruckten. Kurz darauf entdeckte ich die nordamerikanische Pop-Art. Trotz der komplizierten politischen Situation waren die 1960er Jahre in Brasilien eine besonders kreative Phase. Es lag viel Energie in der Luft und überall wurden Ideendebatten ausgetragen.
Die damalige besondere Atmosphäre hat mich sicherlich stark beeinflusst. Wir waren eine Gruppe von Künstlerinnen und Künstlern, die gemeinsam in Rio de Janeiro arbeiteten und dieselbe Formensprache benutzten. Wenn ich zwei von vielen nennen müsste, die mir sehr nahestanden, fiele meine Wahl auf Rubens Gerchman (1942–2008), mit dem ich eine gewisse Vorliebe für einige populäre Themen wie Fussballspieler und gewöhnliche Menschen teile, und Raymundo Colares (1944–1986), dessen Arbeiten mich aufgrund ihrer Dynamik an der Grenze zwischen Pop-Art und Futurismus fesselten.

you exhibited the work *O Presente* (fig. p. 22), a painted wooden box that, when opened, confronted the public with the irreverent caricature of a Brazilian military officer. On the day of the inauguration, before the opening, *O Presente* was withdrawn because it was considered to be anti-government. Did this event influence your subsequent artistic approach to social and political questions?
CV: Overall, I think that I did not approach these questions in a very political or highly critical manner. The central thing for me has always been to be able to work on images that I find interesting, especially on images depicting the people of Brazil. At that time, even the image of the president was interesting to me simply because it was an image related to the people. For instance, I was fascinated by people crossing the street on the zebra crossings, by people stopping at the traffic lights and then moving on as soon as the signal tells them to (fig. pp. 52–53). The popular and urban element was therefore central to my practice as well as a reflection on the anonymity of these fortuitous and transient encounters among people. Working on these subjects allowed me to express my critique against poverty and misery afflicting the man of the street. The role(s) of women in society and the impact of religious beliefs (and obsessions) are also something I was keen on analyzing with my work, as I did for instance in the painting *De tudo aquilo que poderia ter sido e que não foi* (fig. pp. 60–61).

The role(s) of women in society and the impact of religious beliefs (and obsessions) are also something I was keen on analyzing with my work

Die Rolle(n) der Frau in der Gesellschaft und die Auswirkungen religiöser Vorstellungen (und Obsessionen) sind ebenso Themenschwerpunkte, mit denen ich mich in meinen Arbeiten auseinandergesetzt habe

VL: You have just briefly mentioned being inspired by North American Pop Art. As a matter of fact, you are considered one of the major representatives of Brazilian Pop Art during the 1960s. The works you produced during that time critically reflect on Brazilian society and especially on questions of gender relations and female subjectivity. What do you think is the intrinsically characteristic element that distinguishes Brazilian from American Pop Art?
CV: Brazil and the USA are two fundamentally different countries. In Brazil we altered this Western art movement and made it completely ours, first of

VL: Zu dieser Zeit waren Sie wie viele andere Künstlerinnen und Künstler Einschränkungen der zivilen Freiheiten ausgesetzt, einschliesslich der Meinungsfreiheit. Auf der Biennale von São Paulo im Jahr 1967 zeigten Sie die Arbeit *O Presente* (Abb. S. 22), eine bemalte Holzschachtel, die, sobald sie geöffnet wurde, den Betrachter mit der despektierlichen Karikatur eines brasilianischen Militäroffiziers konfrontierte. Am Tag der Einweihung wurde *O Presente* vor der Eröffnung aus der Ausstellung entfernt, da die Arbeit als regierungskritisch betrachtet wurde. Hatte dieses Ereignis Einfluss auf Ihren nachfolgenden künstlerischen Ansatz, der eine Auseinandersetzung mit gesellschaftspolitischen Fragestellungen verfolgt?
CV: Ich denke, dass ich diese Fragestellungen im Allgemeinen nie auf eine besonders politische oder kritische Weise behandelt habe. Für mich war es immer von zentraler Bedeutung, mit Bildern zu arbeiten, die ich interessant fand, insbesondere mit Bildern, die brasilianische Menschen wiedergaben. Damals war sogar das Bild des Präsidenten von Interesse für mich, da es sich um ein Bild handelte, das in Bezug zu den Menschen stand. Mich faszinierten beispielsweise aber auch Personen, die die Strasse auf dem Zebrastreifen überquerten, oder Personen, die an der Ampel innehielten und sich weiterbewegten, sobald das entsprechende Signal erschien (Abb. S. 52–53). Das populäre und urbane Element war folglich grundlegend für meine Praxis, ebenso wie die Reflexion über die Anonymität dieser zufälligen und flüchtigen Begegnungen zwischen Menschen. Durch die Auseinandersetzung mit diesen Themen konnte ich Armut und Elend, die die gewöhnlichen Menschen getroffen haben, anprangern. Die Rolle(n) der Frau in der Gesellschaft und die Auswirkungen religiöser Vorstellungen (und Obsessionen) sind ebenso Themenschwerpunkte, mit denen ich mich in meinen Arbeiten auseinandergesetzt habe, beispielsweise in dem Gemälde *De tudo aquilo que poderia ter sido e que não foi* (Abb. S. 60–61).

VL: Sie haben kurz erwähnt, dass Sie die nordamerikanische Pop-Art beeinflusst hat. Genau genommen gelten Sie als eine der wichtigsten Vertreterinnen der brasilianischen Pop-Art während der 1960er Jahre. Die Arbeiten, die Sie während dieser Zeit realisiert haben, setzen sich mit der brasilianischen

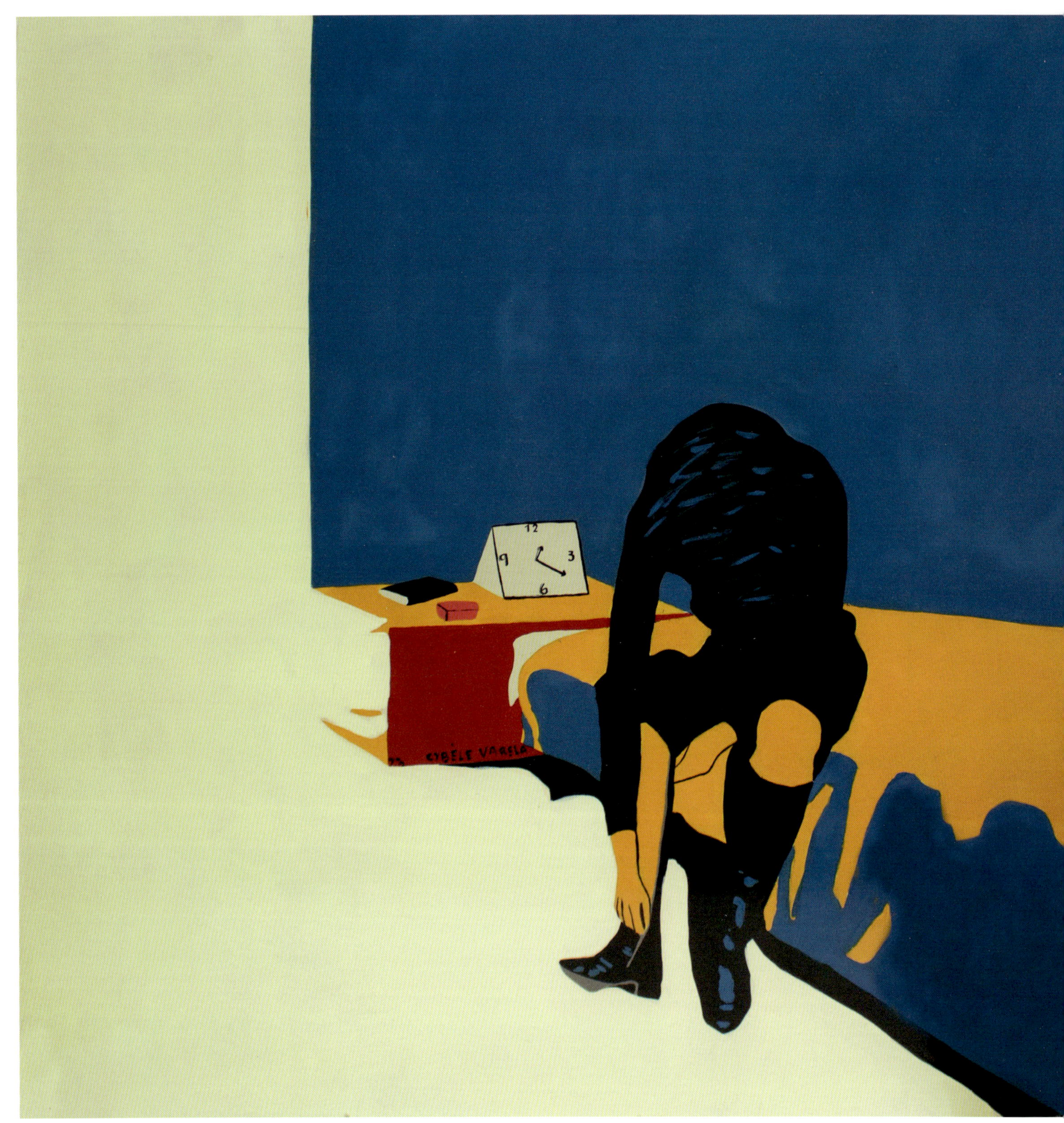

Maison du Brésil
1973

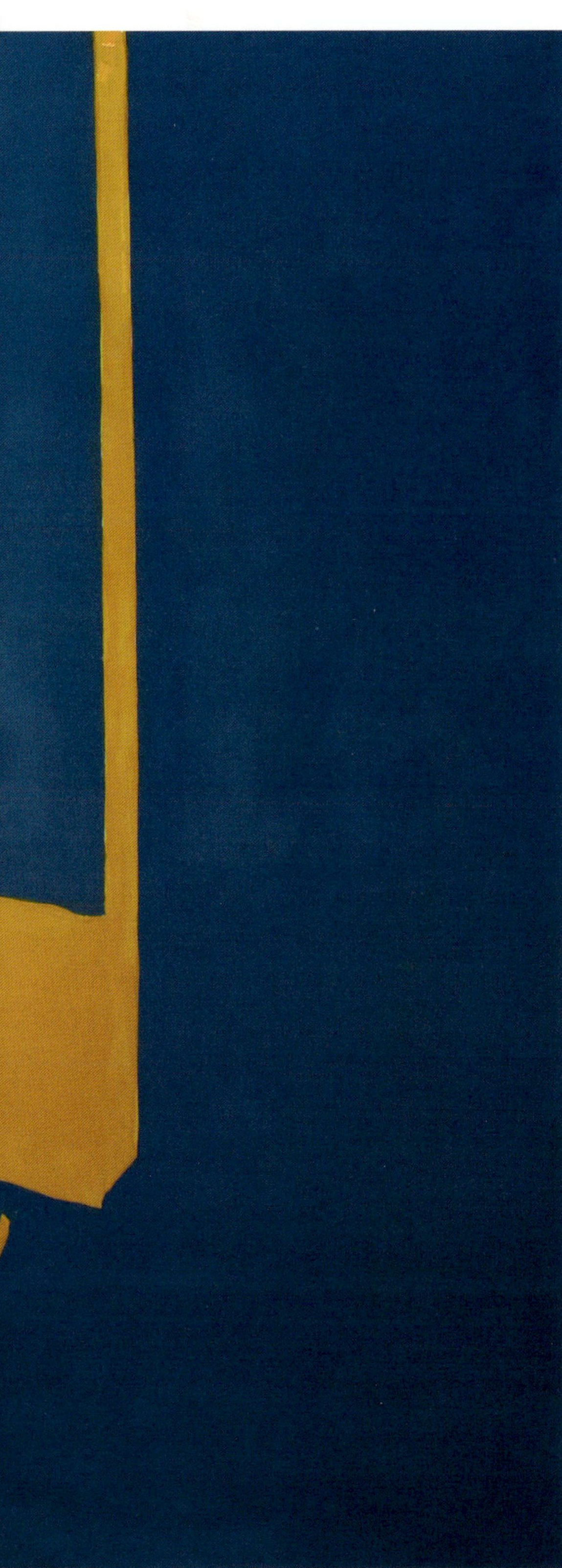

all because we have a different mentality than North Americans, and secondarily because we mixed it with the so-called Tropicalismo movement. American Pop artists were more pragmatic, while Brazilians were, in a way, freer. The influence of Tropicalismo, with its colors, made Brazilian Pop Art "softer" than its American counterpart. In a way, however, I have always preferred British Pop Art to American Pop Art. It seemed to me more elaborated, more ironic, with a critical sense of parody which I found inspiring.

VL: You first arrived in Paris in 1968 thanks to a scholarship obtained from the French government. Those were the days of the student protests and riots. Tell us about your strongest firsthand impressions from that year.
CV: I remember very well that, when I first arrived at the École des Beaux-Arts in Paris, I met a young artist who asked me: "Why did you come to Paris? There is nothing left, we have destroyed everything!". It was in fact a moment of void, people were under

Abstraction does not exist for me. It is an image as well

Für mich gibt es keine Abstraktion. Sie ist gleichfalls ein Bild

Gesellschaft auseinander und insbesondere mit Fragen nach Geschlechterverhältnissen und femininer Subjektivität. Was ist Ihrer Meinung nach das charakteristische Element, das die brasilianische von der amerikanischen Pop-Art unterscheidet?
CV: Brasilien und die USA sind zwei vollkommen unterschiedliche Länder. In Brasilien wandelten wir die westliche Kunstströmung ab und machten daraus etwas ganz Eigenes, da wir eine andere Mentalität als die Nordamerikaner haben und sie zudem mit der Tropicalismo genannten Bewegung vermischten. Die amerikanischen Pop-KünstlerInnen waren pragmatischer, während die brasilianischen irgendwie freier waren. Der Einfluss des Tropicalismo mit seinen Farben machte die brasilianische Pop Art »softer« als ihr amerikanisches Gegenstück. Ich habe jedoch immer die englische Pop-Art der amerikanischen vorgezogen. Sie erschien mir ausgereifter und ironischer, mit einem kritischen Sinn für die Parodie, was ich als inspirierend empfand.

VL: Sie kamen 1968 dank eines Stipendiums der französischen Regierung erstmals nach Paris. In diese Zeit fielen die studentischen Proteste und Aufstände. Erzählen Sie uns etwas über Ihre eigenen Eindrücke aus diesem Jahr.
CV: Ich erinnere mich noch gut daran, wie ich das erste Mal die École des Beaux-Arts in Paris aufsuchte und einem jungen Künstler begegnete, der mich fragte: »Weshalb bist du nach Paris gekommen? Hier ist nichts übrig geblieben. Wir haben alles zerstört!«. Es war wirklich ein Moment der Leere. Die Menschen standen unter Schock. Aus diesem Grund bewarb ich mich um ein zweites Stipendium, um nach Paris zurückzukehren, sobald sich die Situation beruhigt hätte. Ich hatte das Gefühl, Erfahrungen und Kontakte während meines ersten Aufenthalts verpasst zu haben. 1971 wurde ich nach Paris zurückgeschickt und endlich begann ich, die französische Seele zu fühlen und zu verstehen. Während meines zweiten Aufenthalts in Paris studierte ich neben der École du Louvre auch Sozialanthropologie an der École Pratique des Hautes Etudes (EPHE-Sorbonne) unter der Leitung von André Varagnac. Dies war eine sehr wichtige Erfahrung für mich. Das Studium komplettierte meine Ausbildung, indem es meinen Blick auf die Welt erweiterte. Natürlich verbrachte ich

shock. For this reason, I applied for a second scholarship in order to go back to Paris once things had cooled off, as I felt that I had missed some experiences and contacts while there the first time. I was sent back to Paris in 1971 and I finally started feeling and understanding the French soul better. During my second stay in Paris, besides studying at the École du Louvre, I also studied Social Anthropology at the École Pratique des Hautes Etudes (EPHE-Sorbonne) under the guidance of André Varagnac, and this was a very important experience for me. It completed my education by enlarging my vision of the world. Of course, I spent most of my time in Paris visiting museums and art exhibitions.

VL: Once in France you encountered both Conceptual Art and the so called French Narrative Figuration. I believe that, in a way, your first show in Paris was a reaction to these artistic movements interpreted from the perspective of a Brazilian artist…

CV: My first show in Paris was in 1972 at the Galerie Debret. I brought all the pieces from Rio. It was an exercise close to Conceptual Art, but in which the active participation of the public was essential. I had been investigating the ludic aspects of interactivity for some years in Brazil. For that show, I also had produced a piece made of bread, called *Manger*, which in French means "to eat" (fig. p. 35). It was an ephemeral sculpture, that I offered to the guests during the vernissage, as a kind of performance: all was transformed and was meant to disappear in the end, like this always happens in life itself. Back then, other Brazilian artists were also experimenting with the interactive aspects of art, as Lygia Clark (1920–1988), whom I met some years later in Paris.

VL: During the 1970s your work, despite remaining figurative, became more abstract and investigated the interaction between light and shade. What were you seeking to convey with your *Image*-series (figs. pp. 64–66)?

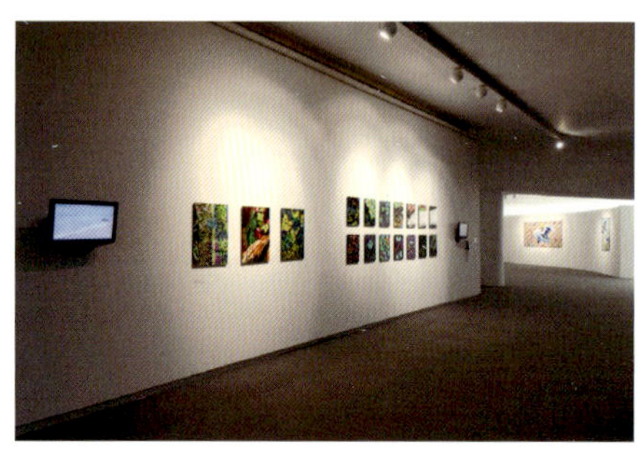

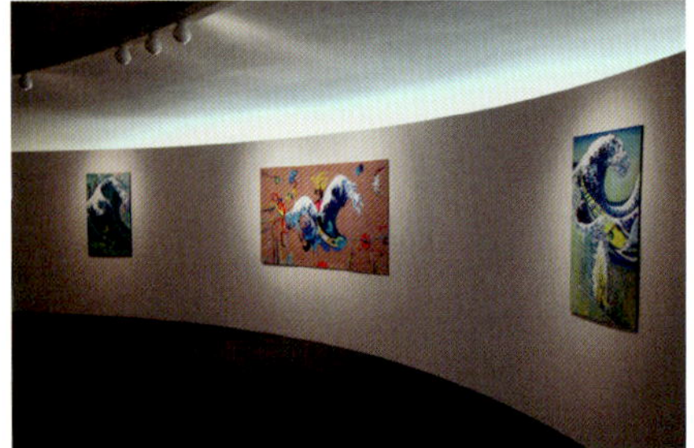

Views of the exhibition *Cybèle Varela. Espaços Simultâneos* at the Museu de Arte Contemporânea in Niterói, 2014

Installationsansichten der Ausstellung *Cybèle Varela. Espaços Simultâneos* im Museu de Arte Contemporânea in Niterói, 2014

Vistas da exposição *Cybèle Varela. Espaços Simultâneos* no Museu de Arte Contemporânea de Niterói, 2014

die meiste Zeit in Paris damit, Museen und Kunstausstellungen zu besuchen.

VL: In Frankreich entdeckten Sie die Konzeptkunst und die französische Narrative Figuration. Meiner Meinung nach war Ihre erste Ausstellung in Paris eine Antwort auf diese Kunstströmungen, die Sie aus der Perspektive einer brasilianischen Künstlerin interpretiert haben…

CV: Meine erste Ausstellung in Paris hatte ich 1972 in der Galerie Debret. Ich brachte alle Arbeiten aus Rio mit. Es handelt sich auch um eine Übung, die der Konzeptkunst nahestand, für die aber die aktive Mitwirkung des Publikums konstitutiv war. Ich habe mich bereits in Brasilien einige Jahre lang mit den spielerischen Aspekten der Interaktivität auseinandergesetzt. Für diese Ausstellung habe ich auch eine Arbeit realisiert, die aus Brot bestand und den Titel *Manger* trug, was im Französischen »essen« (Abb. S. 35) bedeutet. Es handelte sich um eine ephemere Skulptur, die ich den Gästen während der Eröffnung in Form einer Performance anbot: Alles wurde transformiert und sollte am Ende verschwinden, wie es immer im Leben passiert. Damals experimentierten auch andere brasilianische Künstler mit den interaktiven Aspekten der Kunst, darunter Lygia Clark (1920–1988), der ich ein paar Jahre später in Paris begegnet bin.

VL: Während der 1970er Jahre wurden Ihre Arbeiten trotz ihres figurativen Charakters abstrakter und erkundeten verstärkt das Zusammenspiel von Licht und Schatten. Was wollten Sie mit Ihrer *Image*-Serie (Abb. S. 64–66) vermitteln?

CV: Für mich gibt es keine Abstraktion. Sie ist gleichfalls ein Bild. Ich sollte allen meinen Arbeiten den Titel *Image* geben, da für mich alles ein Bild ist. Meine »Fenster«-Serie setzt sich mit dem Wesen der Malerei auseinander. In Paris erforschte ich die Art und Weise, wie das Sonnenlicht durch eine vom Wind bewegte Fensterjalousie in meine Wohnung fallen und Reflexe auf die orangefarbenen Wände werfen würde. Ich war daran interessiert, wie das Sonnenlicht die Wahrnehmung verändert, und, aus meiner Sicht, Sonnenstrahlen selbst zu Bildern werden. Wie Pierre Restany richtig verstanden hat, stellt meine Serie über das Sonnenlicht eine Reflexion über die Ambiguität des Realen dar.

CV: Abstraction does not exist for me. It is an image as well. I should actually give to all of my works the title "Image", because for me everything is an image. My "window" series, was about the very nature of painting itself. In Paris, I used to research the way in which sunlight would filter through a jalousie window moved by the wind entering my flat and create reflections on the orange walls. I was interested in how solar light modifies perception and in my perspective, solar beams became themselves the images. As Pierre Restany had well understood, my series about solar light was actually a reflexion about the ambiguity of the real.

VL: Nature and the bright colors of Brazilian flora are clearly a leitmotif in your work. Is there an ecological concern rooted in your fondness for natural subjects?
CV: Nature is central to my life and to my work. Without it I feel incomplete. I never thought of myself as a militant but what is happening nowadays with the global destruction of biodiversity makes me terribly sad and worry for the future of life on this planet.

VL: Works such as *Image* (figs. pp. 36–37 and 68–69) and *The Artist 1* and *2* (figs. pp. 71–75) reveal the impact of Surrealism and, more specifically René Magritte and Salvador Dalí on your practice. They also point to your ability to simultaneously envision different worlds. Is this "surreal" aspect of your work actually an instrument to achieve a more mystical or spiritual dimension?
CV: I have always been very interested in Indian philosophy and in the oriental spiritual culture. Moreover, when I was very young, I had a fascination for other planets and galaxies, which I developed in my series *Horizontes* in the 1970s and came back to more recently in the show *Espaços Simultaneos*, presented in 2013–14 at the Museu de Arte Contemporânea in Niterói (figs. p. 34).

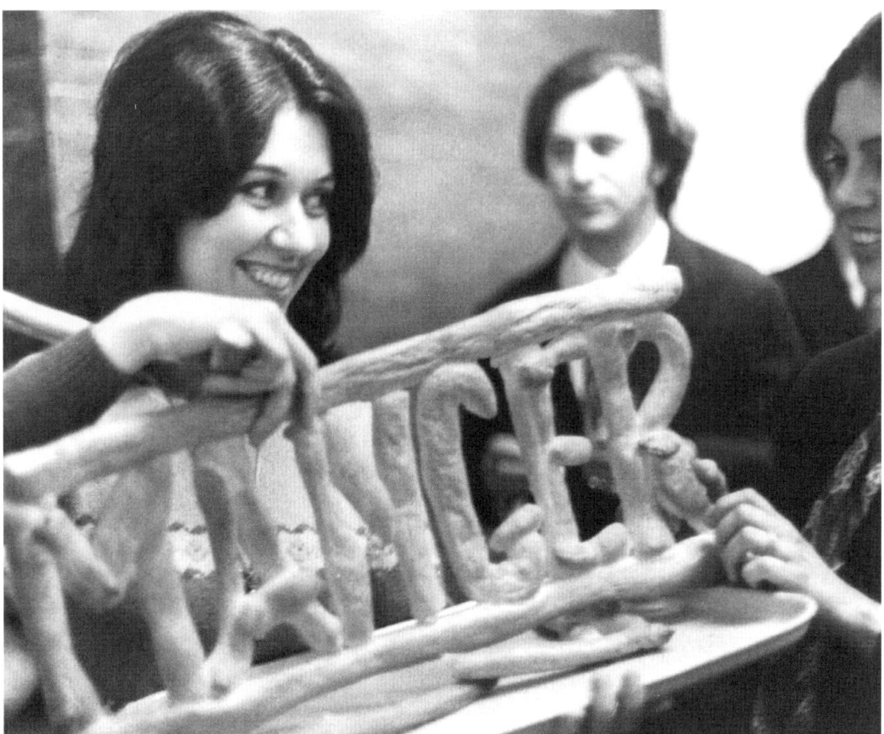

The artist with her work *Manger* at the opening of the Galerie Debret exhibition, Paris, 1972

Die Künstlerin mit ihrem Werk *Manger* an der Eröffnung ihrer Ausstellung in der Galerie Debret, Paris, 1972

A artista com a peça *Manger* durante o vernissage na Galerie Debret, Paris, 1972

VL: Die Natur und die leuchtenden Farben der brasilianischen Flora sind ein Leitmotiv in Ihren Arbeiten. Steht Ihre Vorliebe für Naturthemen in Zusammenhang mit Umweltbelangen?
CV: Die Natur spielt eine zentrale Rolle in meinem Leben und Werk. Ohne sie fühle ich mich unvollständig. Ich habe mich nie für eine Aktivistin gehalten, aber wie heutzutage die Biodiversität weltweit zerstört wird, macht mich sehr traurig, und ich mache mir Sorgen um das zukünftige Leben auf diesem Planeten.

VL: Arbeiten wie *Image* (Abb. S. 36–37 und 68–69) und *The Artist 1* und *2* (Abb. S. 71–75) legen den Einfluss des Surrealismus, und genauer, den von René Magritte und Salvador Dalí auf Ihre künstlerische Praxis nahe. Sie weisen auch auf Ihre Fähigkeit hin, verschiedene Welten gleichzeitig zu betrachten. Ist dieser »surreale« Aspekt in Ihren Arbeiten ein Mittel, um eine mystischere oder spirituellere Dimension zu erlangen?
CV: Ich habe mich schon immer für die indische Philosophie und die östliche spirituelle Kultur interessiert. Als ich noch sehr jung war, haben mich auch andere Planeten und Galaxien interessiert, die ich in meiner Serie *Horizontes*

I used to read books on astronomy and the universe. Sometimes I feel like I do not belong to this planet. The ambiguity of reality fascinates me, the ambiguity of what it is and what it is not. The energies which are exchanged in a communication between human beings, like the one we are having now, are something I always reflect about.

VL: Your work is inspired by both Brazilian and European popular culture and by social issues, especially around questions of identity and gender. Your approach to social critique, however, is never severe and always poetic. I think that your ability to condense even the hardest realities of life into form and color is an intrinsically Brazilian quality…
CV: As I mentioned before, the fact that I approach images in order to unveil their ambiguity is part of my artistic personality. It is a very personal approach, with my work I am researching on me and my 'anima' (soul). I am detached from what I do, I am an external

Image
1980

in den 1970er Jahren entwickelt habe und zu der ich abermals infolge der Ausstellung *Espaços Simultâneos* zurückgekehrt bin, die 2013–14 im Museu de arte contemporânea in Niterói (Abb. S. 34) stattfand. Ich lese seit jeher Bücher über Astronomie und das Universum. Manchmal fühle ich mich, als würde ich nicht zu diesem Planeten gehören. Die Ambiguität der Realität fasziniert mich, die Ambiguität von dem, was ist und was nicht ist. Die Energie, die in der Kommunikation zwischen Menschen, wie der unsrigen, ausgetauscht wird, ist etwas, über das ich immer nachdenke.

VL: Ihr Werk ist von der brasilianischen und europäischen Populärkultur und von gesellschaftlichen Themen beeinflusst, insbesondere von Fragen nach Identität und Geschlecht. Sie nähern sich jedoch nie auf strenge, sondern poetische Weise an gesellschaftskritische Aspekte an. Ihre Fähigkeit, auch die härteste Lebensrealität in Formen und Farben zu verdichten, ist ein typisch brasilianisches Merkmal…
CV: Wie ich zuvor erwähnt habe, ist es ein Teil meiner künstlerischen Persönlichkeit, Bilder zu verwenden, um ihre Ambiguität offenzulegen. Es handelt sich um einen sehr persönlichen Ansatz. Mit meinen Arbeiten recherchiere ich über mich und meine »anima« (Seele). Ich bin losgelöst von dem, was ich tue. Ich beobachte die Realität von aussen und was ich in meinen Arbeiten zeige, ist nie eine direkte Reflexion, sondern eine indirekte Beobachtung.

VL: Auch nach Ihrer Übersiedlung nach Europa und in den folgenden Jahrzehnten Ihrer Laufbahn bis heute charakterisiert sich ihr Werk durch eine grosse Leidenschaft und Aufmerksamkeit für Farben, Bewegung und Ornament. Was sind die Wurzeln Ihres Interesses für das dekorative Element in der Kunst?
CV: Ich liebe alles, was populär und folkloristisch ist. Ich liebe Strassenmärkte, Händler, die alle möglichen Waren verkaufen, wie Blumen, Puppen (ich habe sogar eine Puppensammlung!) oder alten Töpferwaren. Als ich in Rom lebte, zogen mich die sogenannten »bancarelle« (Strassenstände) magisch an. Ich denke, dass der Ursprung meines Interesses für ornamentale Elemente in der Kunst in diesem Aspekt meiner Persönlichkeit begründet liegt.

observer of realities, and what I show in my work is never a direct reflection but rather an indirect observation.

VL: Even after moving to Europe and during the following decades of your career till today, your work has been characterized by a dedication to and attention for color, movement and ornament. What is the root of your interest for the decorative element in art?
CV: I love anything that is popular and folkloristic. I love street markets, people selling goods of different kinds, like flowers, dolls (I even have a collection of dolls!) or old pottery. When I was living in Rome, for instance, I was especially attracted by the so-called "bancarelle" (side-of-the-road stalls). I think the origin of my attention for the ornamental elements in my art is rooted in this aspect of my personality.

VL: When we were discussing which title to give to this retrospective exhibition, you suggested to make a reference to music, as rhythm and sound are central values in your work. *Tropicalismo Remixed* takes on this suggestion and is a playful reference both to your beginnings amid the artists of the Tropicalismo group in Rio de Janeiro and to your ability to reinvent and "remix" all the ingredients that characterize your oeuvre and culminate in your own style. How do you include music in your creative process?
CV: Music is central to my practice. In Brazil, I studied classical singing and I have always worked listening to classical music. I still like to listen to and sing Richard Wagner when I am in my atelier. I also play guitar and, back in the days, when I was still an art student in Paris, I remember that I used to meet up with other artists and play popular songs together, including bossa nova songs. Nevertheless, when I work I only want to work accompanied by classical music.

Image
1989

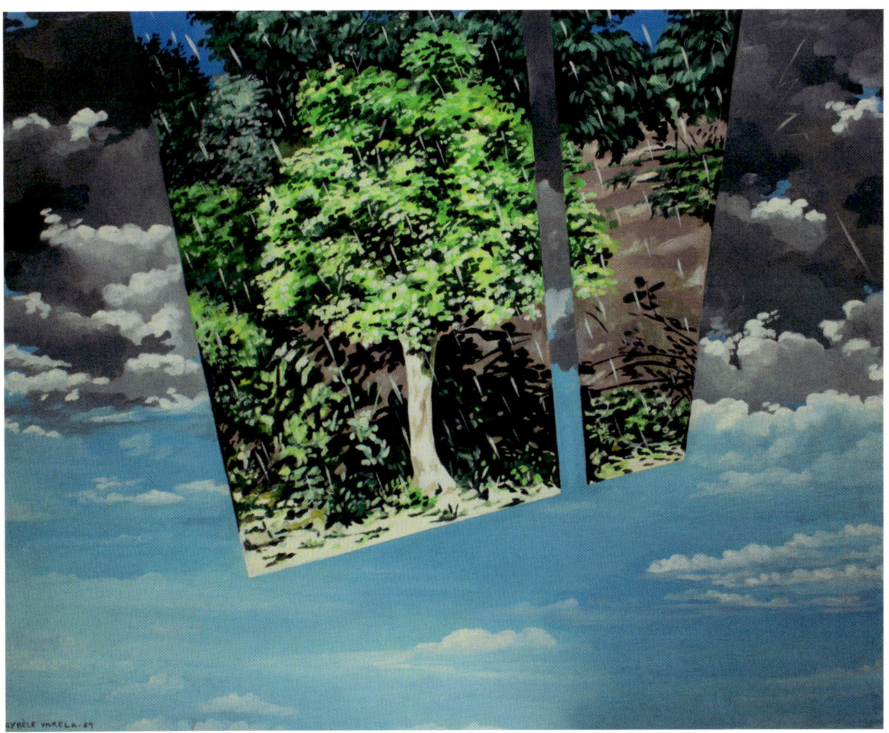

VL: Als wir über den Titel für diese Retrospektive diskutiert haben, haben Sie vorgeschlagen, auf die Musik Bezug zu nehmen, da Rhythmus und Ton zentrale Werte in Ihrem Werk sind. *Tropicalismo Remixed* übernimmt diese Anregung und versteht sich als spielerischen Verweis auf Ihre Anfänge zwischen den dem Tropicalismo verbundenen Künstlerinnen und Künstlern in Rio de Janeiro und Ihre Fähigkeit, alle Elemente, die Ihr Œuvre charakterisieren und in Ihrem eigenen Stil kulminieren neu zu erfinden und zu »mischen«. Wie fliesst die Musik in Ihren kreativen Prozess ein?
CV: Musik ist für meine künstlerische Praxis von grosser Relevanz. In Brasilien studierte ich klassischen Gesang. Ich höre beim Arbeiten immer klassische Musik. Ich höre und singe immer noch gerne Richard Wagner, wenn ich in meinem Atelier bin. Ich spiele auch Gitarre. Als Studentin in Paris habe ich mich mit anderen Künstlerinnen und Künstlern getroffen, um gemeinsam beliebte Songs zu spielen, darunter Bossa-Nova-Songs. Wenn ich jedoch arbeite, möchte ich nur klassische Musik um mich haben.

VL: Even if you are known mostly as a painter, both photography and video have been taking an increasingly important role in your work as they are naturally related to questions of light and movement. How do you integrate these different media and approaches?
CV: Generally, when I have an idea for a project, I develop it over some years. For instance, I worked on my series devoted to the "cangaçeiros" (figs. pp. 93-99) for about four years. I started working with photography and video in the 1970s as a way to complement my work with painting. It has allowed me to discover new aspects which I had not taken into account when I was working only with painting. I am not a professional photographer in the strict sense of the word. I use this media as a vehicle to new discoveries. All of my photographs are reworked extensively; they are composed layering different elements. I do not use photography in order to show something that I see, but rather as an instrument capable of discovering the poetry of the world. With video, on the other hand, I have pursued on another level my research on movement, which I had started in the 1960s with my puzzles and box form works.

VL: We are now standing together in your new home and atelier, literally surrounded by much of your life's work. Many of the most salient phases of your artistic biography are visualized and reunited in this impressive space. Now that you can look back at over 50 years of artistic achievement, what do you think are the most important milestones in your career thus far?
CV: It is not easy to answer this question. I think that every single moment in my life was important and left a visible sign on my work. Each one of my projects and researches has impacted my work. They all have been important milestones along my journey.

VL: Looking towards the future, what inquiries are occupying your attention nowadays? Are you working on new projects?

VL: Auch wenn Sie hauptsächlich als Malerin bekannt sind, haben die Fotografie und das Video eine zunehmend wichtige Rolle in Ihrem Werk gespielt, da sie mit Fragen nach Licht und Bewegung in einem Zusammenhang stehen. Wie führen Sie die verschiedenen Medien und Ansätze zusammen?
CV: Wenn ich eine Idee für ein Projekt habe, entwickle ich diese normalerweise mehrere Jahre lang. Ich habe mich beispielsweise mit meiner Serie, die sich den »Cangaçeiros« widmet (Abb. S. 93–99), vier Jahre beschäftigt. Ich begann in den 1970er Jahren mit Fotografie und Video zu arbeiten, um meine Auseinandersetzung mit der Malerei zu komplettieren. Die Medien Fotografie und Video haben es mir ermöglicht, neue Aspekte zu entdecken, die ich in der Arbeit mit der Malerei nicht berücksichtigt habe. Ich bin keine professionelle Fotografin. Ich verwende das Medium als Mittel, um neue Entdeckungen zu machen. Alle meine Fotografien werden umfassend überarbeitet und setzen sich aus verschiedenen Schichten von Elementen zusammen. Ich verwende die Fotografie nicht, um etwas zu zeigen, was ich sehe, sondern als ein Instrument, das es ermöglicht, die der Welt innewohnende Poesie einzufangen. Dank des Videos habe ich dagegen meine Recherche über die Bewegung, die ich in den 1960er Jahren mit meinen Puzzles und Schachteln begonnen habe, auf eine ganz neue Ebene gehoben.

VL: Wir befinden uns jetzt gemeinsam in Ihrem neuen Zuhause und Atelier, wo Sie Ihr Lebenswerk umgibt. Viele Ihrer wichtigsten Schaffensphasen sind in diesem beeindruckenden Raum vertreten. Wenn Sie jetzt auf Ihre über 50-jährige künstlerische Laufbahn zurückblicken, welche sind dann die wichtigsten Meilensteine Ihrer Karriere?
CV: Es fällt mir nicht leicht, auf diese Frage zu antworten. Ich denke, dass jeder einzelne Moment in meinem Leben von Bedeutung war und seine Spuren in meinem Werk hinterlassen hat. Alle meine Projekte und Recherchen haben meine Arbeiten beeinflusst Sie alle waren bedeutsame Meilensteine auf meiner Reise.

VL: Wenn Sie in die Zukunft blicken, welche Fragen beschäftigen Sie heute? Arbeiten Sie an neuen Projekten?
CV: Ich mache mir noch keine Gedanken um das nächste Projekt, da ich noch an der Serie *Unknown* arbeite (Abb. S. 100–05). Wie ich

CV: I cannot think about the next project yet, as I am still working on the *Unknown* series (figs. pp. 100–05). As I said, I generally carry on a project idea for four to five years. The topics of migration and change are at the core of this series of paintings of "unknown" people, animals and objects. Maybe it is also about my own migration, as I have lived in so many different countries and moved so many times. I have to continue reflecting on these ideas. My destination, like the title of the works is still "unknown".

This Interview was conducted in French in Cybèle Varela's apartment and atelier in Madrid, on September 16, 2017. Translated into English by Valentina Locatelli.

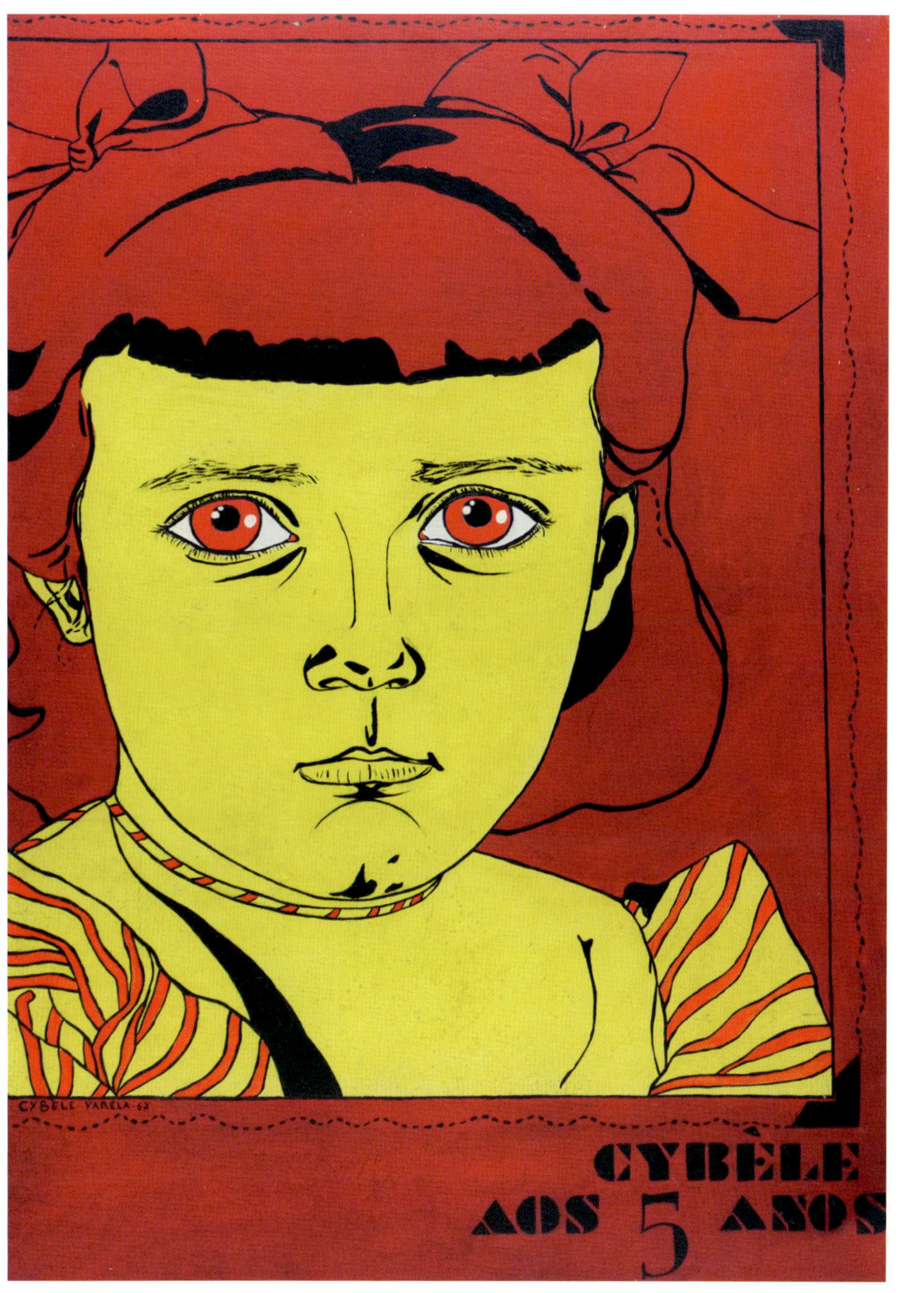

bereits erwähnt habe, beschäftige ich mich normalerweise vier, fünf Jahre lang mit einem Projekt. Die Themen der Migration und des Wandels stehen im Mittelpunkt dieser Bilderserie von »unbekannten« Menschen, Tieren und Objekten. Vielleicht geht es auch um meine eigene Migration, da ich in so vielen verschiedenen Ländern gelebt habe und so oft umgezogen bin. Ich muss diese Ideen vertiefen. Mein Ziel ist, wie der Werktitel nahelegt, noch »unbekannt«.

Dieses Interview wurde am 16. September 2017 in Cybèle Varelas Wohnung und Atelier in Madrid auf Französisch geführt.

Cybèle aos 5 anos
1967

Daniel Faust
Prefácio

A primeira retrospectiva de Cybèle Varela na Suíça insere-se de forma especial no conceito da Fundação Brasilea, sediada em Basileia: a emigração e criação de raízes em lugares distantes do país de origem. A representação de recordações do Brasil que trazem sua cultura, o colorido e a alegria de viver. Imagens da beleza deslumbrante da natureza do Brasil, de suas diversidades e discrepâncias sociais, abrangendo também as correntes socioculturais.
A obra de Cybèle Varela é uma observação do Brasil à distância desde a Europa, onde a artista passou a maior parte de sua vida. É, ao mesmo tempo, uma observação no próprio local, na Europa, com olhos brasileiros. O *Tropicalismo Remixed* de Varela é Pop Art latino-americana, que visita o Surrealismo e é sempre permeado pelos desenvolvimentos culturais europeus da segunda metade do século XX.
As peças-chave de *Tropicalismo Remixed* de Basileia são dois puzzles criados especialmente para a exposição (ils. pp. 10, 12-13), inspirados em várias obras dos anos 60, por exemplo, *Um passeio feliz* (1970; il. p. 23). A falta de uma peça do puzzle permite deslocar e modificar a representação, a *realidade*. O observador é tentado e convidado a posicionar os quadrados para reconstruir de forma imaginária a *verdadeira representação*. Pop Art surrealista que procura a interação do observador.
Em Basileia, são apresentadas mais de 30 obras em diferentes suportes. A exposição divide-se em capítulos cronológicos, que estruturam tematicamente a obra de Varela e que pretendem ser representativos das fases de criação mais importantes da artista. O Tropicalismo e a Pop Art da sua fase inicial de criação, nos anos 60 e 70; a *Figuração Narrativa* e a investigação conceitual de realidades representadas nos quadros, fotografias e vídeos dos anos 70 e 80. Seguem-se autorretratos criados entre os anos 70 e a atualidade, motivo de diálogo sobre a auto-representação na arte contemporânea. Outro capítulo aborda o fenômeno brasileiro dos cangaceiros, os fora da lei que rondavam o sertão do Nordeste, e das suas figuras mais célebres, Lampião e Maria Bonita (1960-2000). A série *Unkown* (2015-2016) encerra a exposição e é uma reflexão da artista sobre a fragmentação social e pessoal, bem como sobre a alienação.
A apresentação desta exposição na Suíça, onde a artista viveu durante 15 anos e expôs regularmente de forma individual, e na nossa Fundação Brasilea, especialmente dedicada aos artistas brasileiros, surge como consequência natural para todos aqueles que têm estado atentos à obra de Cybèle Varela.
As curadoras Ariane Varela Braga e Valentina Locatelli conseguiram, com sucesso, e em estreita colaboração com Cybèle Varela, lançar um olhar completo e inédito sobre sua obra. A elas, o nosso reconhecimento e agradecimento. Alem do mais, gostariamos de agradecer a Giulia Lamoni pelo seu ensaio sobre a artista. Agradecemos também o trabalho da equipe da editora Silvana Editoriale em Milão, responsável pela organização criativa deste catálogo e pela tradução dos textos em três idiomas. Um agradecimento muito especial à Fundação artEDU e a Embaixada do Brasil em Berna, que tornaram possível a exposição *Cybèle Varela: Tropicalismo Remixed* e a edição do catálogo que a acompanha, graças ao apoio financeiro prestado.

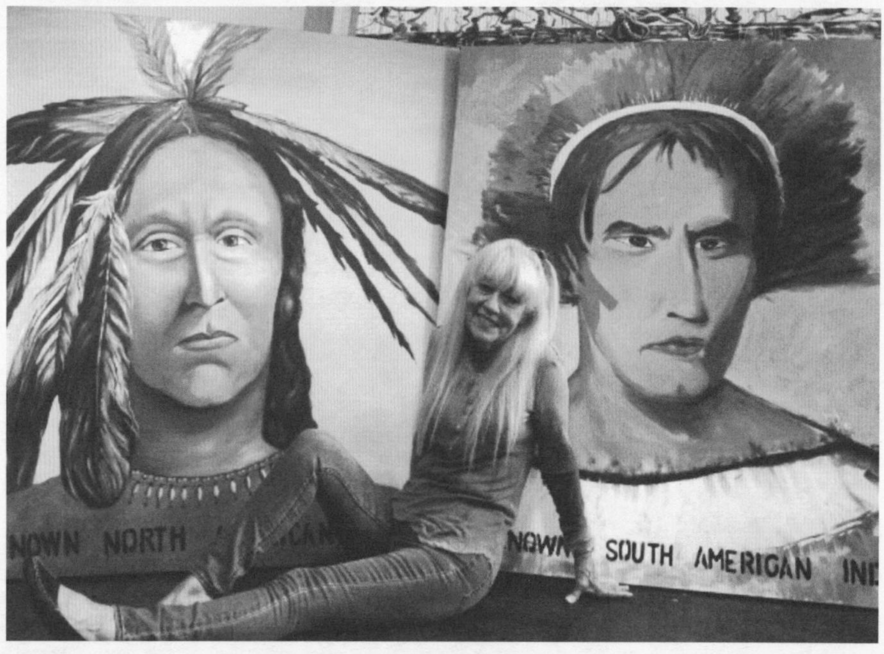

Cybèle Varela in her studio with two works from her series *Unknown*, 2016

Cybèle Varela in ihrem Atelier mit zwei Werken der Serie *Unknown*, 2016

Cybèle Varela no seu ateliê com duas obras da sua serie *Unknown*, 2016

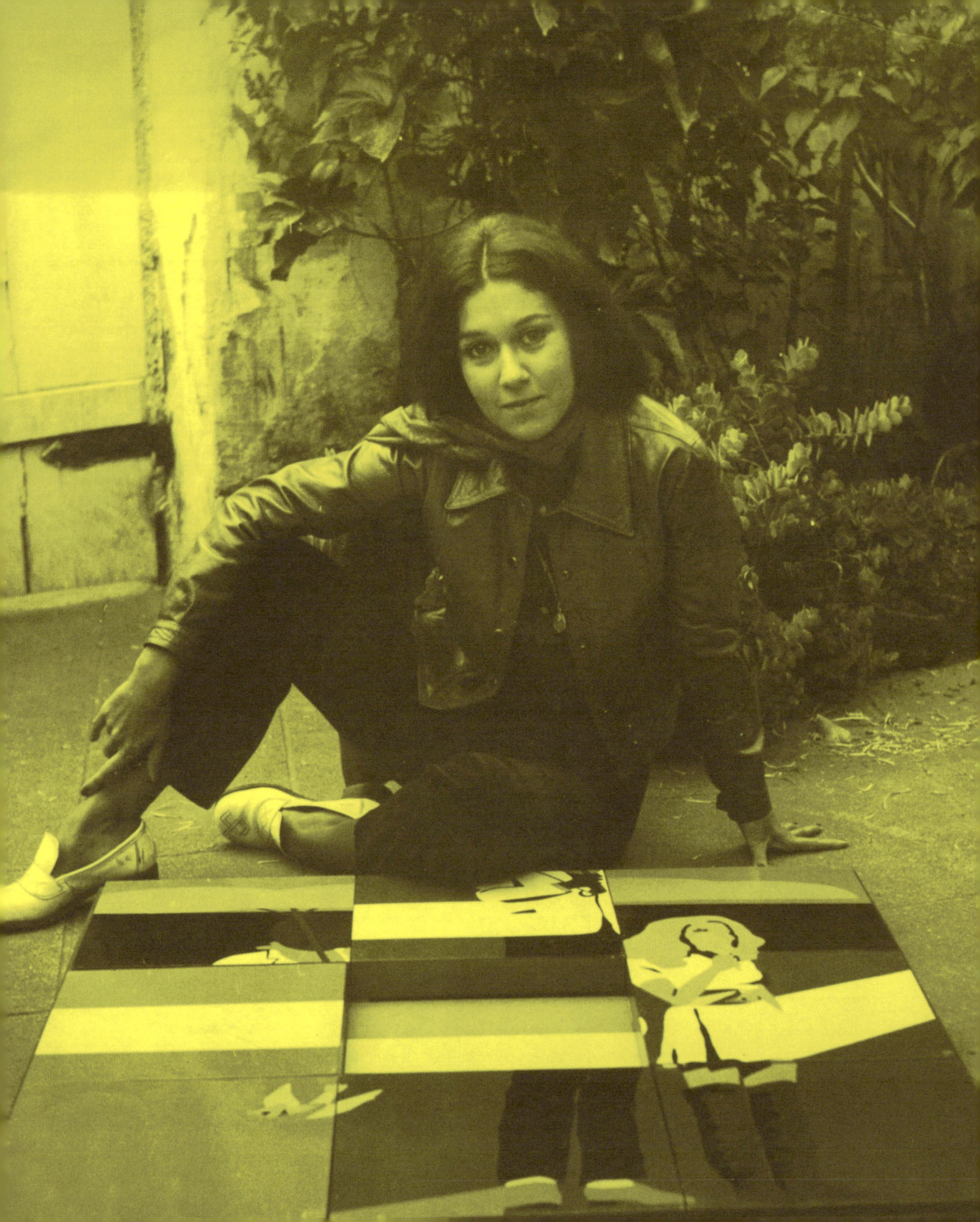

Valentina Locatelli
Ariane Varela Braga

Cybèle Varela: Tropicalismo Remixed Uma introdução

'Tropicalismo' (ou 'Tropicália') indica um movimento artístico de curta duração que surgiu no Brasil no final da década de 1960. Em 1972, já se podia considerar concluído. O termo deriva diretamente de uma instalação ambiental criada em 1967 por Hélio Oiticica (1937-1980), à época um dos maiores protagonistas do panorama brasileiro das artes visuais. O Tropicalismo, todavia, foi um fenômeno cultural de amplo alcance, que teve ressonância em todos os setores criativos, da arte à música, do teatro à moda, acompanhado por um sentimento comum de experimentação e crítica social. O movimento estava atrelado à ideia de "antropofagia", literalmente um canibalismo cultural que emergiu no Brasil no final dos anos vinte, como reação ao colonialismo cultural,[1] e esboçava a mistura da cultura tradicional e da arte brasileira, com as manifestações internacionais da Pop e Op Art.

Foi neste contexto vibrante que Cybèle Varela (n. 1943, Petrópolis, RJ) deu início à sua carreira no Brasil. A artista participou das mais importantes exposições e bienais da época, e tornou-se em breve uma das figuras-chave do Tropicalismo e da Pop Art brasileira,[2] antes de se mudar para Paris no começo dos anos setenta. Engajada em um prolífico intercâmbio artístico com muitos colegas, quer no Brasil, quer no exterior, com o passar dos anos Cybèle Varela desenvolveu uma linguagem crítica, mas nunca marcada por ideologia e com um toque de sutil ironia. Entre suas fontes de inspiração preferidas estão as pessoas comuns e sua relação com o ambiente urbano; o anonimato da vida nas grandes cidades e os papéis impostos pelas restrições de gênero e expectativas sociais. Pintora antes de tudo, com seus objetos em formato de caixas e pinturas quebra-cabeça sobre madeira, adere à mesma abordagem alegre e interativa que consagrou internacionalmente os artistas brasileiros. Ao mesmo tempo, as experimentações vídeo e fotográficas foram fundamentais para sua pesquisa sobre a interação da luz, sombra e movimento.[3]

O título desta mostra, *Tropicalismo Remixed*, é uma referência divertida à música e procura recriar aquela juvenil atmosfera de otimismo que caracterizava os inícios da longa jornada artística de Cybèle Varela, deixando nítido rastro na sua produção sucessiva. Um Tropicalismo "*remixed*" é um Tropicalismo que foi alterado, modificado de sua condição original, para criar algo novo e audaz. Este bem equilibrado sentimento de continuidade e renovação é, precisamente, o que caracteriza a obra de Varela.

Cybèle Varela: Tropicalismo Remixed apresenta uma seleção das mais emblemáticas pinturas da artista, objetos e vídeos, desde a década de 1960 até os dias de hoje. A exposição na Fundação Brasilea em Basel – Suíça, é a primeira retrospectiva de Varela na Europa. Representa também a ocasião de reavaliar a relação da artista com a Suíça, onde viveu entre 1978 e 1993, e de examinar de que forma o encontro e a apropriação da cultura europeia influenciaram seu trabalho. Ao examinar os principais momentos do desenvolvimento artístico de Varela e apresentando-os em capítulos organizados por ordem cronológica, a exposição quer dar novo destaque às numerosas realizações da artista. Além disso, analisa a contribuição de Cybèle Varela no panorama artístico, internacional e latino-americano, desde a Pop Art e a Arte Conceitual até a Figuração Narrativa e a Videoarte.

Nos últimos 60 anos, o impulso criativo de Varela seguiu várias trilhas, sempre profundamente ligadas umas às outras, como vários capítulos do mesmo enredo: como explica a mesma artista, após ter desenvolvido um conceito por quatro, cinco anos, ela ressente a urgência de passar para o sucessivo, em uma continuação natural de suas reflexões anteriores. A exposição está construída sobre esta ideia de continuidade e de mutação. Começando pelos trabalhos iniciais da artista, da década de 1960, que demonstram claramente a influência do Tropicalismo e da Pop Art, traz os objetos e as pinturas pertencentes à produção inicial de Varela, combinados com versões revisitadas de obras já não mais existentes, como *Souvenir de Rio 2* (il. pp. 6-7) e duas pinturas quebra-cabeça (ils. pp. 10, 12-13). A segunda parte da mostra é dedicada à pesquisa conceitual da realidade e à sua representação, declinada através de uma série de pinturas, fotos e vídeos desde os anos setenta até os anos oitenta (ils. pp. 64-69, 84-87). Obras que giram ao redor da imagem da artista como mulher (ils. pp. 71-75), e também os 'cangaceiros' (ils. pp. 93-99) são representados nesta retrospectiva. Enfim, *Cybèle Varela: Tropicalismo Remixed* revela pela primeira vez as mais recentes séries de Varela, *Unknown* (ils. 100-105), que abordam questões de identidade, memória e migração.

1 A raiz deste conceito remonta ao *Manifesto Antropófago* de Oswald de Andrade (1928).
2 Em 2015, a obra de Varela obteve referência na inovadora exposição *The World Goes Pop*, organizada pela Tate Modern em Londres. Ver Giulia Lamoni, "Unfolding the 'Present': Some Notes on Brazilian 'Pop'", in Jessica Morgan e Flavia Frigeri [eds.], *The World Goes Pop*, cat. expo., Tate Modern, Londres, 2015, pp. 70-71.
3 Ver Camille Morineau (ed.), *elles@centrepompidou, artistes femmes dans la collection du Musée national d'art moderne*, cat. expo., Centre Pompidou, Paris, 2009, p. 222.

Cybèle Varela with one of her puzzle-works in the late 1960s

Cybèle Varela mit einem ihrer Puzzle-Arbeiten, Ende der 1960er Jahre

Cybèle Varela com uma de suas obras-puzzle no final dos anos 1960

Giulia Lamoni

Baralhando as cartas e multiplicando as imagens. Algumas notas acerca da obra de Cybèle Varela

Criado por Cybèle Varela em 1967, *Telefone Real* é um objeto de madeira em forma de telefone (il. p. 21). Modesto e inofensivo, quase um jogo para crianças, o telefone pintado em cores berrantes esconde contudo um núcleo surpreendente. Ao levantar o fone, o público abre inadvertidamente seu sistema de discagem redondo, revelando assim um interior de espelhos que multiplicam a imagem de uma carta de baralho ao fundo: um rei de ouros. Que este objeto, aparentemente banal e pouco sofisticado, possa constituir um ponto de partida particularmente desafiante para uma exploração do itinerário artístico de Cybèle Varela – das suas migrações geográficas, culturais e formais entre a escultura, fotografia, vídeo e, sobretudo, pintura – poderá parecer contraditório. Contudo, *Telefone Real* – cujas coordenadas estéticas se inscrevem nos desdobramentos do "realismo crítico" brasileiro do final dos anos sessenta, com o seu enfoque na transformação da pintura em objeto e da contemplação em participação ativa do espectador[1] – materializa um conjunto de opções formais e conceituais que marca, embora de modo diferente, o trabalho da artista ao longo de todo seu percurso.

Se 1967, ano de criação desta peça, é um momento significativo para Cybèle Varela – o Museu de Arte Contemporânea de São Paulo atribui-lhe o importante prêmio da exposição "Jovem Arte Contemporânea" destinado aos artistas com menos de 35 anos – é também o ano em que um conjunto de obras de arte *pop* norte-americana é exposto no Brasil, na Bienal de São Paulo, impulsionando um debate muito vivo no âmbito da crítica de arte local. Assim, por um lado, a seleção de artistas brasileiros é considerada demasiadamente ampla e tecnicamente medíocre. Por outro, é defendida pela sua juventude feroz e diversa, por sua tentativa de envolver o espectador, tornando-o participante, mesmo quando o custo disso é a destruição das próprias obras[2]. Ao oposto, a representação *pop* dos Estados Unidos é elogiada como muito sofisticada e bem montada. Neste mesmo evento, a polícia obriga a retirar da exposição o objeto em forma de caixa de Cybèle Varela, *O Presente* (1967, il. p. 22)[3], por razões políticas.

O Presente, tal como *Telefone Real*, afirma antes de tudo o compromisso da artista com um envolvimento mais alargado do espectador. Ao mesmo tempo, a resistência perante o regime militar implantado no país desde 1964 materializa-se através da ironia e da caricatura, tal como no trabalho de outros artistas de sua geração. O *Presente* alude tanto ao presente como dom – a caixa parece de fato um presente embrulhado – quanto ao tempo presente, marcado por uma opressão política destinada a agravar-se. Assim, ao abrir a caixa, o participante descobre a caricatura de um militar e as palavras de um hino de tom nacionalista. De forma semelhante, o título *Telefone Real* indica ao mesmo tempo a figura "real", de poder, que se esconde no telefone – o rei de ouros – e a forma com que este poder tentava dominar a realidade brasileira daqueles anos. A coexistência de preocupações formais, que envolvem o questionamento da própria obra de arte e de sua materialidade, e de uma atenção para o mundo social e político configura-se assim, desde meados dos anos sessenta, como umas das linhas mestras que perpassam a obra da artista. Em 1970, por ocasião de sua exposição individual na galeria Copacabana Palace no Rio de Janeiro, a própria artista sugeria esta dupla orientação: "Procuro a abertura de novos espaços, talvez com um sentido de liberdade total. Também me interessa muito o tempo em relação à forma"[4].

Na produção "tropicalista" da artista, do final dos anos sessenta e início dos anos setenta[5] – onde se insere a obra *Telefone Real* – concentrada na exploração do ambiente urbano e suburbano e do gosto e da cultura popular, o crítico Frederico Morais lia, em 1968, uma "[...] nostalgia de um Brasil telúrico, rural, tropical, nostalgia daqueles que morando nos subúrbios vivem ainda sentimentalmente no campo e no passado."[6]

Se este enfoque cria uma linha de diálogo particularmente forte com artistas cujo trabalho explora os meandros da cidade, como o carioca Rubens Gerchman (1942-2008), o interesse nas relações entre movimento e forma – talvez algum resquício de um legado neoconcreto apropriado e antropofagicamente transformado – e entre figuração e abstração geométrica, aproxima em certa medida sua prática àquela do artista da mesma geração, e amigo, Raymundo Colares (1944-1986). Assim, em pinturas sobre madeira como *Cinco moças passeando* (1967, il. p. 30) ou *Cenas de rua* (1968; il. pp. 58-59), a representação do ambiente urbano é marcada por linhas que se repetem – faixas de pedestres ou linhas abstratas – que ao mesmo tempo constroem o espaço e desvendam a ilusão da representação pictórica. Em peças de chão em forma de puzzle, como *Um passeio feliz* (1970; il. p. 23), o próprio espectador, ao movimentar os fragmentos que compõem a imagem, participa da criação e da destruição de uma composição que nunca se deixa prender numa lógica mimética.

Esta ambiguidade, que caracteriza a passagem de Cybèle Varela pelo "realismo crítico" brasileiro – que devora linguagens vernáculas e internacionais para desenvolver uma reflexão crítica sobre "o contexto sócio-politico-cultural" brasileiro[7] – é articulada numa linguagem pictórica calculadamente simplificada, em aparência pouco refinada, que utiliza materiais industriais e através da qual a artista assume ironicamente o papel de "*popista* do subdesenvolvimento"[8], para utilizar uma

Cybèle Varela with one of her box-form works in the mid-1960s

Cybèle Varela mit einem ihrer Werke in Box-Form, Mitte der 1960er Jahre

Cybèle Varela com um de seus trabalhos em formato de caixa, em meados da década de 1960

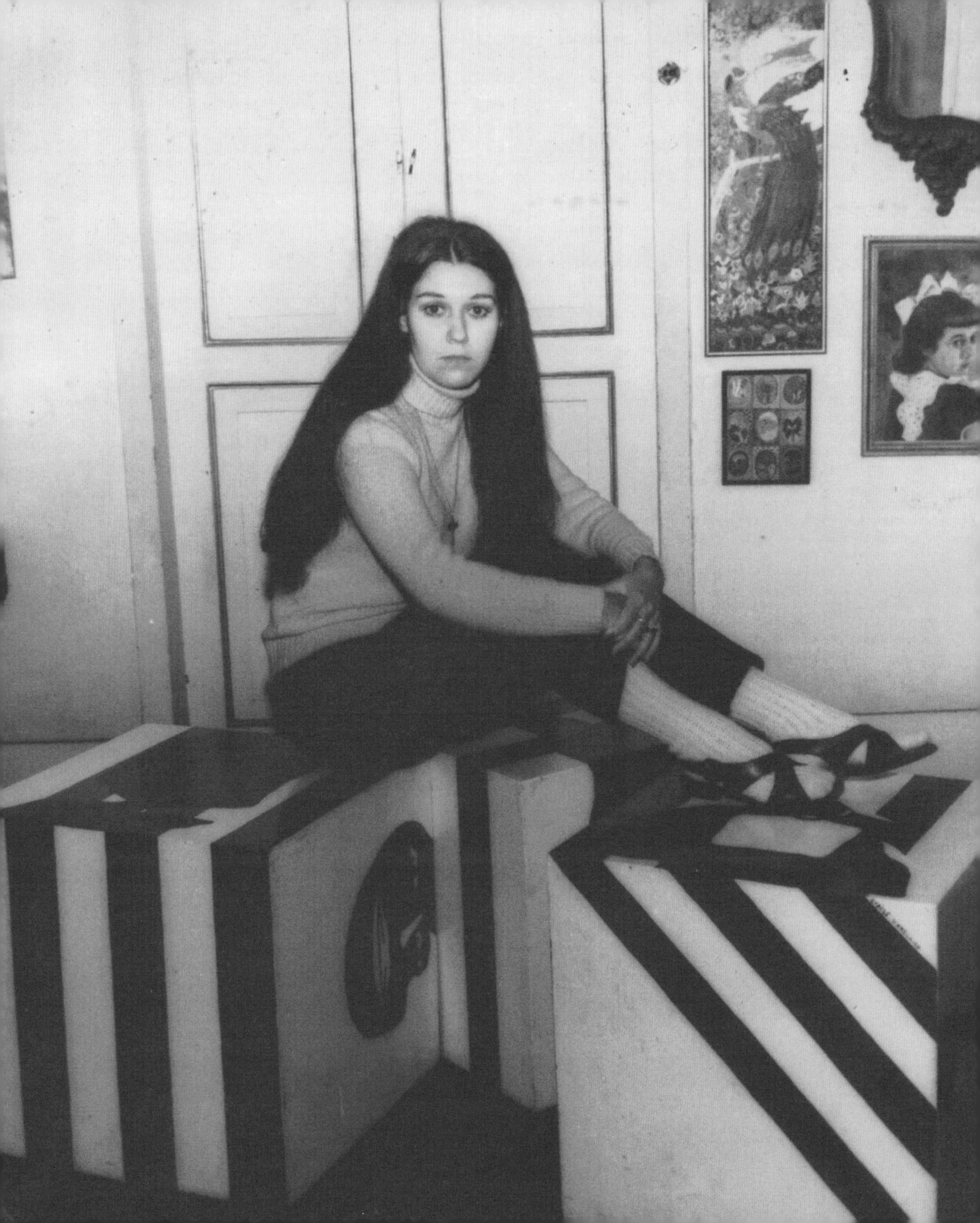

famosa fórmula de Mário Pedrosa. Contudo, tanto a utilização de espelhos e a atenção aos desdobramentos da imagem e da luz em *Telefone Real* quanto a repetição da figura e das linhas nas paisagens urbanas e suburbanas dos anos sessenta, prefiguram uma investigação acerca dos efeitos da luz no espaço e dos poderes da representação, que irá desabrochar nos anos setenta.

Neste sentido, parece significativo evocar o diálogo com o artista argentino Julio Le Parc (n. 1928) em Paris, para onde Cybèle Varela viaja em 1968-1969 graças a uma bolsa do governo francês. Ao chegar à capital francesa no outono de 1968 – à altura da dissolução do Groupe de Recherche d'Art Visuel do qual Le Parc é membro ativo – a artista descobre uma cidade em plena efervescência. O encontro com as experiências cinéticas do argentino e com o ambiente artístico parisiense mais alargado parece resultar, em um primeiro momento, em uma radicalização da sua pesquisa acerca da relação forma/movimento e do envolvimento do espectador através do recurso à brincadeira. Assim, ao expor na Galerie Debret em Paris em 1972, depois de ter voltado à cidade graças a uma segunda bolsa de estudos, a artista cria um ambiente lúdico habitado por objetos-jogos manipuláveis, marcados por inscrições ora poéticas, ora irônicas, que não deixa de lembrar, em alguns de seus aspectos, as "salas de jogo" criadas pelo próprio G.R.A.V. a partir de 1963. Existe contudo, nesta proposta de Cybèle Varela, um deslizamento do plano perceptivo para o plano poético que, mais uma vez, remete a um processo de apropriação, digestão e transformação dos impulsos que vêm de um conjunto de novos encontros e situações. Ironicamente, uma obra em pão é servida e comida durante a inauguração: é a própria palavra "*manger*" (comer) que é transformada em objeto comestível, de compartilhamento coletivo (il. p. 35).

Mas a estadia em Paris, que se prolonga e acaba por resultar em um processo migratório de longa duração, alimenta igualmente o compromisso da artista com a luz e a sombra e aprofunda seu questionamento da ilusão dentro da própria representação pictórica que obras anteriores já sugeriam. É a própria vivência do seu afastamento do Brasil a impulsionar a figuração de espaços interiores, provavelmente domésticos, em que paisagens brasileiras se tornam presenças ambíguas, irreais como uma representação de cartaz. Assim, em pinturas como *O tucano* e *Pantanal* (ambos de 1973; ils. p. 25), a projeção da sombra começa a funcionar como elemento de construção e revelação espacial. Nesta medida, embora a artista tenha participado, em meados dos anos setenta, de eventos coletivos importantes, em Paris, como o Salon de Mai e o Salon Comparaisons, e em exposições de grupo com, entre outros, artistas associados à figuração narrativa como Jacques Monory (n. 1924) e Antonio Recalcati (n. 1938), seu percurso dentro do panorama dos realismos nos anos setenta é fortemente singular e focado, como observa Pierre Restany em 1975, em um "método linguístico"[9] – "O real de Cybèle Varela existe só ao nível da linguagem,"[10] afirma o crítico. De fato, a série de trabalhos intitulados *Image* (ils. pp. 36-37, 64-66), entre o final dos anos setenta e o inicio dos oitenta, revela um aprofundamento desta indagação linguística não só no âmbito da pintura mas também do vídeo e da fotografia. Como se constrói o espaço de uma imagem? Onde se situa a fronteira entre figuração e abstração geométrica? A limitação do campo de pesquisa – a representação de uma paisagem em um espaço interior atravessado pela luz, uma árvore e o céu com suas nuvens, os bancos vermelhos dos jardins do Museu Imperial de Petrópolis – permite à artista ensaiar possíveis respostas a estas e a outras perguntas.

Embora esta pesquisa ganhe espaço no trabalho de Cybèle Varela nos anos oitenta e noventa, a linha política de *Telefone Real* continua a atravessar sua produção, ora de forma sutil ora, pelo contrário, mais abertamente. O olhar fortemente irônico da artista registra, no Brasil do final dos anos sessenta, claros sinais de mudança nas relações de gênero e marcos de emancipação feminina e libertação do corpo – por exemplo na encenação de um encontro entre freiras e jovens vestindo minissaias em *De tudo aquilo que poderia ter sido e que não foi* (1967; il. pp. 60-61). Paralelamente, a atribuição de poder às figuras femininas em obras mais recentes, desde a artista da série *The Artist* (1999, ils. pp. 71-75) até à guerreira ecologista, quase uma heroína de quadrinhos, em trabalhos como *O que é verdade é verdade* (2010, il. p. 81) e *Another Wonderful Summer* (2013, ils, p. 26), responde a desafios contemporâneos de igualdade e justiça social de um ponto de vista tanto político como simbólico. Contudo, talvez seja em seu compromisso com a cultura popular brasileira e com a própria história política, social e cultural da América Latina – marcada por um passado colonial cujos desdobramentos ainda afetam o presente – que vai se esboçando uma linha de continuidade mais profunda. Na série de pinturas recentes intitulada *Unknown* (2015-2016, ils. pp. 100-105) são precisamente estas as histórias que se materializam e cruzam através de retratos de objetos e personagens anônimo. De alguma forma, este posicionamento, que "[...] constata mas que também contesta dialeticamente"[11] os mitos da cultura popular em todas suas formas – desde os cangaceiros até os rosários coloridos – nunca deixou de ser "tropicalista", mesmo quando deixou de sê-lo.

1 Ver especialmente o catálogo da exposição *Nova Objetividade Brasileira*, Museu de Arte Moderna do Rio de Janeiro, abril de 1967.

2 Ver especialmente Mário Schemberg, "A representação brasileira na IX Bienal de São Paulo", *Correio da Manhã*, 4º Caderno, Rio de Janeiro, 17 de setembro de 1967, p. 3 e Mário Pedrosa, "Bienal e participação... do povo", *Correio da Manhã*, 4º Caderno, Rio de Janeiro, 8 de outubro de 1967, p. 1. Para uma discussão mais ampla ver: Giulia Lamoni, "Unfolding the 'Present': Some Notes on Brazilian 'Pop'", in Jessica Morgan, Flavia Frigeri (eds.), *The World Goes Pop*, cat. expo., Tate Modern, Londres, 2015, pp. 59-71.

3 A obra foi retirada antes mesmo da abertura ao público da Bienal. Posteriormente, a obra foi destruída pela própria artista, existindo contudo um registro fotográfico.

4 Antônio Bento, "Espaço com ritmo", *Última Hora*, Rio de Janeiro, 29 de abril, 1970.

5 Para uma exploração do contexto mais amplo em que esta prática se inscreve ver: Paulo Sérgio Duarte, *Anos 60, Transformações da arte no Brasil*, Rio de Janeiro, 1998; Daisy Peccinini, *Figurações, Brasil anos 60*, São Paulo, 1999; Paulo Reis, *Arte de vanguarda no Brasil, os anos 60*, Rio de Janeiro, 2006.

6 Frederico Morais in "Cybèle Varela, Pintura", Folha de sala da exposição da artista na galeria Goeldi, Rio de Janeiro, junho e julho de 1968.

7 Adoto aqui a leitura de Frederico Morais, notadamente sua utilização da metáfora antropofágica, articulada em vários escritos, entre eles o texto aqui citado "Cybèle Varela, Pintura", Folha de sala da exposição da artista na galeria Goeldi, Rio de Janeiro, junho e julho de 1968.

8 Mário Pedrosa, "Do Pop americano ao sertanejo Dias", *Correio da Manhã*, 4º Caderno, Rio de Janeiro, 29 de outubro de 1967, p. 1.

9 "... sa méthode linguistique." Pierre Restany, "Le réel au niveau du langage", *Cybèle Varela, Pinturas*, cat. expo, Galeria Bonino, Rio de Janeiro, 1975, não paginado. Trad. do autor.

10 "Le réel de Cybèle Varela n'existe qu'au niveau du langage." Trad. do autor. Ibidem.

11 Frederico Morais in "Cybèle Varela, Pintura", Folha de sala da exposição da artista na galeria Goeldi, Rio de Janeiro, junho e julho de 1968.

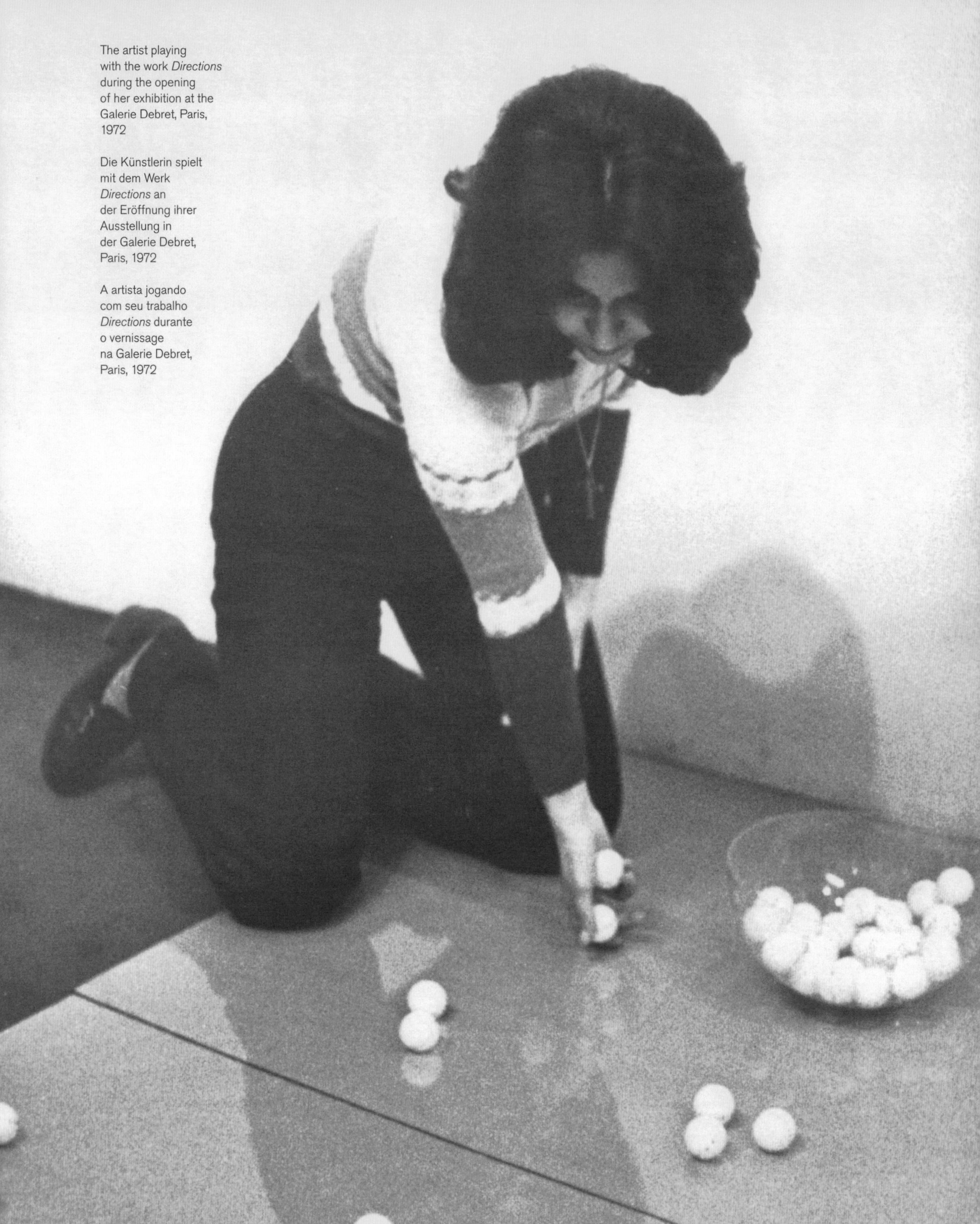

The artist playing
with the work *Directions*
during the opening
of her exhibition at the
Galerie Debret, Paris,
1972

Die Künstlerin spielt
mit dem Werk
Directions an
der Eröffnung ihrer
Ausstellung in
der Galerie Debret,
Paris, 1972

A artista jogando
com seu trabalho
Directions durante
o vernissage
na Galerie Debret,
Paris, 1972

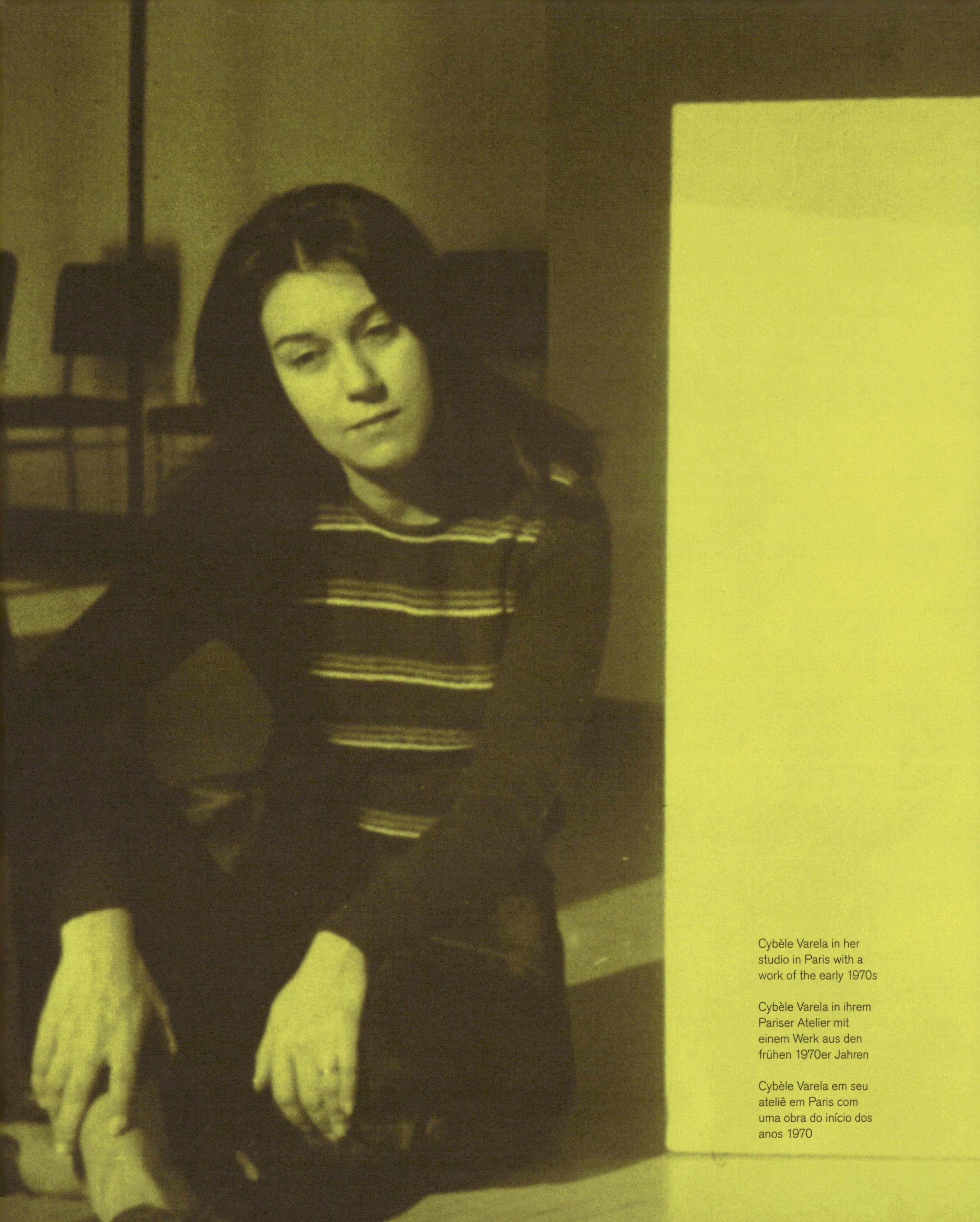

Cybèle Varela in her studio in Paris with a work of the early 1970s

Cybèle Varela in ihrem Pariser Atelier mit einem Werk aus den frühen 1970er Jahren

Cybèle Varela em seu ateliê em Paris com uma obra do início dos anos 1970

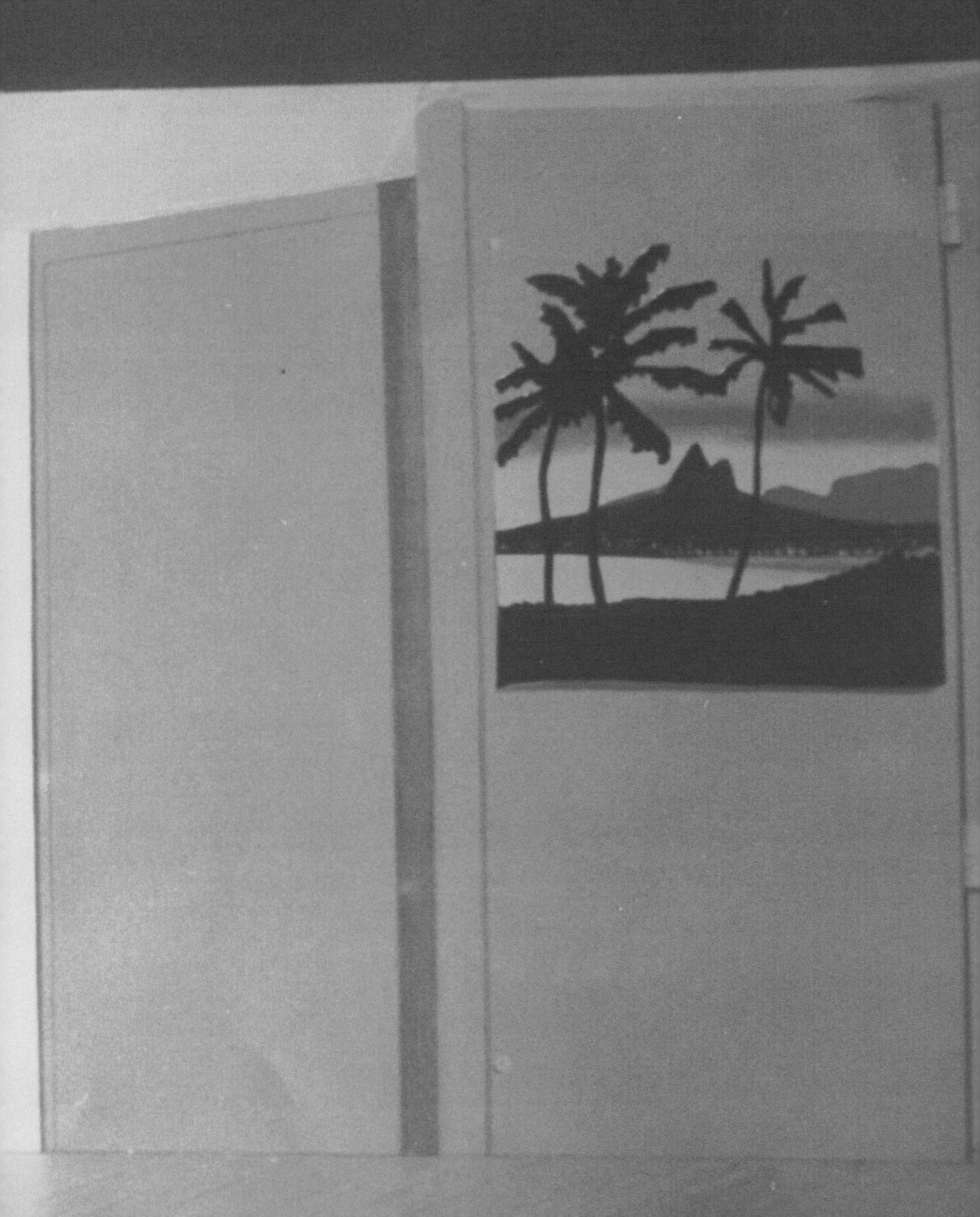

Valentina Locatelli

Uma conversa com Cybèle Varela

VL Cybèle, você deixou Petrópolis pela primeira vez em 1968 e desde então viveu quase continuamente na Europa. Recentemente, mudou-se de Roma para Madri e, antes de Roma, passou um longo tempo entre Genebra e Paris. De que forma cada um desses lugares tem marcado sua obra?
CV: Todos esses lugares, com suas grandes diferenças culturais e de mentalidade, deixaram algum rastro em mim e no meu trabalho. No Brasil, quando era criança, literalmente eu respirava as cores da paisagem local. Lembro-me de ter tido uma revelação, certo dia, quando passeava pelo jardim de meus avós. Via as várias cores da terra, as várias camadas de cor e comecei a coletar amostras. O azul intenso do céu, o verde luxuriante das árvores, tudo isso teve um forte impacto na garotinha que era então. A diversidade das pessoas comuns ao andar nas ruas é também uma das mais fortes lembranças de minha infância. "Folclore brasileiro" seja provavelmente a maneira certa para expressar aquilo que deixava marcas em mim, naquele momento.
Mais tarde, já em Paris, fiquei especialmente interessada pela atmosfera cultural da cidade. As lembranças do Brasil começavam a ser filtradas pelas impressões dadas pela capital francesa e, consequentemente, me vi envolvida numa profunda reflexão sobre a arte enquanto expressão cultural. Meu trabalho se tornou um pouco mais auto-reflexivo.
Quando mudei para Genebra, em 1978, o cenário natural da cidade, com o lago, orientou novamente minha atenção para a natureza. Com base em uma foto de uma árvore contraposta ao azul do céu, tirada em Paris, trabalhei na ideia de desenvolver e mudar formas e formatos e na divisão de espaço e imagens. Por mais estranho que possa parecer, na Suíça encontrei novamente aqueles céus límpidos que me lembravam do Brasil (ils. pp. 68-69).
Por outro lado, minha experiência em Roma, algo como quarenta anos depois, foi bem diferente. Marcou o início de um novo diálogo com os antigos mestres, especialmente os renascentistas. Realmente, acredito que a Itália tenha me ajudado a desenvolver certa atenção para os detalhes, mas o peso de seu passado histórico é, às vezes, intenso demais e dificulta a pesquisa contemporânea. Acabei de chegar a Madri, portanto ainda não sei de que forma este lugar terá impacto na minha prática artística, mas, até mesmo antes de saber que teria morado aqui, pintei uma série com animais pré-históricos (ils. p. 76) inspirada na tela de Francisco de Goya, *El quitasol* (1777, Museo del Prado, Madri). De certa forma, é como se eu tivesse sido atraída aqui.

VL: Poderia nos contar como foram os inícios de sua carreira no Brasil? Quais foram os artistas brasileiros que, então, mais admirava e que lhe serviram de inspiração?
CV: Comecei a pintar quando tinha sete, oito anos, copiando trabalhos de Jean-Honoré Fragonard e dos Impressionistas franceses. Mas o início oficial de minha carreira, a meu ver, coincide com a atribuição de meu primeiro prêmio, aos 16 anos, uma "Menção Honrosa" concedida pela Associação dos Artistas Brasileiros, no Museu Nacional de Belas Artes (MNBA) do Rio de Janeiro.
Na época, minha maior fonte de inspiração era a obra de um grande pintor, João Batista da Costa (1865-1926) que trabalhou em minha cidade natal, Petrópolis. Ele pintava maravilhosas paisagens utilizando as mesmas cores da terra que haviam me impressionado quando criança. Logo depois, comecei a me interessar pela Pop Art norte-americana. Os anos sessenta, no Brasil, apesar da situação política complexa, foram um momento excelente para a criatividade. Havia muita energia ao redor dos debates de ideias. Acredito que a atmosfera peculiar daquele período tenha me inspirado grandemente. Nós éramos um grupo de artistas, trabalhávamos todos no Rio de Janeiro e servíamo-nos da mesma linguagem. Se tiver que nomear dois entre muitos, posso dizer que estava muito próxima de Rubens Gerchman (1942-2008), com quem compartilhava a predileção pelos tópicos populares, como jogadores de futebol e pessoas nas ruas, e também Raymundo Colares (1944-1986), cujo trabalho atraia-me por seu dinamismo, no ponto de interseção entre Pop Art e Futurismo.

VL: Àquela época, teve que enfrentar, como vários colegas, restrições às suas liberdades civis, incluindo a liberdade de expressão. Na Bienal de São Paulo de 1967, você expôs a obra *O Presente* (il. p. 22), uma caixa de madeira pintada que, quando aberta, exibia ao público uma irreverente charge de um oficial militar brasileiro. No dia da inauguração, antes da abertura, *O Presente* foi retirada, por ser considerada uma obra contra o Governo. Este evento influenciou sua abordagem sucessiva às questões políticas e sociais?
CV: Em primeiro lugar, acredito que minha abordagem a essas questões não era particularmente política ou crítica. O ponto central, para mim, era sempre trabalhar em coisas que achava interessantes, especialmente em imagens que representavam o povo brasileiro. Naqueles anos, até a imagem do presidente era interessante, para mim, simplesmente porque era uma imagem relativa ao povo. Por exemplo, era fascinada pelas pessoas que atravessavam a rua nas faixas de pedestres, pelas pessoas que paravam nos sinais de trânsito e que se moviam tão logo o sinal abria (il. pp. 52-53). O elemento popular e urbano, portanto, era central na minha prática, bem como a reflexão sobre a anonimidade desses encontros fortuitos e passageiros entre as pessoas. Trabalhar sobre estes temas me permitiu expressar minha crítica contra a pobreza e a

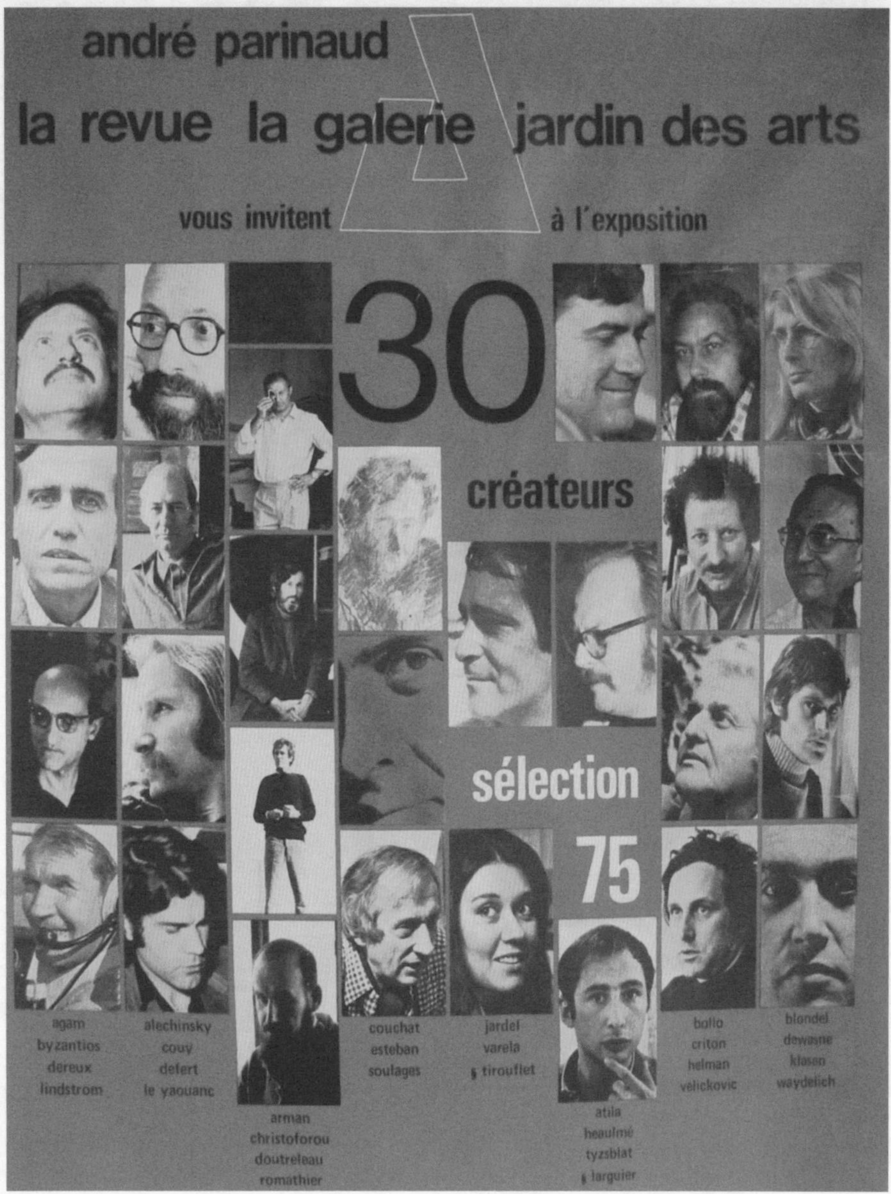

Poster of the travelling exhibition *30 Créateurs – Sélection 75*, France, 1975

Plakat der Wanderausstellung *30 Créateurs – Sélection 75*, Frankreich, 1975

Cartaz da exposição itinerante *30 Créateurs – Sélection 75*, França, 1975

miséria que afligem o homem da rua. O papel, ou os papéis, da mulher na sociedade e o impacto das crenças religiosas (e suas obsessões) são também algo que estava interessada em analisar, na minha obra, como fiz, por exemplo, na pintura *De tudo aquilo que poderia ter sido e que não foi* (1967, il. pp. 60-61).

VL: Antes, você citou rapidamente a inspiração que lhe deu a Pop Art americana. De fato, você é considerada um dos maiores representantes da Pop Art brasileira durante a década de 1960. As obras que realizou nesse período refletem sobre a sociedade brasileira e especialmente sobre questões de gênero e de subjetividade feminina. Qual você acha que seja o elemento intrinsecamente característico que diferencia a Pop Art brasileira daquela norte-americana?

CV: Fundamentalmente, Brasil e Estados Unidos são países diferentes. No Brasil, modificamos este movimento artístico ocidental, tornando-o completamente nosso, primeiro porque temos uma mentalidade diferente da dos norte-americanos, e segundo porque misturamos seus elementos com aquele que denominamos movimento Tropicalista. Os expoentes da Pop Art americana eram mais pragmáticos, enquanto que os brasileiros eram, de certa forma, mais livres. A influência do Tropicalismo, com suas cores, tornou a Pop Art brasileira mais "suave" daquela americana. De certa maneira, todavia, eu sempre preferi a Pop Art inglesa à americana. Acho-a mais elaborada, mais irônica, com um senso crítico de paródia no qual encontro inspiração.

VL: Sua primeira chegada a Paris foi em 1968, graças a uma bolsa de estudos concedida pelo Governo francês. Aqueles, foram os dias dos protestos e revoltas estudantis. Fale-nos sobre as primeiras e fortes impressões daquele ano.
CV: Lembro muito bem que, quando cheguei à École des Beaux-Arts em Paris, encontrei um jovem artista que me perguntou: "Por que veio a Paris? Não sobrou nada, destruímos tudo!". Com efeito, vivia-se um momento vazio, as pessoas estavam chocadas. Por esta razão, me candidatei para uma segunda bolsa de estudos, de modo a retornar a Paris quando as coisas tivessem se acalmado, porque tinha a sensação que havia perdido a chance de viver experiências e contatos, da primeira vez. Retornei em Paris em 1971 e finalmente comecei a sentir e compreender melhor a alma francesa. Durante minha segunda permanência em Paris, além dos estudos na École du Louvre, estudei também Antropologia Social na École Pratique des Hautes Etudes (EPHE-Sorbonne) sob a orientação de André Varagnac. Foi, para mim, uma experiência muito importante. Completou minha formação, ampliando minha visão do mundo. E, claro, passei muito tempo em Paris visitando museus e exposições de arte.

VL: Na França, você conheceu tanto a Arte Conceitual quanto a denominada Figuração Narrativa francesa. Acredito que, de certa maneira, sua primeira mostra em Paris foi uma reação a esses movimentos artísticos, interpretados desde o ponto de vista de uma artista brasileira …
CV : Minha primeira exposição em Paris foi em 1972, na Galerie Debret. Trouxera todas as peças do Rio. Foi um exercício próximo à Arte Conceitual, mas, nele, a participação do público era essencial. Por alguns anos, no Brasil, pesquisara a respeito dos aspectos lúdicos da interatividade. Para essa mostra, realizara também uma peça feita de pão, cujo título era *Manger*, que, em português , significa "comer" (il. p. 35). Era uma escultura efêmera que oferecia aos visitantes durante o vernissage, como uma espécie

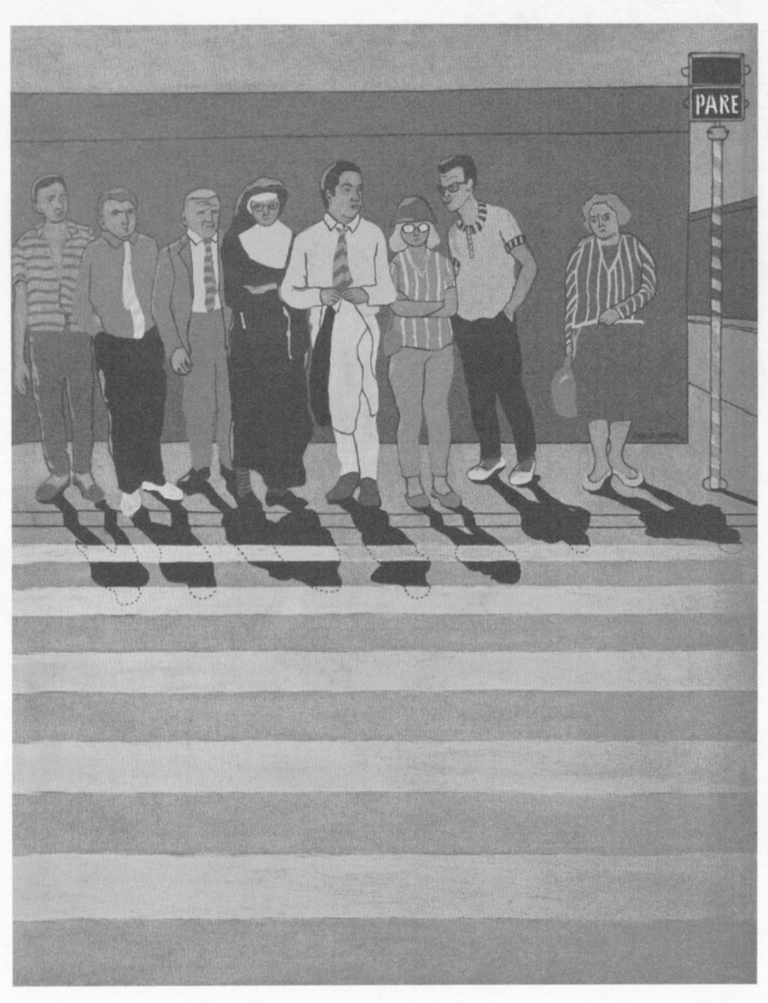
PARE

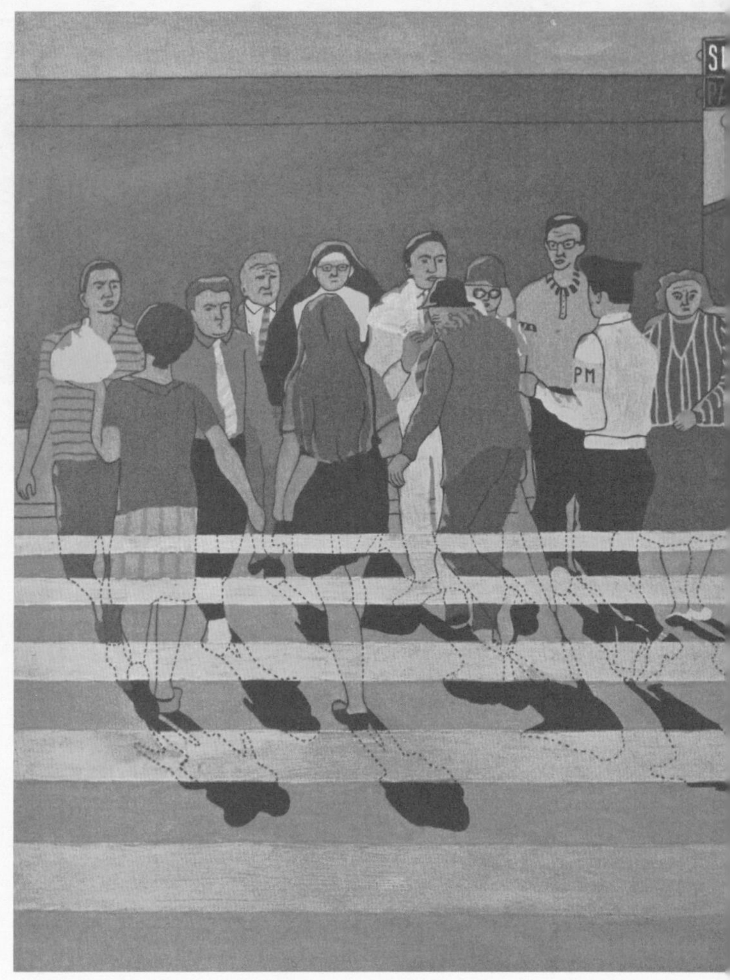
PM

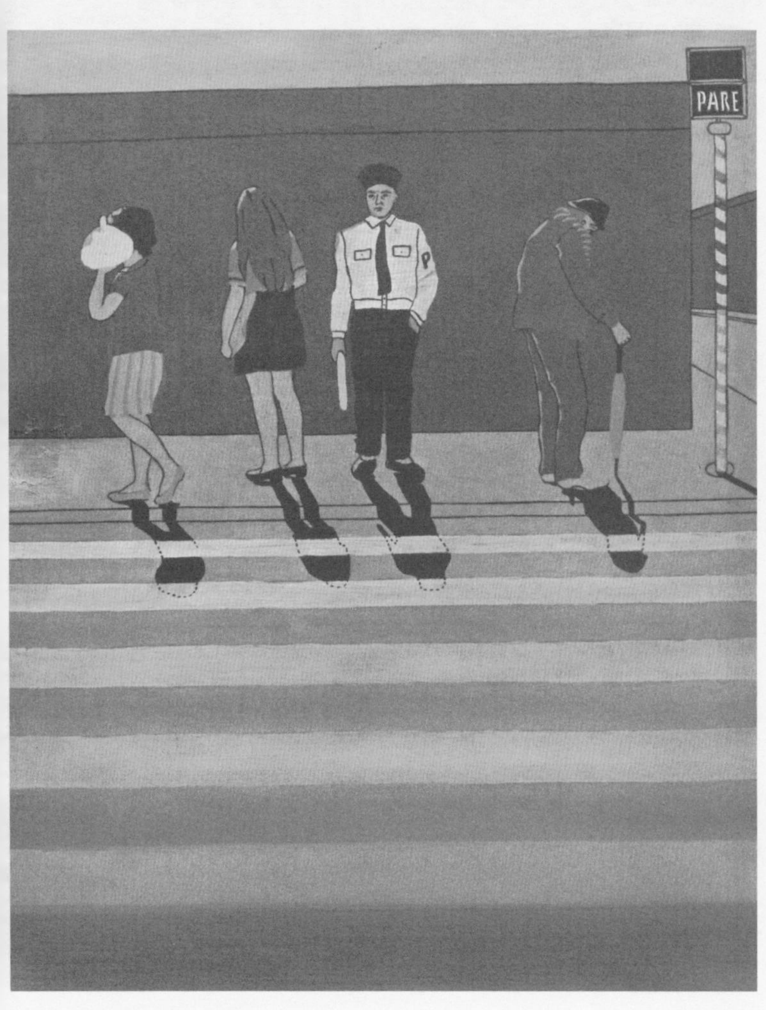

Pedestres
1967

de performance: tudo se transformava e estava destinado, no final, a desaparecer, como acontece na própria vida. Naquela época, outros artistas brasileiros experimentavam algo relativo aos aspectos interativos da arte, como Lygia Clark (1920-1988), a quem encontrei alguns anos mais tarde em Paris.

VL: Durante a década de 1970, sua obra, embora permanecendo figurativa, tornou-se mais abstrata e investigou a interação entre luz e sombra. O que procurava transmitir com sua série *Image* (ils. pp. 64-66)
CV: A abstração, para mim, não existe. Trata-se sempre de imagens. Na verdade, deveria dar a todos meus trabalhos o título *Image*, imagem, porque para mim tudo é uma imagem. Minha série *Image* estava estruturada ao redor da própria natureza da pintura em si. Em Paris, costumava procurar identificar a maneira com que a luz do sol, filtrando através das persianas movidas pelo vento, entrava no meu apartamento e criava reflexos nas paredes cor de laranja. Como percebeu muito bem Pierre Restany, a série sobre luz solar era, de fato, uma reflexão sobre a ambiguidade do real.

VL: A natureza e as cores brilhantes da flora brasileira são claramente uma das linhas-mestras de sua obra. Seu interesse tão profundo pelos temas naturais encerra uma preocupação com o meio-ambiente?
CV: A natureza é um elemento central de minha vida e meu trabalho. Sem ela, sentir-me-ia incompleta. Nunca pensei em mim mesma como uma militante, mas aquilo que está acontecendo, hoje, em relação à destruição global da biodiversidade, torna-me terrivelmente triste e preocupada com o futuro da vida neste planeta.

VL: Obras como *Image* (ils. pp. 36-37, 68-69) e *The Artist 1* e *2* (ils. pp. 71-74) revelam o impacto do Surrealismo na sua prática artística e, mais especificamente, de René Magritte e Salvador Dalí. Além disso, revelam sua habilidade a imaginar, simultaneamente, mundos diferentes. Este aspecto "surreal" de sua obra é, de fato, um instrumento para alcançar uma dimensão mais mística ou espiritual?
CV: A filosofia indiana e a cultura espiritual oriental sempre me interessaram muito. Além disso, quando era muito jovem, tinha verdadeiro fascínio por outros planetas e galáxias, que desenvolvi em minha série *Horizontes*, dos anos setenta, e retornou recentemente na mostra *Espaços Simultâneos*, apresentada em 2013-2014 no MAC de Niterói (ils. p. 34). Costumava ler livros sobre astronomia e sobre o universo. Às vezes, sentia-me alheia a este planeta, como se não lhe pertencesse. A ambiguidade da realidade fascina-me, a ambiguidade daquilo que é e daquilo que não é. As energias que são trocadas em uma comunicação entre seres humanos, como está acontecendo agora, entre você e eu, é algo que sempre despertou minha atenção.

VL: Sua obra é inspirada tanto na cultura popular e nas questões sociais brasileiras quanto europeias, especialmente quando aborda questões de identidade e gênero. Sua aproximação à crítica social, todavia, nunca é severa, mas sempre poética. Acredito que a sua habilidade em condensar até as realidades mais duras em formas e cores seja uma qualidade intrinsecamente brasileira...
CV: Como disse antes, o fato de lidar com imagens para desvendar sua ambiguidade é parte da minha personalidade artística. É uma abordagem muito pessoal, com meu trabalho eu investigo a mim mesma e a minha alma. Estou afastada daquilo que faço, sou um observador externo das realidades, e aquilo que mostro no meu trabalho nunca é uma reflexão direta, mas sempre uma observação indireta.

VL: Mesmo depois ter se mudado para a Europa e durante as décadas sucessivas de sua carreira, até hoje, sua obra tem sido caracterizada por uma dedicação e atenção à cor, ao movimento e ao ornamento. Qual é a raiz de seu interesse para o elemento decorativo na arte?
CV: Eu amo tudo quanto seja popular e folclórico. Amo os mercados de rua, as pessoas fazendo compras de várias coisas, como flores, bonecas (a propósito, eu tenho uma coleção de bonecas!) ou louças antigas. Quando vivia em Roma, por exemplo, eu tinha uma atração especial pelas chamadas "bancarelle" (bancas dos ambulantes, nas ruas ou nos mercados). Acho que a origem de minha atenção para os elementos ornamentais na minha arte esteja ligada a este aspecto de minha personalidade.

VL: Quando falávamos a respeito do título a ser dado à sua exposição retrospectiva, você sugeriu que fizéssemos uma referência à música, já que ritmo e som são aspectos centrais de sua produção artística. *Tropicalismo Remixed* acolhe sua sugestão e é uma referência jocosa aos seus inícios, no meio dos artistas do grupo Tropicalismo no Rio de Janeiro, mas também à sua habilidade de reinventar e 'remixar' todos os ingredientes que caracterizam sua obra e têm em seu próprio estilo seu ponto de culminância. Como inclui a música em seu processo criativo?
CV: A música é um elemento central de minha prática artística. No Brasil, estudei canto lírico e sempre trabalhava ouvindo música clássica. Ainda hoje, ouço e canto Richard Wagner quando estou no meu ateliê. Além disso, toco violão e, no passado, quando era uma estudante de arte em Paris, lembro que encontrava amiúde outros artistas e com eles tocávamos músicas populares, incluindo a bossa-nova. Todavia, quando trabalho, só ouço música clássica.
VL: Embora sua fama esteja mais ligada à pintura, também a fotografia e os vídeos assumiram um papel cada vez mais relevante na sua obra, por estarem naturalmente ligados às questões da luz e do movimento. Como integra esses meios e abordagens diferentes?
CV: Geralmente, quando surge uma ideia para um projeto, desenvolvo-a por diversos anos. Por exemplo, trabalhei na minha série dedicada aos cangaceiros (ils. pp. 93-99) por cerca de quatro anos. Comecei trabalhando com fotos e vídeo na década de 1970, como uma maneira de complementar meu trabalho com pintura. Isso me permitiu descobrir novos aspectos que não tinha levado em conta ao dedicar-me somente à pintura. Não sou fotógrafa profissional no sentido estreito da palavra. Utilizo esta forma de expressão como veículo rumo a novas descobertas. Todas minhas fotos passam por um processo de reelaboração intenso; são formadas por camadas de elementos diferentes. Não uso a fotografia para mostrar algo que vejo, mas como um instrumento capaz de descobrir a poesia no mundo. Com o vídeo, por outro lado, levei adiante, em outro nível, minha pesquisa sobre movimento, que comecei nos anos sessenta com meus quebra-cabeças e trabalhos em formato de caixa.

VL: Agora, estamos juntas em sua nova casa e novo ateliê, literalmente rodeadas por grande parte do trabalho de toda sua vida. Muitas das fases mais relevantes de sua biografia artística são visualizadas e reunidas nesse espaço impressionante. Quando olha atrás, para mais de 50 anos de realizações artísticas, quais acredita que tenham sido os marcos mais importantes de sua carreira, até agora?
CV: Não é uma pergunta cuja resposta seja fácil. Penso que cada momento de minha vida foi importante e deixou uma marca visível no meu trabalho. Cada um de meus projetos e pesquisas teve impacto na minha obra. Todos foram marcos, e marcos importantes, ao longo de minha caminhada.

VL: Olhando para o futuro, quais são as questões que despertam sua atenção, hoje? Está trabalhando em novos projetos?
CV: Ainda não posso pensar no próximo projeto, já que continuo trabalhando na série *Unknown* (ils. pp. 100-105). Como disse, geralmente levo adiante uma ideia por quatro a cinco anos. Os tópicos da migração e da mudança são o coração desta série de pinturas de pessoas desconhecidas, "unknown", assim como de animais e objetos. Talvez, tenha algo a ver com minha própria migração, já que vivi em tantos países diferentes e me mudei tantas vezes. Tenho que refletir mais sobre essas ideias. Meu destino, como o titulo desses trabalhos, é ainda "unknown", desconhecido.

Esta entrevista foi realizada em francês, no apartamento e ateliê de Cybèle Varela, em Madri, no dia 16 de setembro de 2017.

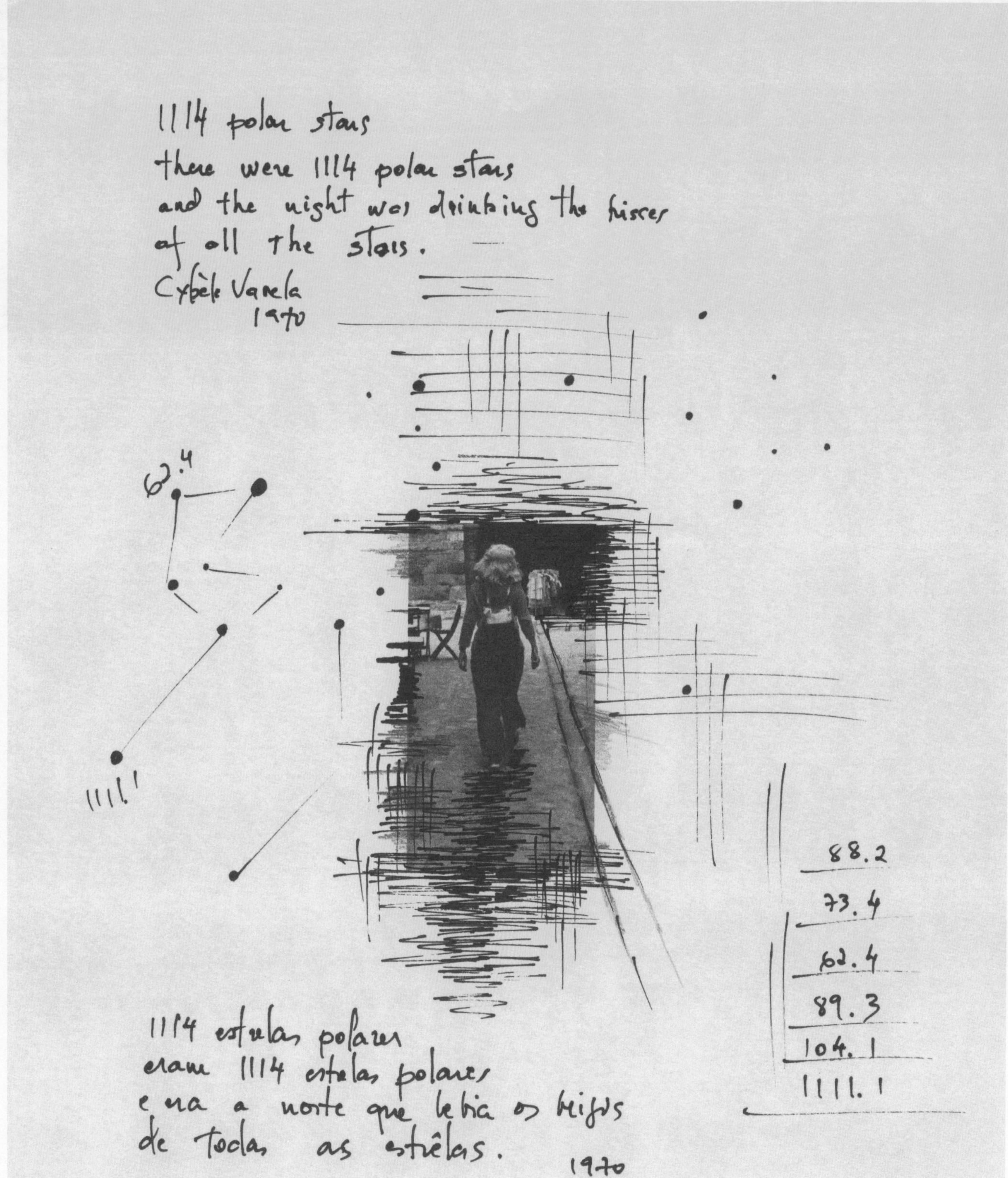

1114 estrelas polares
1997

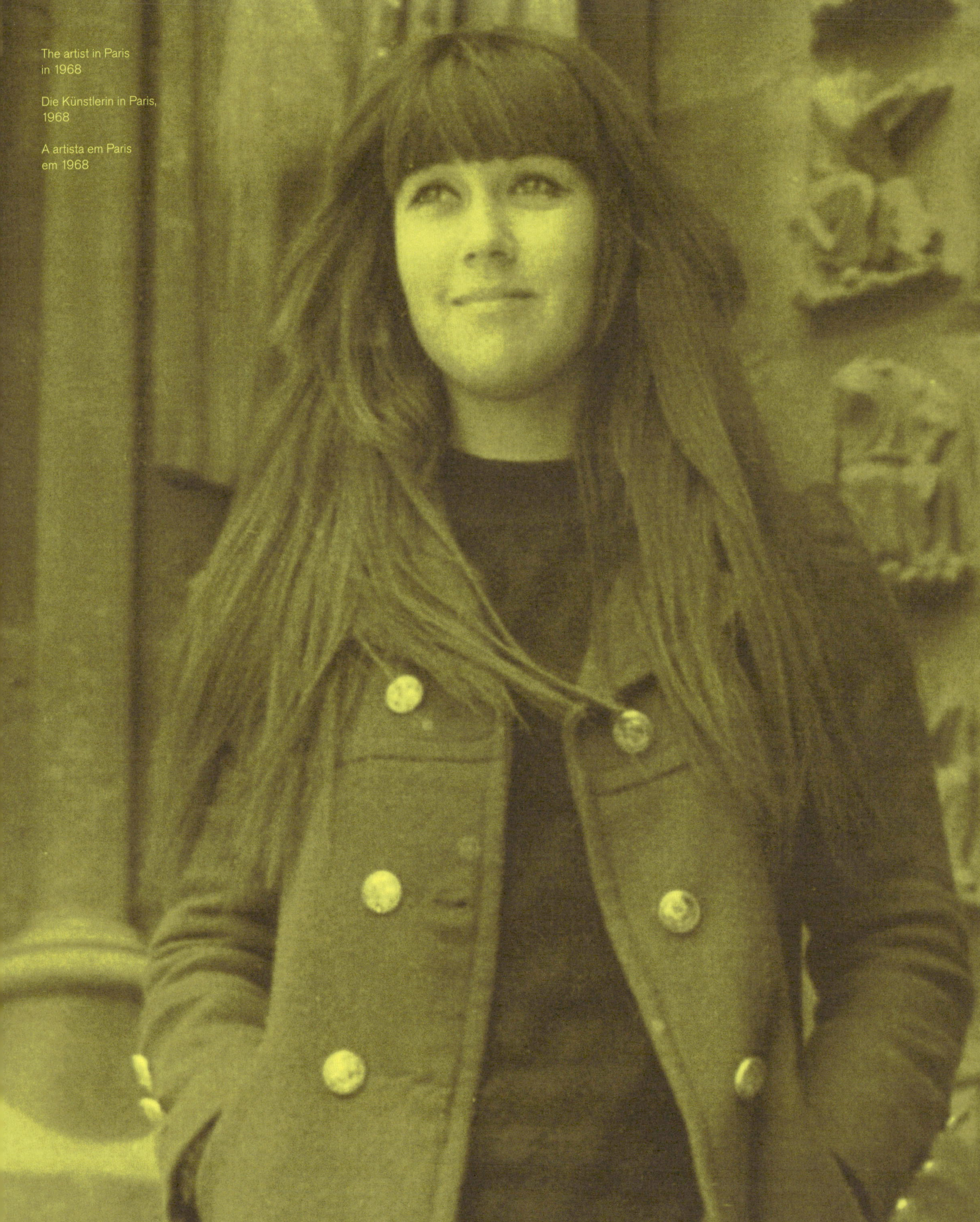

The artist in Paris
in 1968

Die Künstlerin in Paris,
1968

A artista em Paris
em 1968

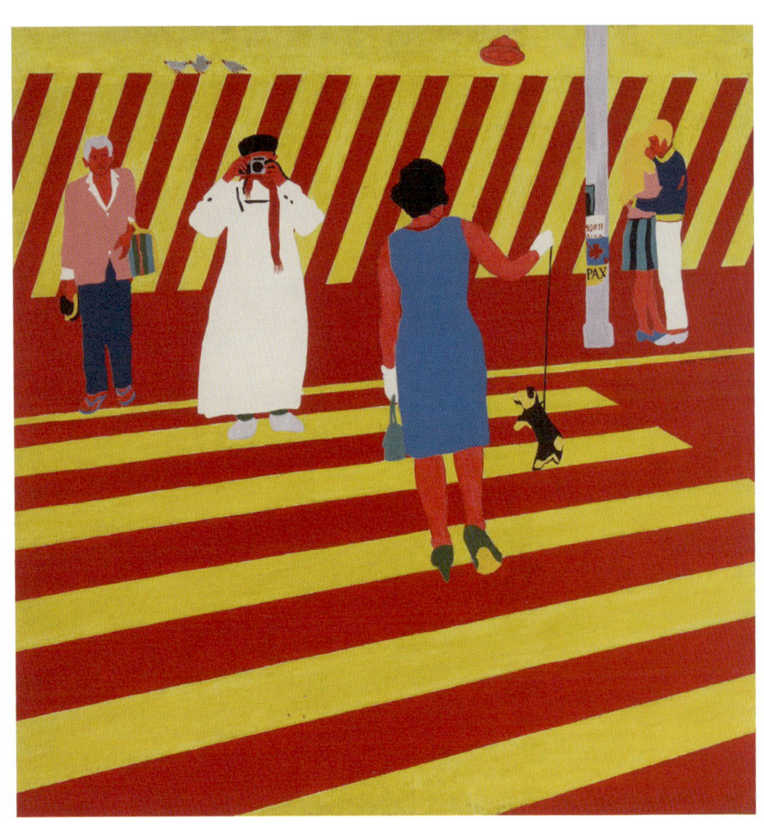
PAX

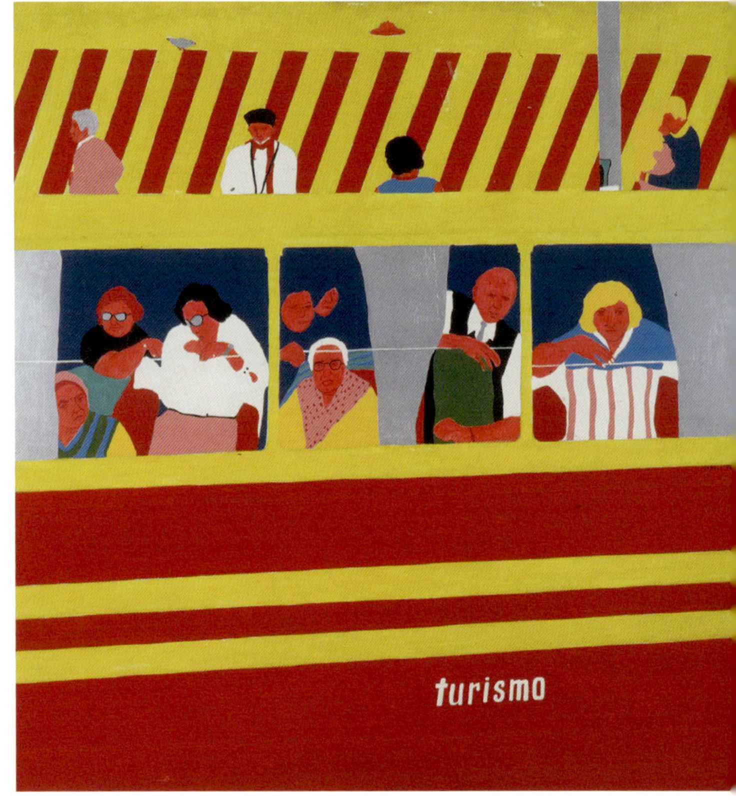
turismo

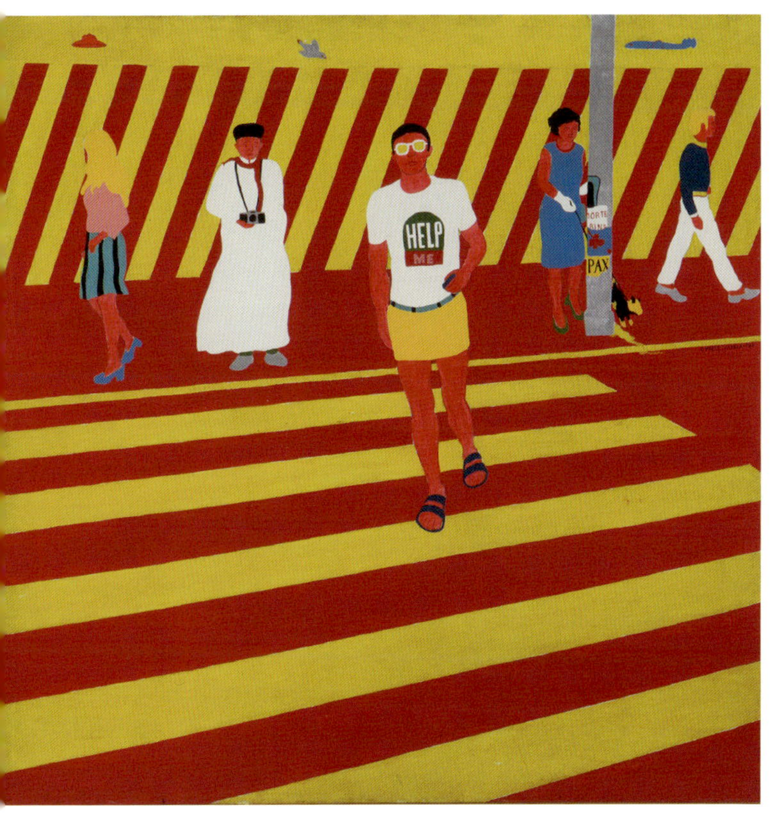

"The starting point for Cybèle Varela's work is absurd life. Using this frequently mocked absurd, she constructs a real system of movement, where colour and space act as great wings to freedom and clarity."

Walmir Ayala, Rio de Janeiro, April 1979

Cenas de rua
1968

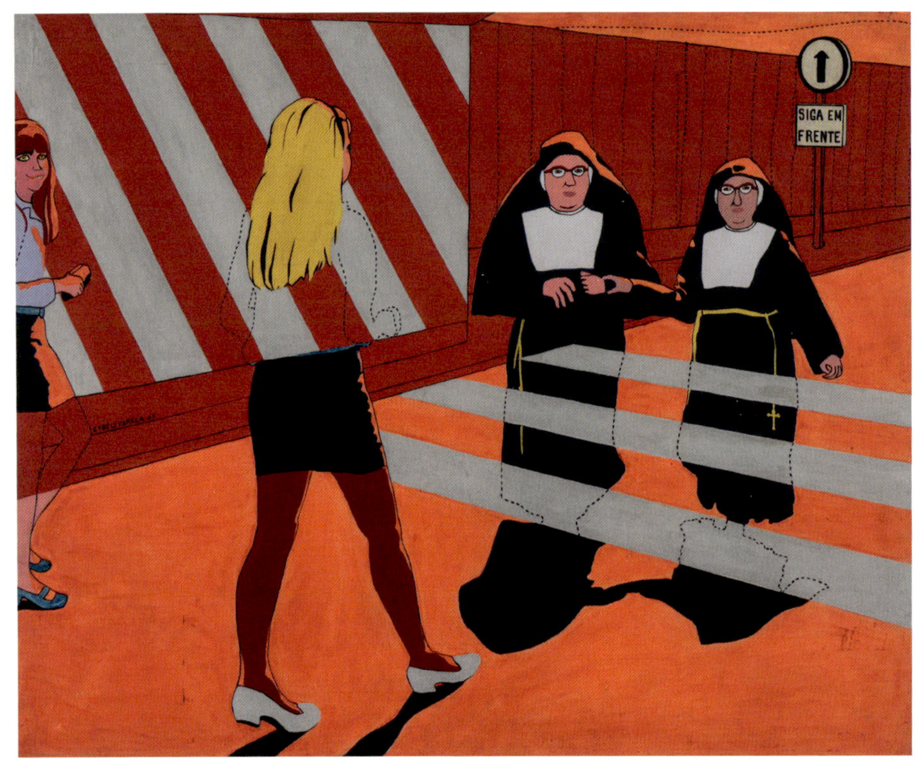

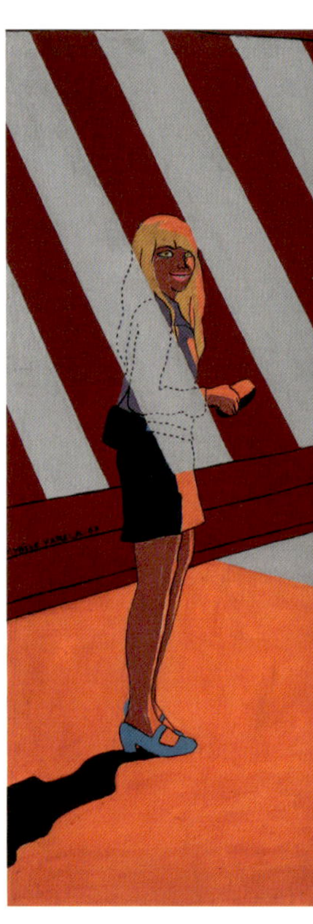

De tudo aquilo que poderia ter sido e que não foi
1967

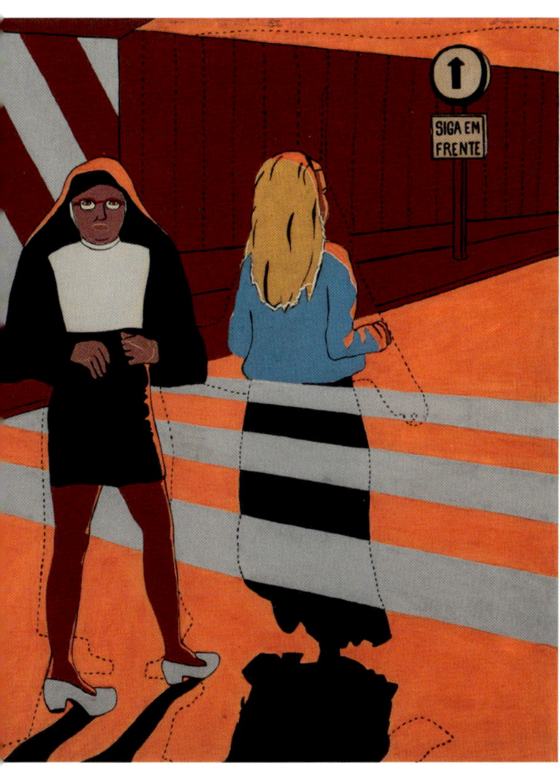

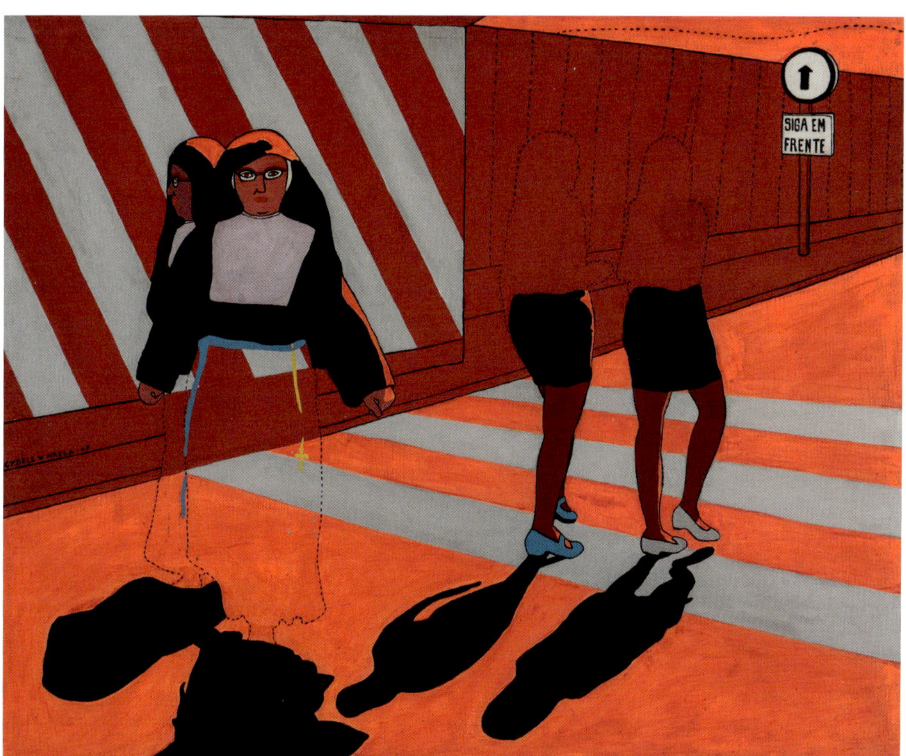

»Der Ausgangspunkt für das Schaffen von Cybèle Varela ist das absurde Leben. Aus dieser häufig verspotteten Absurdität konstruiert sie ein regelrechtes Bewegungsmuster, in dem die Farbe und der Raum als grosse Flügel der Freiheit und der Klarheit fungieren.«

Walmir Ayala, Rio de Janeiro, April 1979

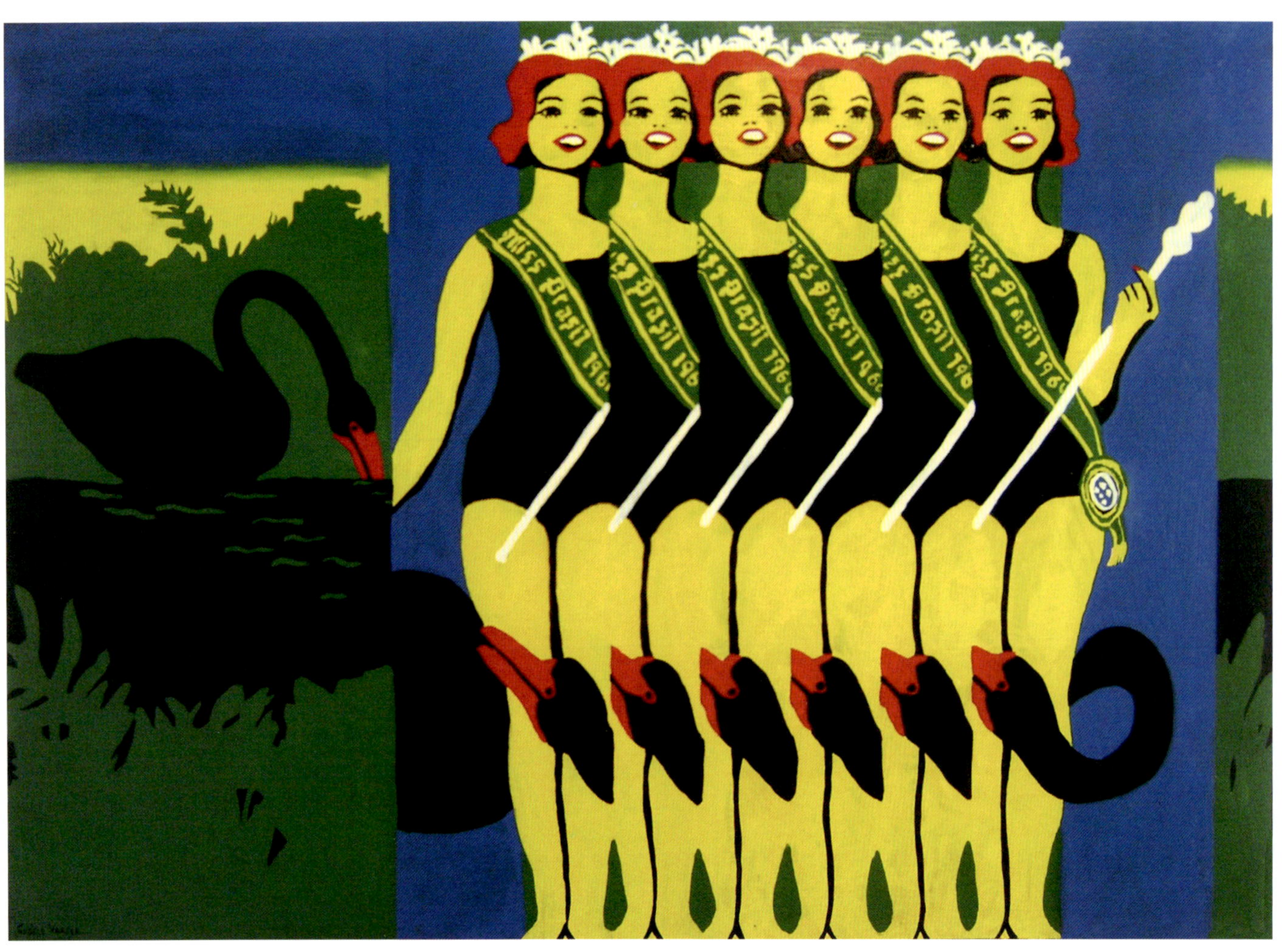

"O ponto de partida do trabalho de Cybèle Varela é a vida absurda. Deste absurdo frequentemente ironizado ela constrói um verdadeiro esquema de movimento, no qual a cor e o espaço funcionam como grandes asas de liberdade e nitidez."

Walmir Ayala, Rio de Janeiro, abril 1979

Miss Brasil e o cisne
1968

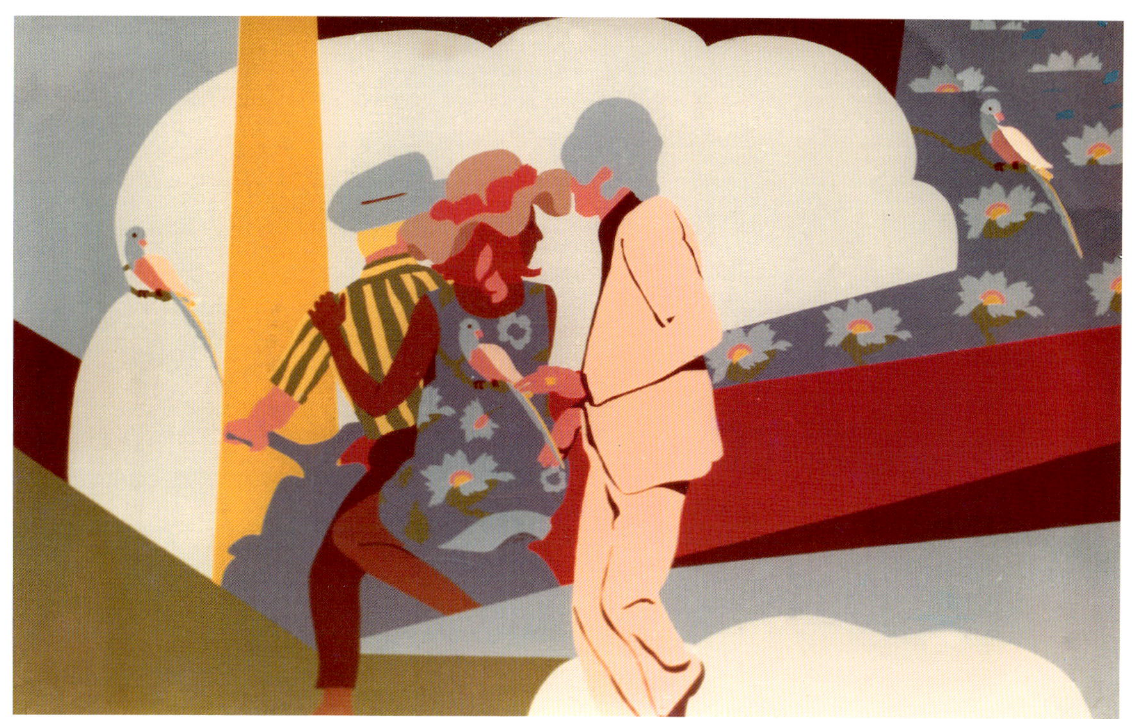

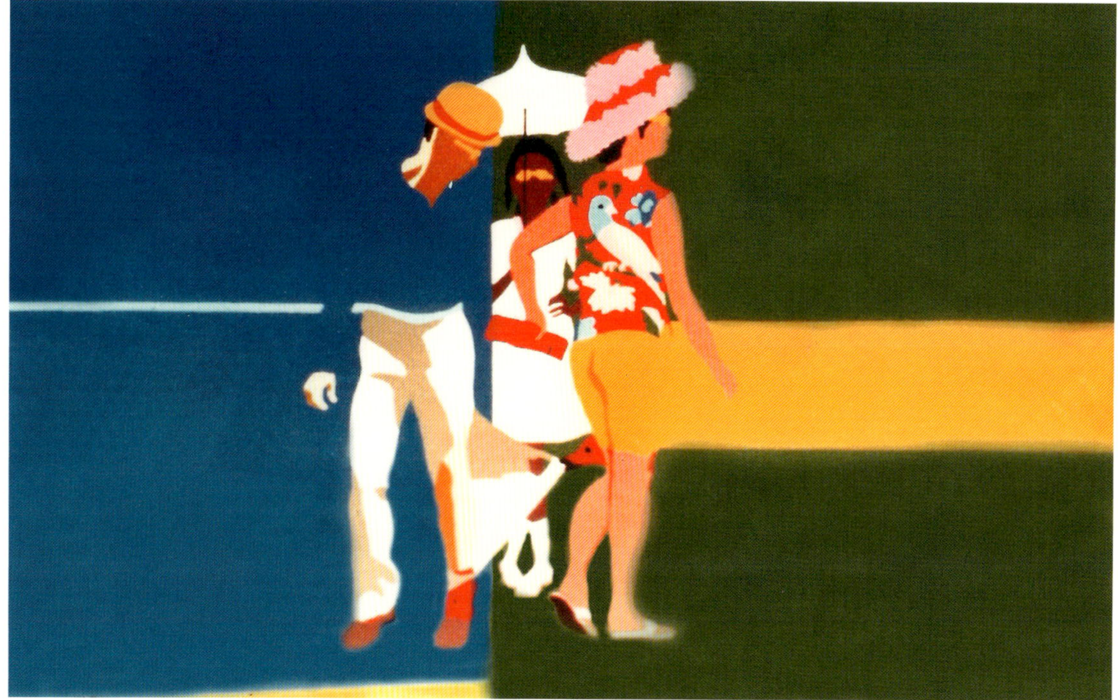

O papagaio
1969

O encontro
1969

"Cybèle Varela doesn't paint landscapes. The complete banality of the mirror-image is for her nothing but a pretext. (...) The multiplicative relationship of light/shade has an effect upon the representative unity of the image (something like a landscape) and this is how Cybèle Varela's painting restores the pluridimensional reality of the signified field. Reality for Cybèle Varela only exists on a linguistic level."

Pierre Restany, Paris, May 1975

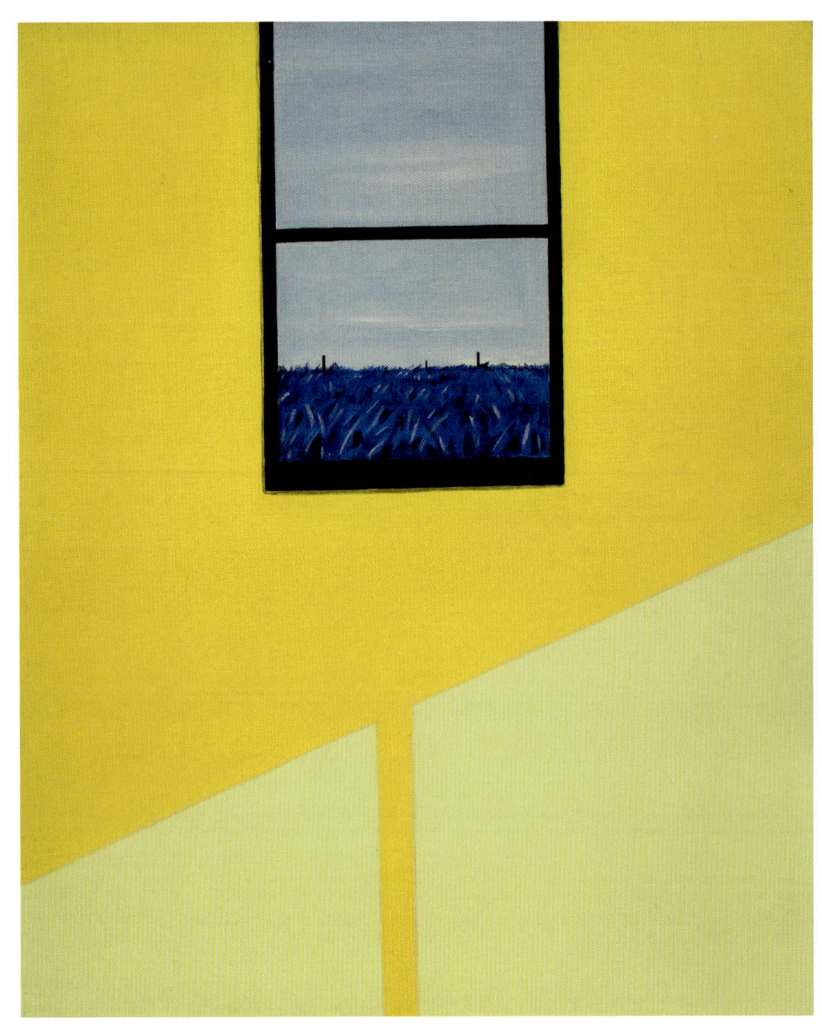

Image 1, 2, 3
1975

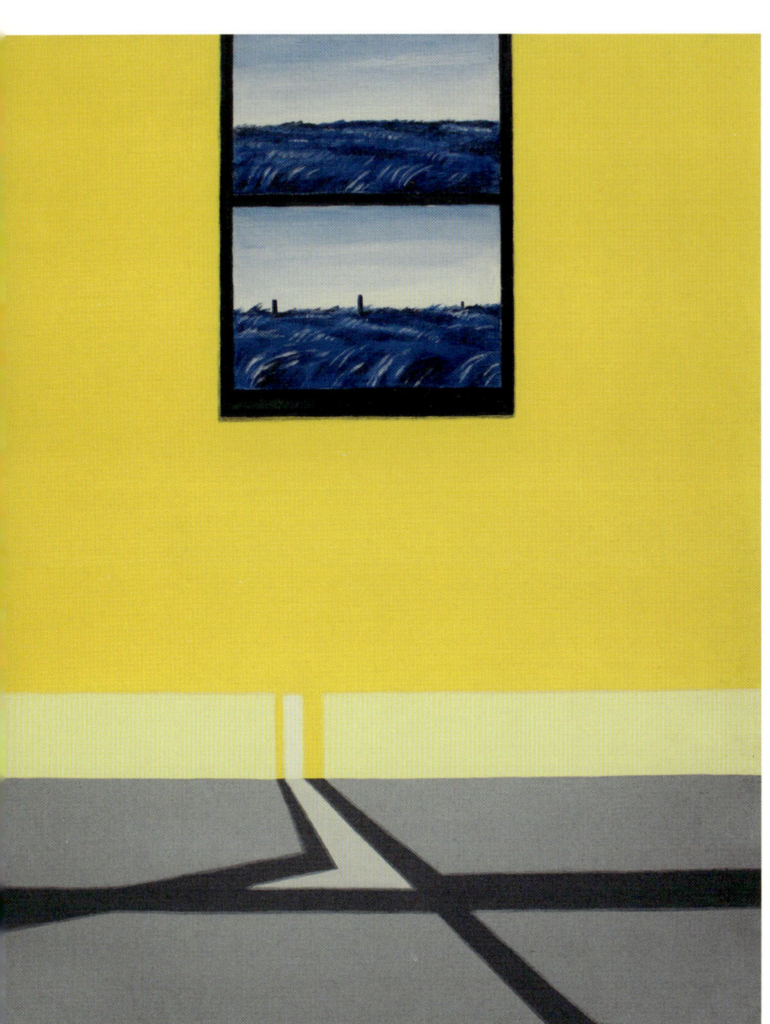

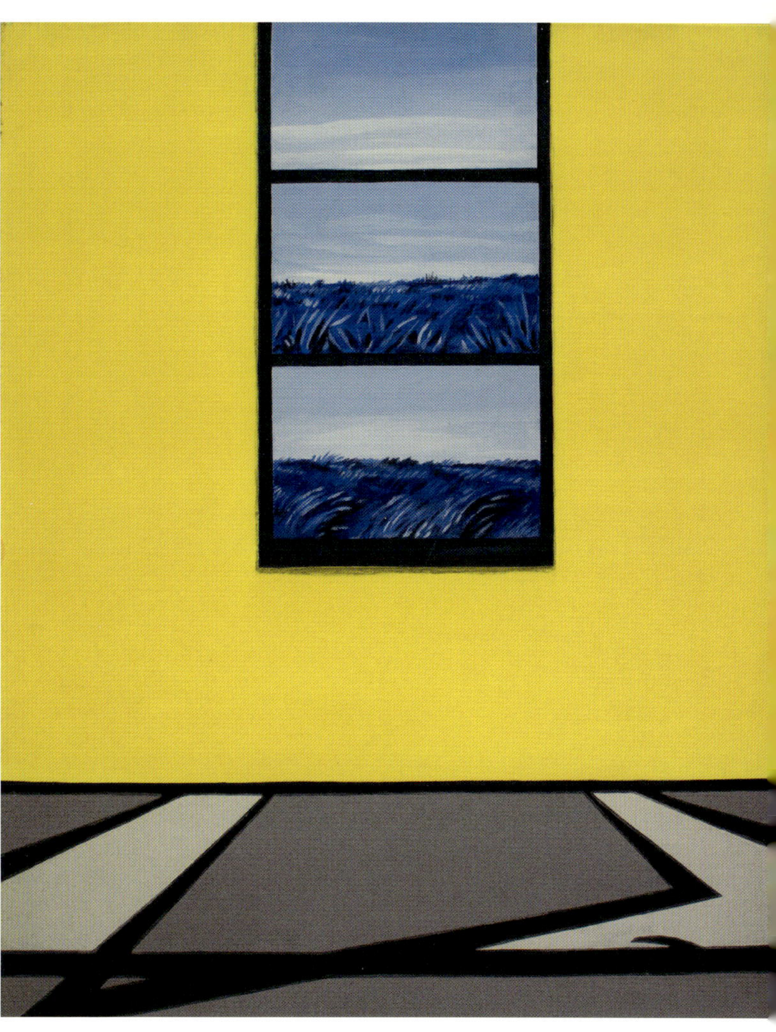

»Cybèle Varela malt keine Landschaften. Die totale Banalität des Spiegelbilds ist nur ein Vorwand. (...)Das vielfältige Verhältnis Schatten/Licht beeinflusst die darstellerische Einheit des Bildes (so etwas wie eine Landschaft), und so widerspiegelt die Malerei von Cybèle Varela die mehrdimensionale Wirklichkeit der Bedeutungsebene. Das Reale existiert bei Cybèle Varela lediglich auf der sprachlichen Ebene.«

Pierre Restany, Paris, Mai 1975

"Cybèle Varela não pinta paisagens. A total banalidade da imagem especular é somente um pretexto. (...) A relação múltipla sombra/luz age sobre a unidade representativa da imagem (algo como uma paisagem) e é deste modo que a pintura de Cybèle Varela nos restitui a realidade pluridimensional do campo significativo. O real de Cybèle Varela existe apenas ao nível da linguagem."

Pierre Restany, Paris, maio 1975

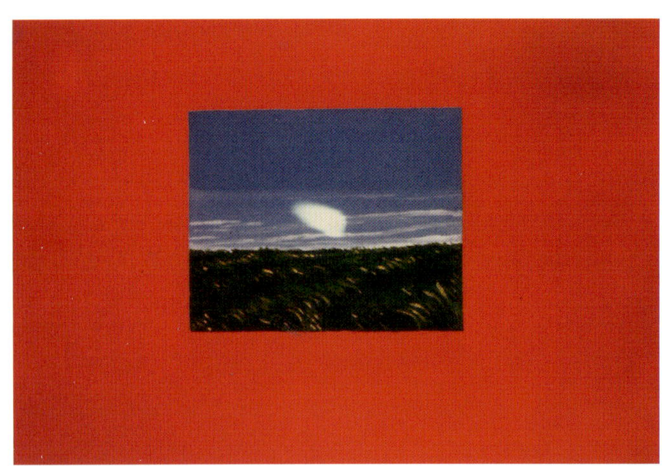

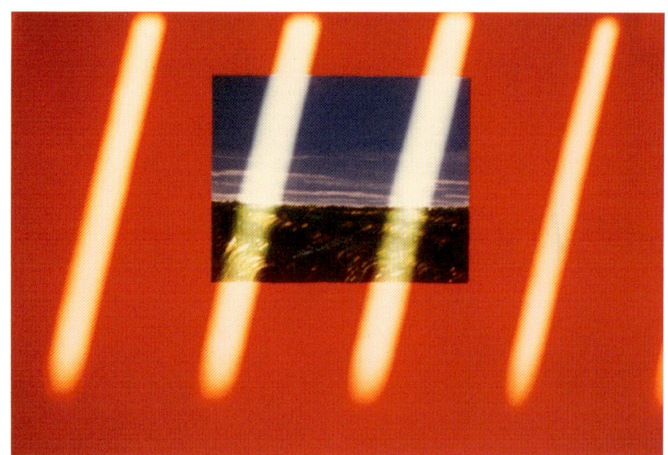

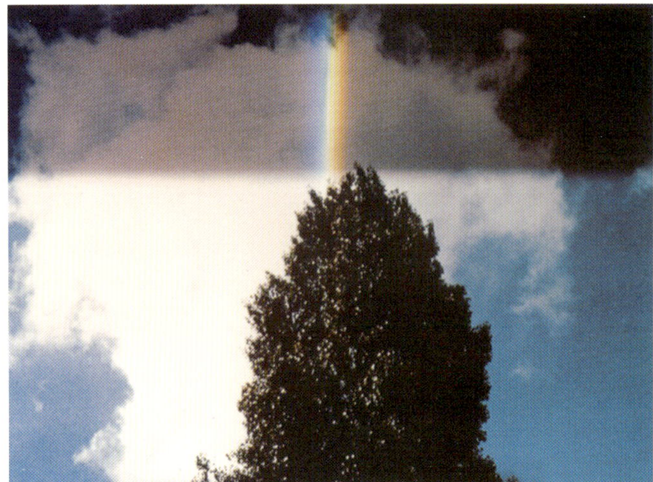

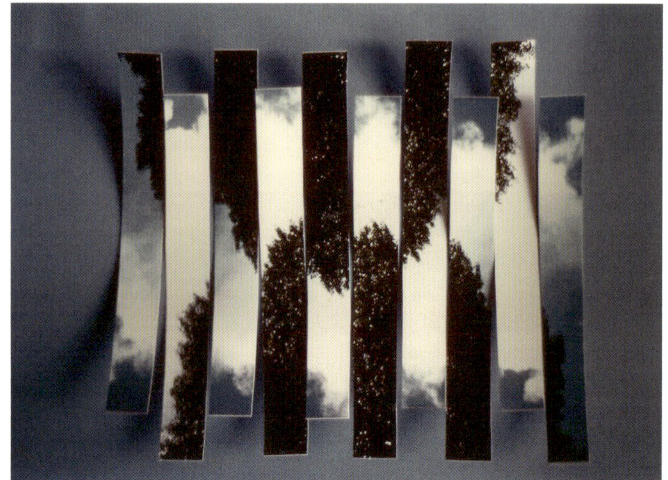

Image
1977

Image
1977

Image
1980

Image
1980

Once in Paris, Cybèle Varela began placing nature at the centre of her paintings. She translated her colorful memories of Brazil's tropical fauna and flora in the form of painted posters pinned onto the walls of her studio at the Cité Internationale des Arts (figs. p. 25). Unexpected elements, such as an electrical plug and the reflection of the solar beams filtering through a jalousie window, enable the viewer to break the fiction and remind him or her of the subtle illusion that is at play here. For the man of the city, nature only exists as representation. It is an object amongst others in a domestic interior. In her series simply entitled *Image* (figs. pp. 64–65), Brazil's luxuriant forests are replaced by the sight of North European fields under cultivation. These are however no mere landscapes. What really interests the artist is not the landscape itself. Actually, these works are only a pretext for Varela to develop a reflection on the ambiguity of the real.
In her *Image* paintings later produced in Switzerland, the artist further investigated the representation of movement, light and time. The fragmented vision of trees, clouds and skies (figs. pp. 36–37, 68–69) transforms nature into geometrical spatial architectures which seem on the point of breaking, reminding us of nature's vulnerability. AVB

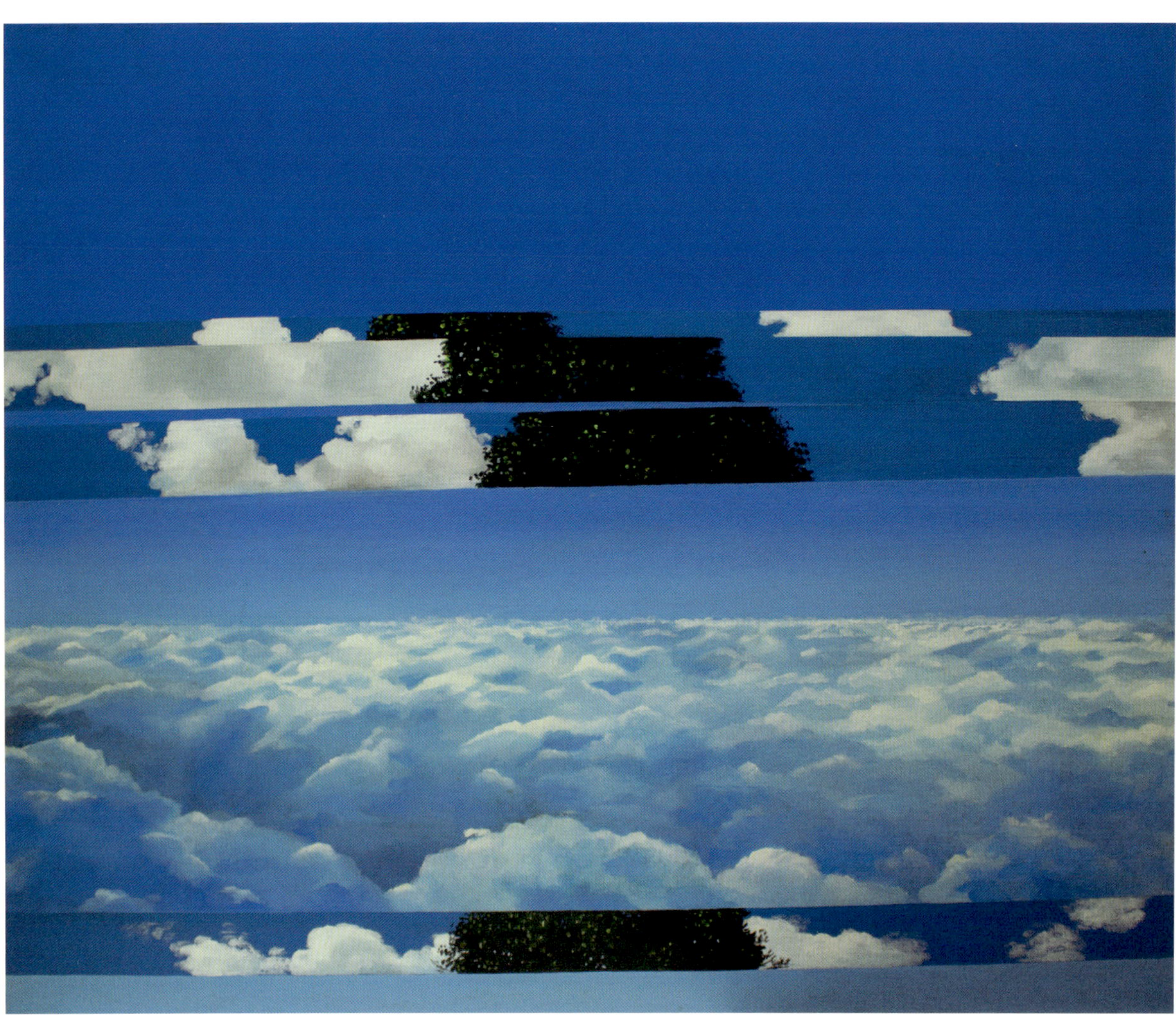

In Paris begann Cybèle Varela die Natur ins Zentrum ihrer Malerei zu rücken. Sie übertrug ihre Erinnerungen an die farbenfrohe brasilianische Fauna und Flora auf eine Art von gemalten Plakaten, die sie an den Wänden ihres Ateliers in der Cité Internationale des Arts (Abb. S. 25) anbrachte. Unerwartete Elemente wie ein Elektrostecker oder der Reflex der durch eine Jalousie fallenden Sonnenstrahlen ermöglichen es dem Betrachter, die Fiktion zu durchbrechen, wobei er oder sie an den subtilen Illusionismus erinnert werden, der hier am Werk ist. Für Stadtmenschen existiert die Natur nur als Repräsentation. Sie ist ein Objekt wie jedes andere in einem häuslichen Interieur. In Varelas Serie, die den schlichten Titel *Image* (Abb S. 64–65) trägt, werden Brasiliens üppige Wälder durch den Anblick von nordeuropäischen kultivierten Feldern ersetzt. Es handelt sich nicht mehr um reine Landschaften. Was die Künstlerin wirklich interessiert, ist nicht die Landschaft selbst. Diese Arbeiten sind vielmehr ein Vorwand für Varela, um eine Reflexion über die Ambiguität des Realen zu entwickeln.

In den nachfolgend in der Schweiz entstandenen Bildern der *Image*-Serie widmet sich Varela verstärkt der Darstellung von Bewegung, Licht und Zeit. Die fragmentierte Wiedergabe von Bäumen, Wolken und Himmeln (Abb. S. 36–37 und 68–69) verwandelt die Natur in geometrisch-räumliche Architekturen, die einzustürzen scheinen und uns die Vulnerabilität der Umwelt in Erinnerung rufen. AVB

Image
1982

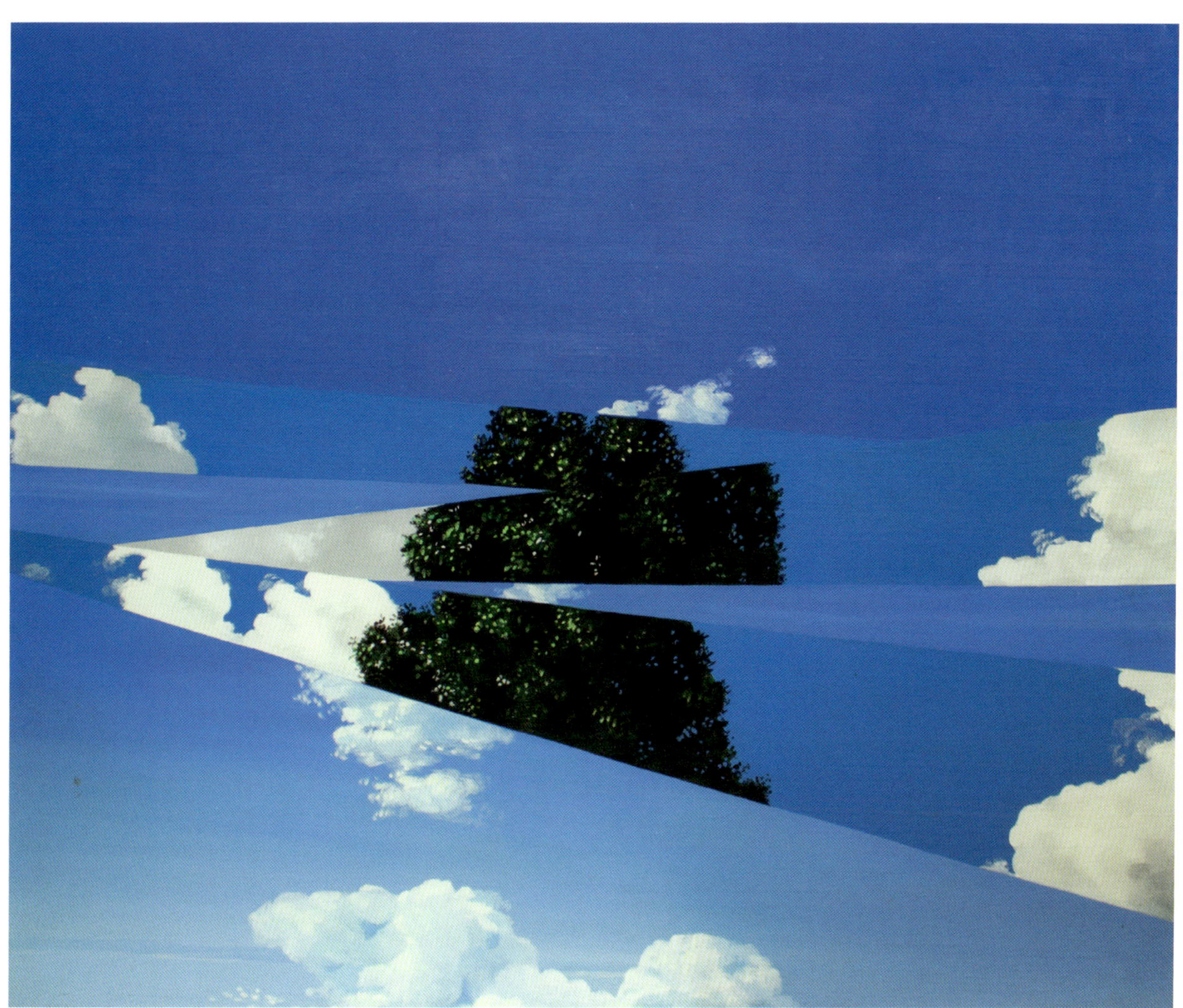

Image
1982

Uma vez em Paris, Cybèle Varela começou a posicionar a natureza na essência de suas pinturas. Traduziu suas coloridas lembranças da fauna e da flora tropicais do Brasil em cartazes pintados e afixados nas paredes de seu estúdio na Cité Internationale des Arts (il. p. 25). Elementos inesperados, como uma tomada elétrica e o reflexo dos raios do sol filtrando através da persiana de uma janela, obrigam o observador a quebrar a ficção e lembrar-se da sutil ilusão que, naquele momento, está em jogo. Para o homem metropolitano, a natureza existe somente como representação. É um objeto no meio dos outros, em ambientes domésticos. Na sua série intitulada simplesmente *Image* (ils. pp. 64-65), as florestas luxuriantes do Brasil são substituídas pela vista dos campos cultivados da Europa do Norte.

Todavia, não estamos, aqui, diante de simples paisagens. Na verdade, essas obras são apenas um pretexto para que Varela leve adiante uma reflexão sobre a ambiguidade do real. Nas suas pinturas *Image*, realizadas posteriormente na Suíça, a artista pesquisaria ulteriormente a representação do movimento, da luz e do tempo. A visão fragmentada de árvores, nuvens e céus (ils. pp. 36-37, 68-69) transforma a natureza em arquiteturas espaciais geométricas que parecem estar em ponto de ruptura, lembrando-nos da vulnerabilidade da natureza. AVB

In 1996, Cybèle Varela realized an impressive cycle of frescoes for her house in Thoiry (France; fig. p. 75). Her compositions, dominated by anamorphic images and trompe-l'oeil, were inspired both by real life and classical sources. On the ceiling of the living room, for instance, she copied the illusory oculus painted by Andrea Mantegna in the Camera picta at the Ducal Palace in Mantua (1465–74), ironically adding a portrait of her dog Jyp to the circle of putti. Varela worked long hours on these frescoes, and had to climb up on a tall ladder in order to reach the ceiling. In the vertical dyptichs *The Artist 1* and *The Artist 2* (figs. pp. 71–74), she records this strenuous task as a moment in her life suspended between reality and dream. The artist protagonist, clearly Varela's herself, is represented at work, but her sumptuous Renaissance dress and the pink wig suggests another identity. This idealistic vision of artistic freedom and independence is disturbed by the voyeristic scenes playing in the background of the canvas: the artist is here represented as a common woman occupied in the many activities of her daily routine, such as ironing or cooking a meal. Varela's statement about the role and aspirations of women in society could not be clearer. VL

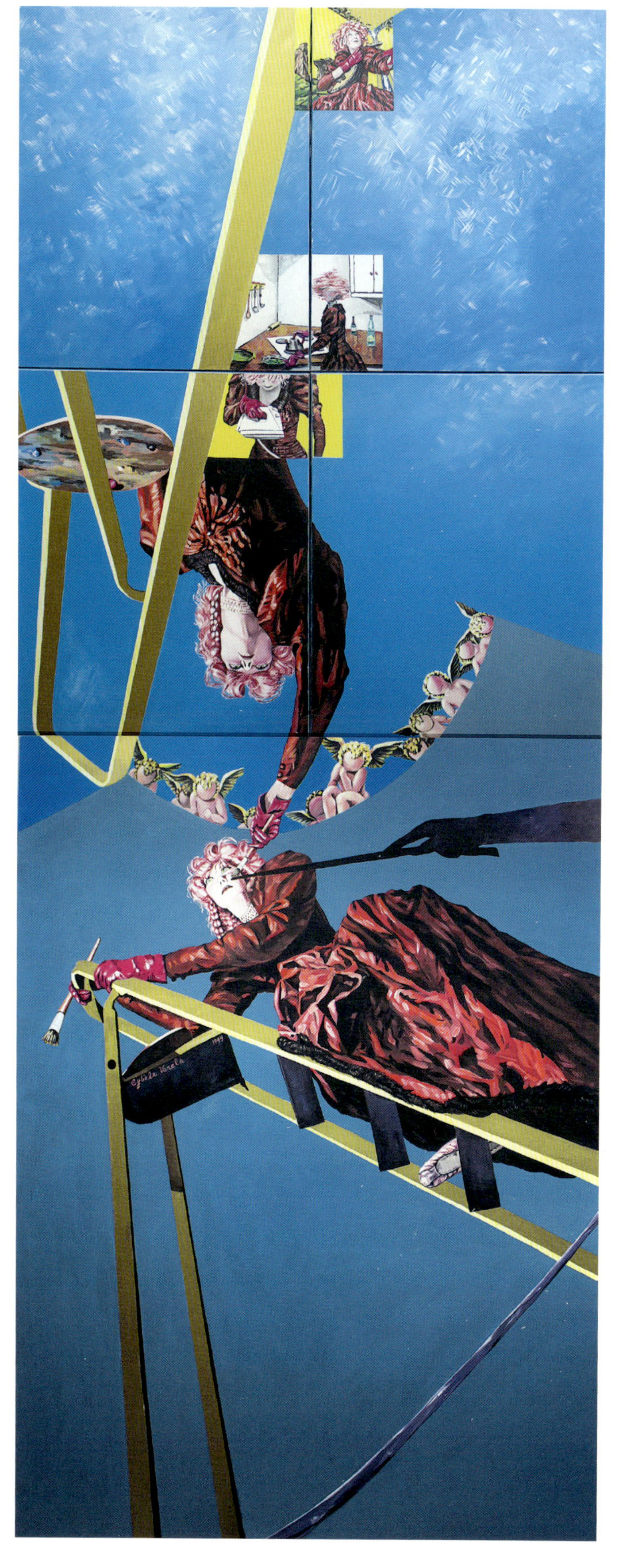

The Artist 2
1999

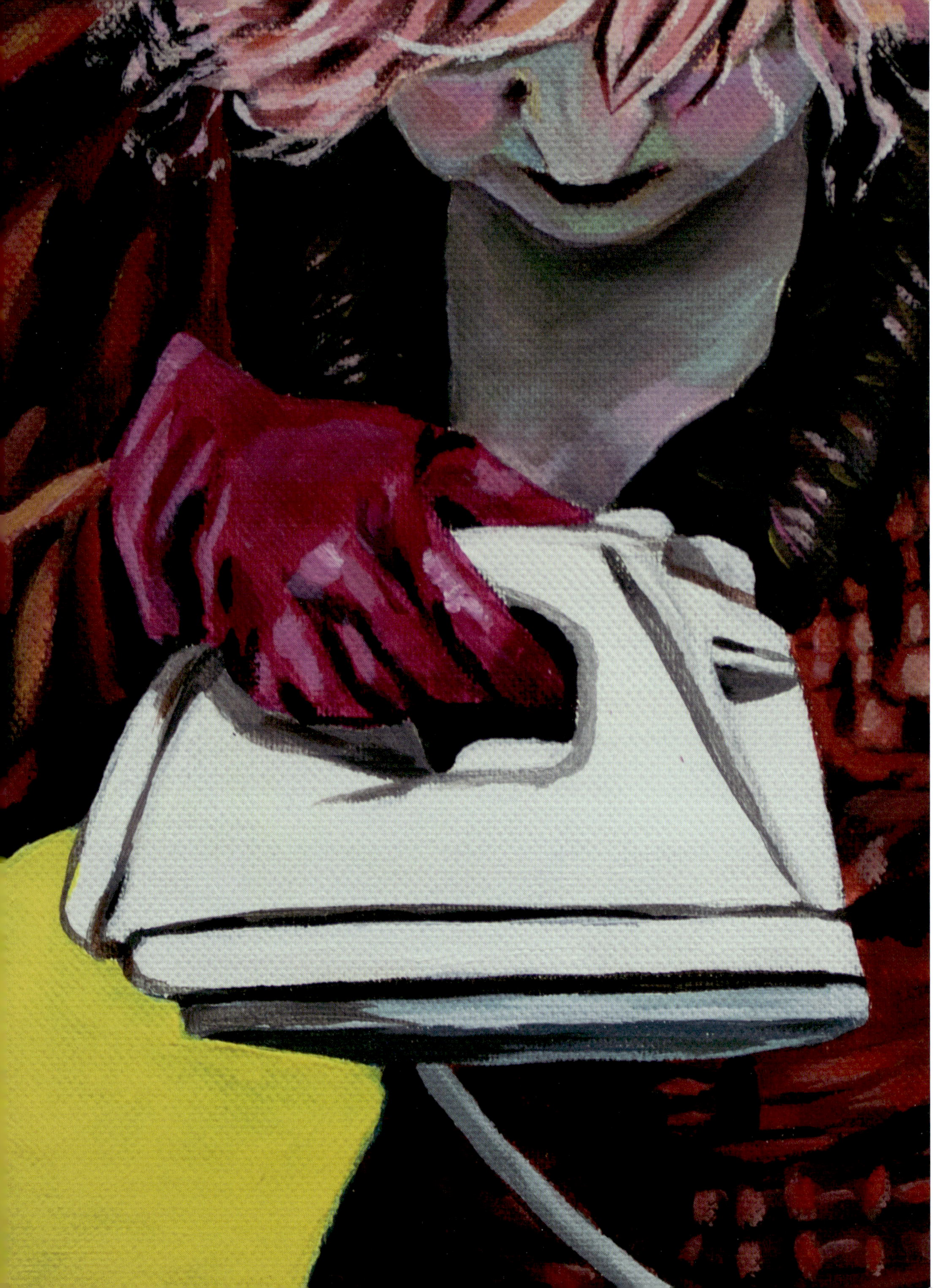

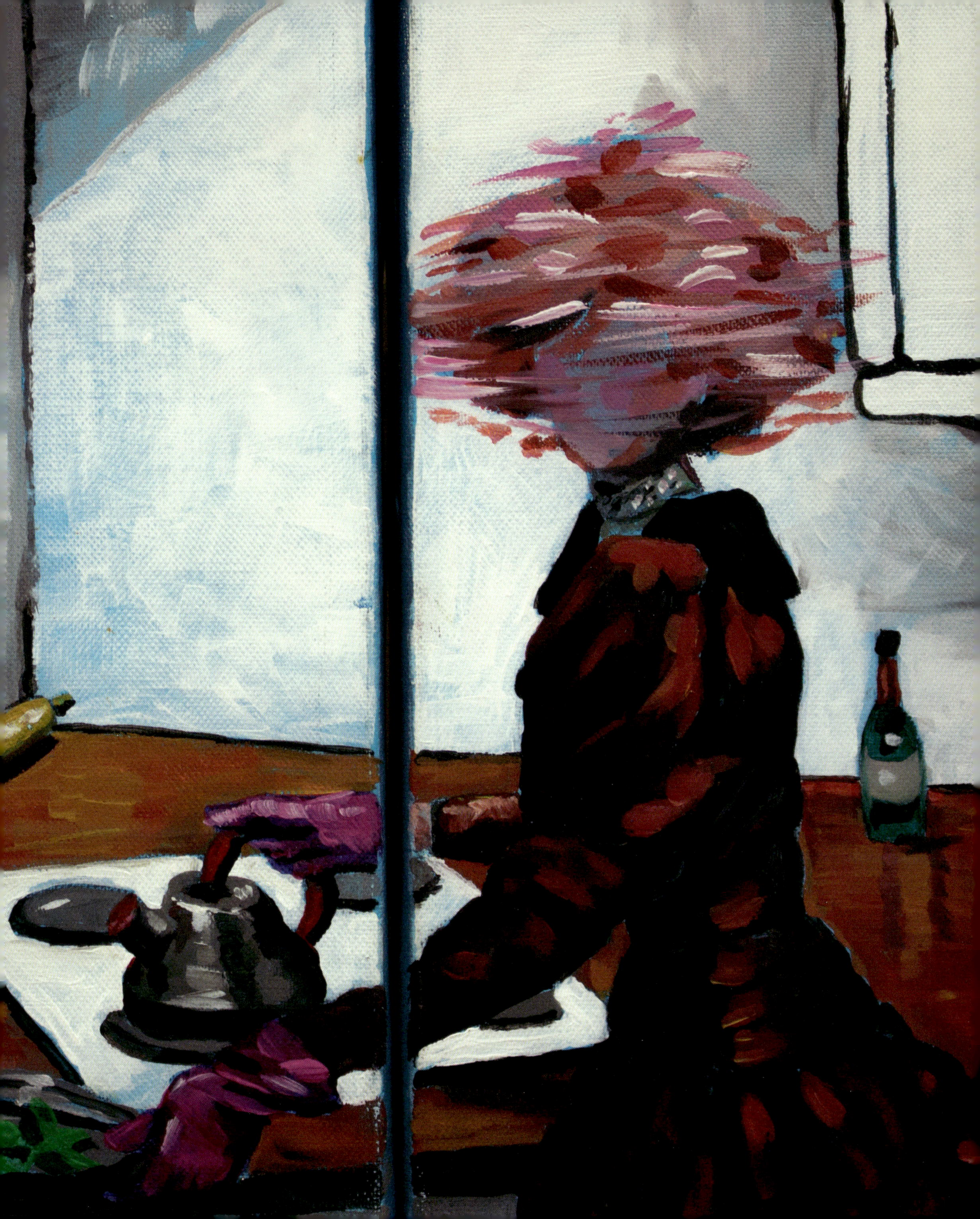

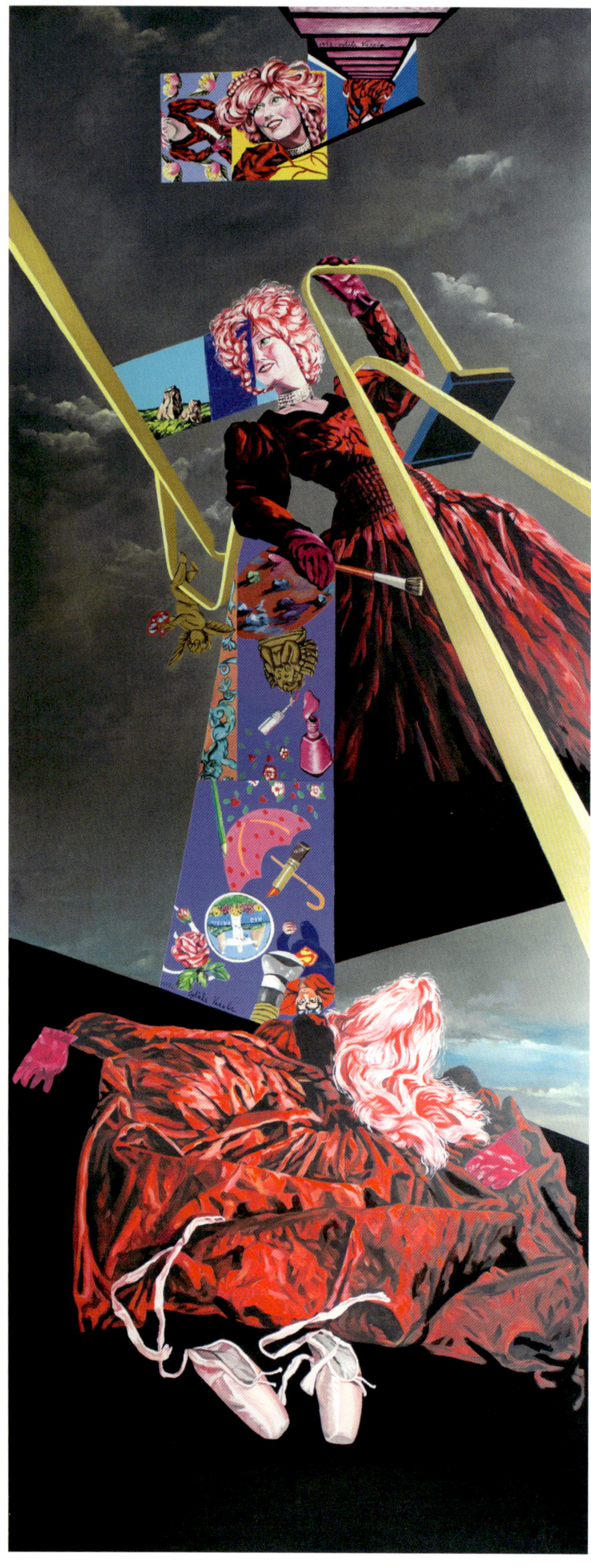

Im Jahr 1996 realisierte Cybèle Varela einen beeindruckenden Freskenzyklus für ihr Haus in Thoiry (Frankreich; Abb. S. 75). Ihre von anamorphen Bildern und der Trompe-l'oeil-Technik beeinflussten Kompositionen wurden von der Lebensrealität und klassischen Quellen geprägt. Auf der Wohnzimmerdecke kopierte sie beispielsweise das von Andrea Mantegna in der Camera picta im Mantovaner Herzogspalast gemalte illusionistische Oculus, wobei sie dem Putti-Reigen ironischerweise ein Porträt ihres Hundes Jyp hinzufügte. Varela verwendete viel Zeit auf diese Fresken, wobei sie eine hohe Leiter hinaufklettern musste, um die Decke zu erreichen. In den vertikalen Diptychen *The Artist 1* und *2* (Abb. S. 71–74) erinnert sie sich an diese mühsame Aufgabe als einen Moment in ihrem Leben, der zwischen Realität und Traum oszillierte. Die Künstler-Protagonistin ist Varela selbst bei der Arbeit, ihr prächtiges Renaissancegewand legt jedoch zusammen mit der rosa Perücke eine andere Identität nahe. Diese idealistische Vorstellung künstlerischer Freiheit und Unabhängigkeit wird durch die voyeuristischen Szenen gestört, die sich im Bildhintergrund abspielen: Die Künstlerin präsentiert sich hier als ganz gewöhnliche Frau, die von den zahlreichen Alltagstätigkeiten wie Bügeln und Kochen in Beschlag genommen wird. Varelas Statement zur Rolle und den Bestrebungen der Frauen in der Gesellschaft könnte nicht eindeutiger ausfallen. VL

The Artist 1
1999

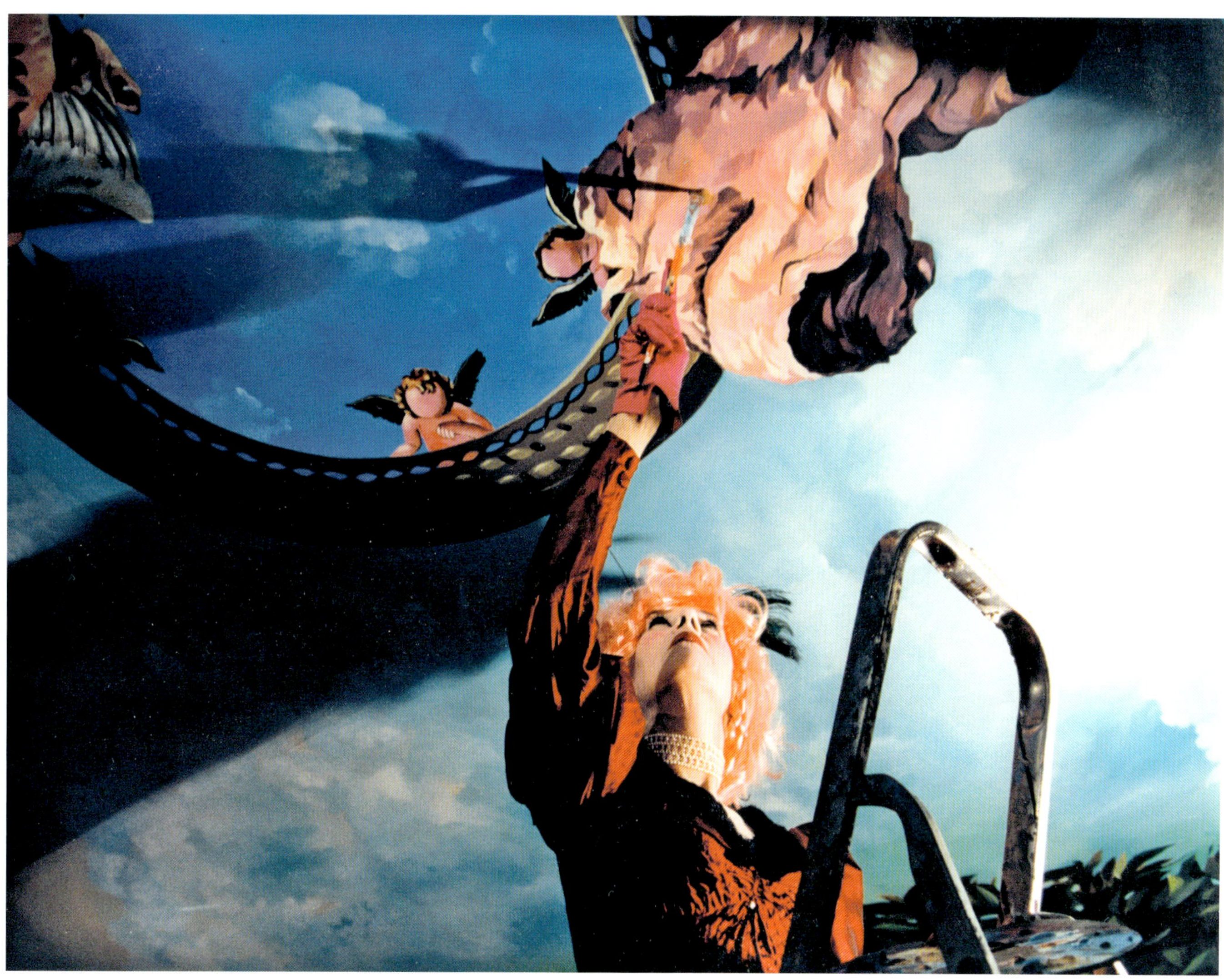

The artist staging herself while painting a fresco on the ceiling of her house in Thoiry, France, 1999

Die Künstlerin inszeniert sich selbst, während sie ein Fresko an der Decke ihres Hauses in Thoiry, Frankreich, malt, 1999

A artista se representando enquanto pinta sua casa em Thoiry, na França, 1999

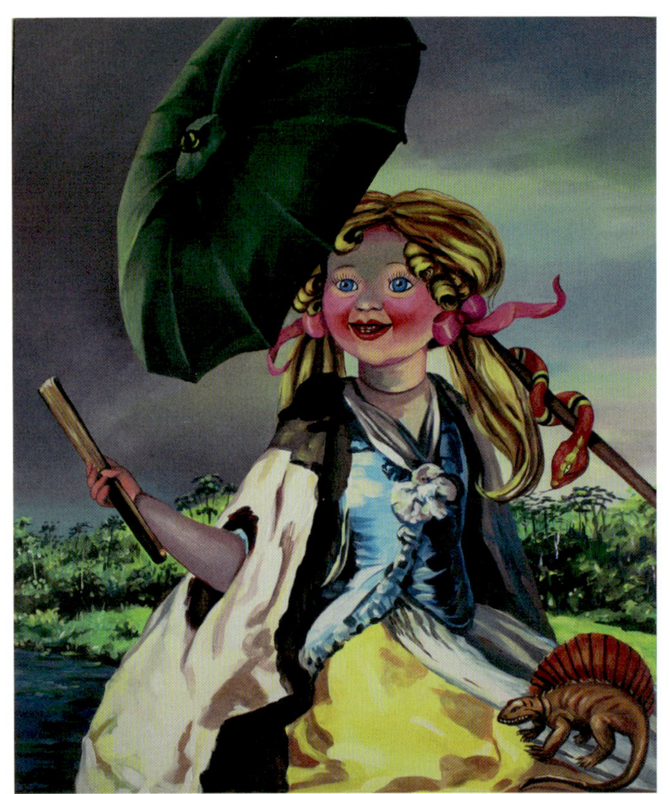
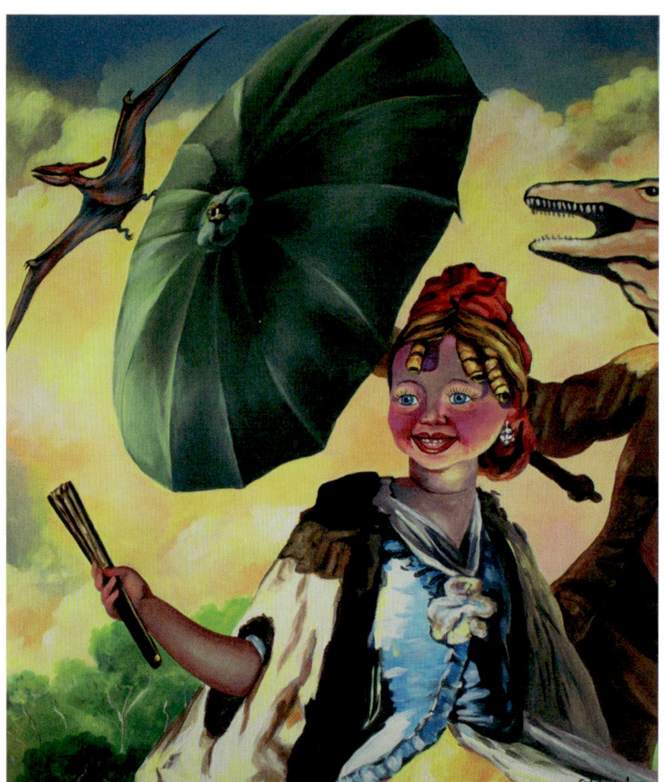
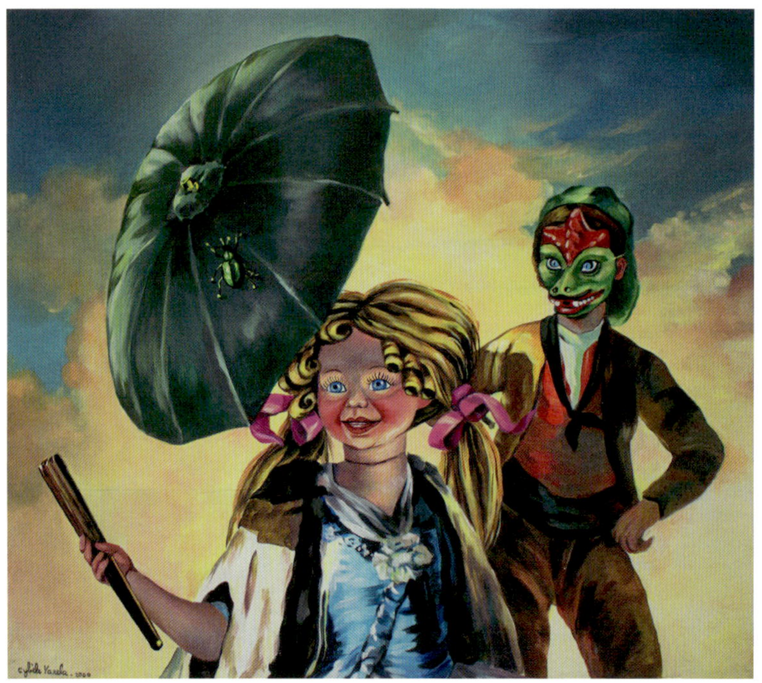

L'ombrello 1, 2, 3
2000

Em 1996, Cybèle Varela realizou um impressionante ciclo de afrescos para sua casa em Thoiry (França; il. p. 75). Suas composições, dominadas pelas imagens anamórficas e *trompe-l'oeil*, inspiravam-se tanto na vida real quanto nas fontes clássicas. No teto da sala de estar, por exemplo, a artista reproduziu o óculo fictício pintado por Andrea Mantegna na Camera picta, os aposentos dos esposos no Palácio Ducal em Mântua (1465-1474), adicionando ironicamente um retrato de seu cachorro Jyp ao círculo dos *putti*. Varela trabalhou por longas horas a estes afrescos, e tinha que subir numa alta escada para alcançar o teto. Nos dípticos verticais *The Artist 1* e *2* (ils. pp. 71-74), ela deixou gravada esta tarefa extenuante como um momento em que sua vida estaria suspendida entre sonho e realidade. A artista protagonista, claramente a mesma Varela, é representada ao trabalho, mas seu suntuoso vestido renascentista e sua peruca cor-de-rosa sugerem outra identidade. Esta visão idealista da liberdade e da independência artísticas é perturbada pelas cenas voyeurísticas representadas no pano de fundo da tela: a artista é aqui representada como uma mulher comum ocupada nas tarefas diárias, como passar roupa ou cozinhar. Não poderia ser mais clara a opinião de Varela a respeito do papel e das aspirações das mulheres na sociedade.
VL

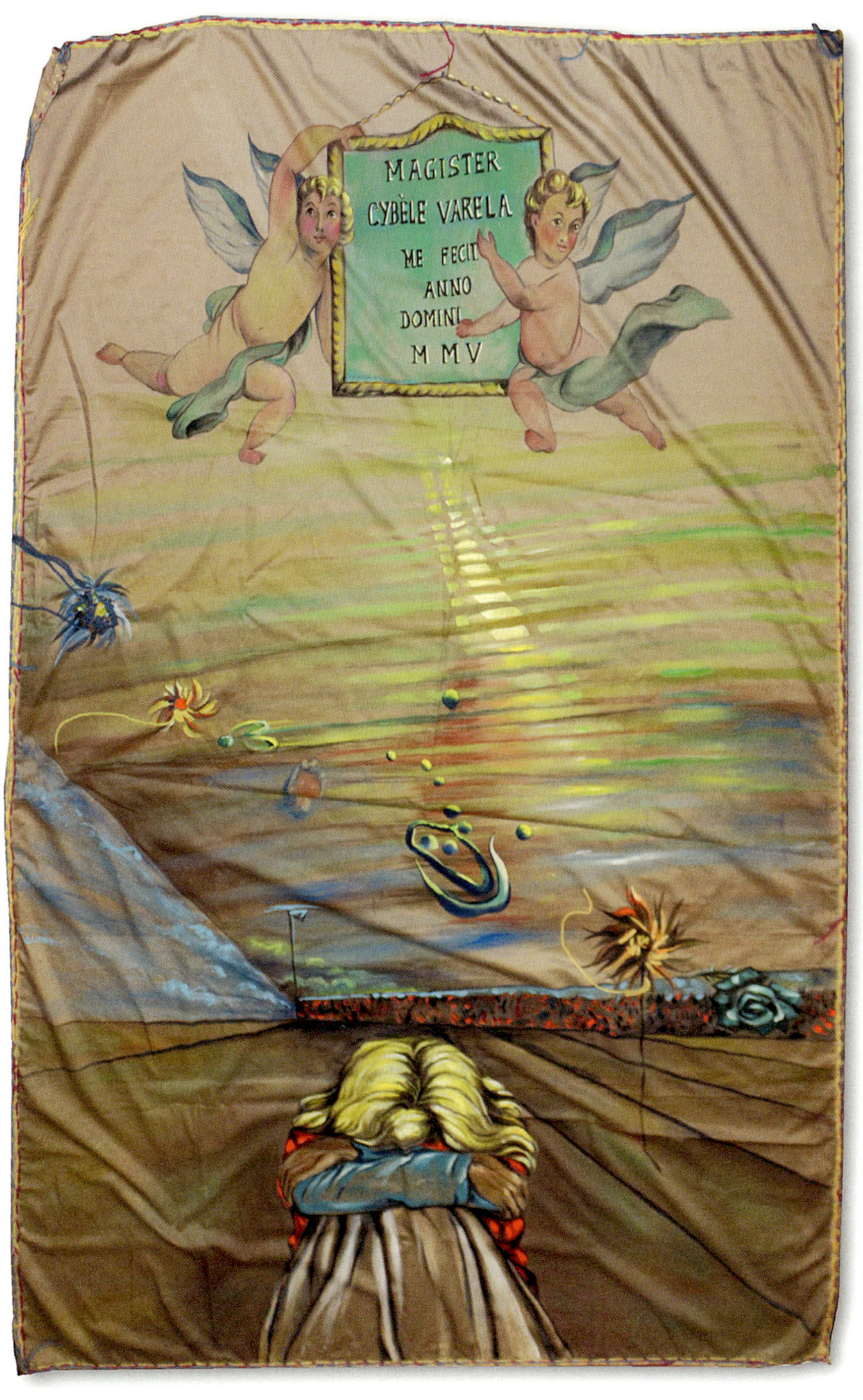

O caminho
2005

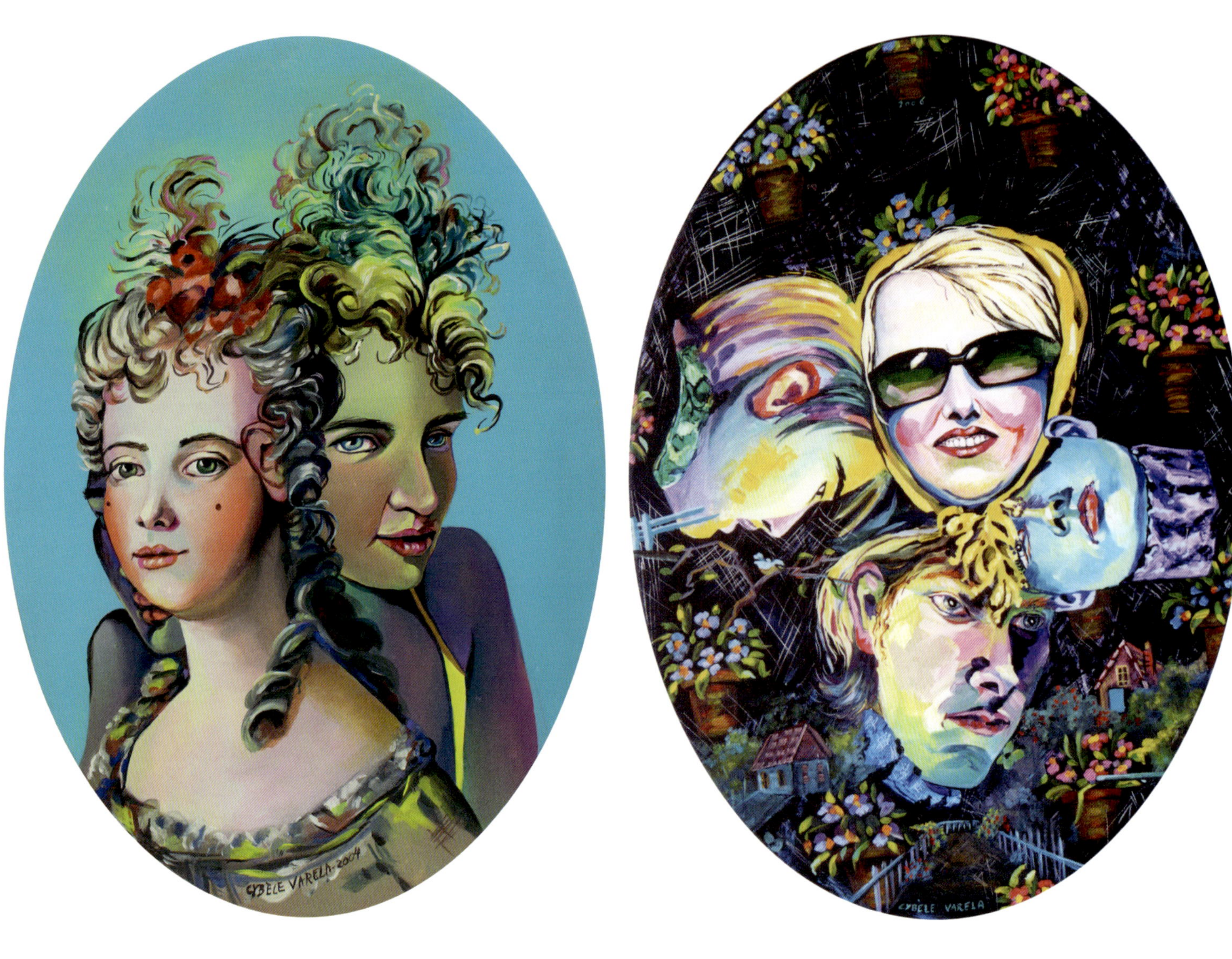

Tre amici
2006

T.C.G.H.
2006

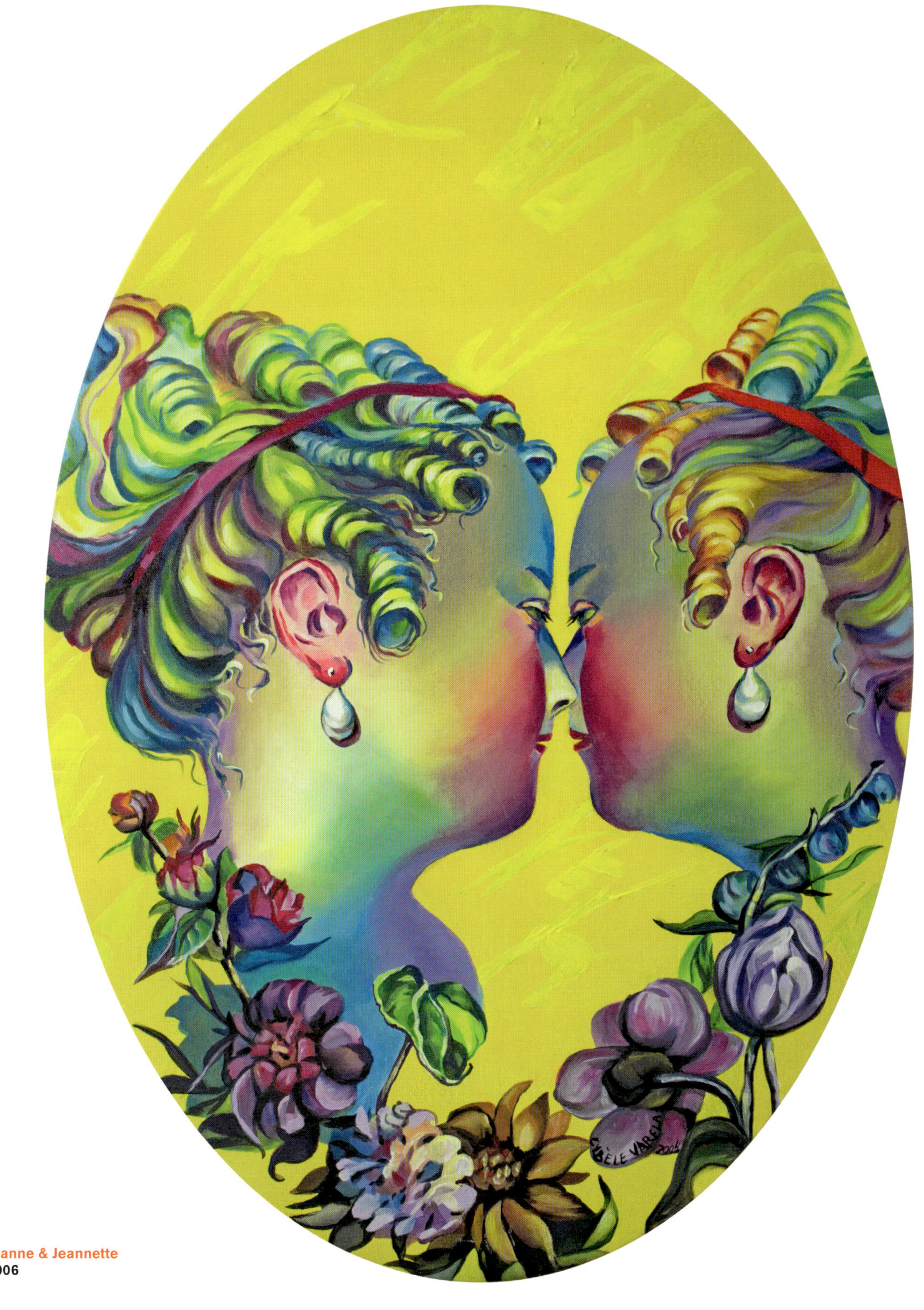

Jeanne & Jeannette
2006

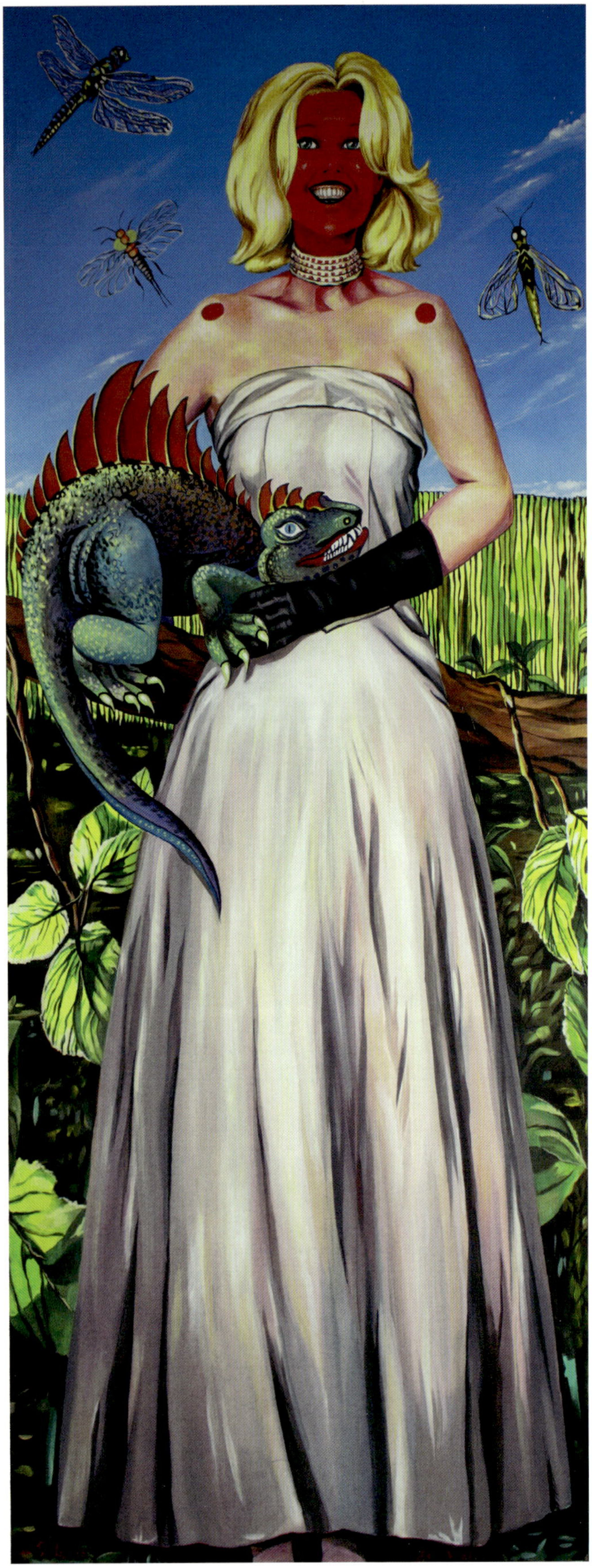

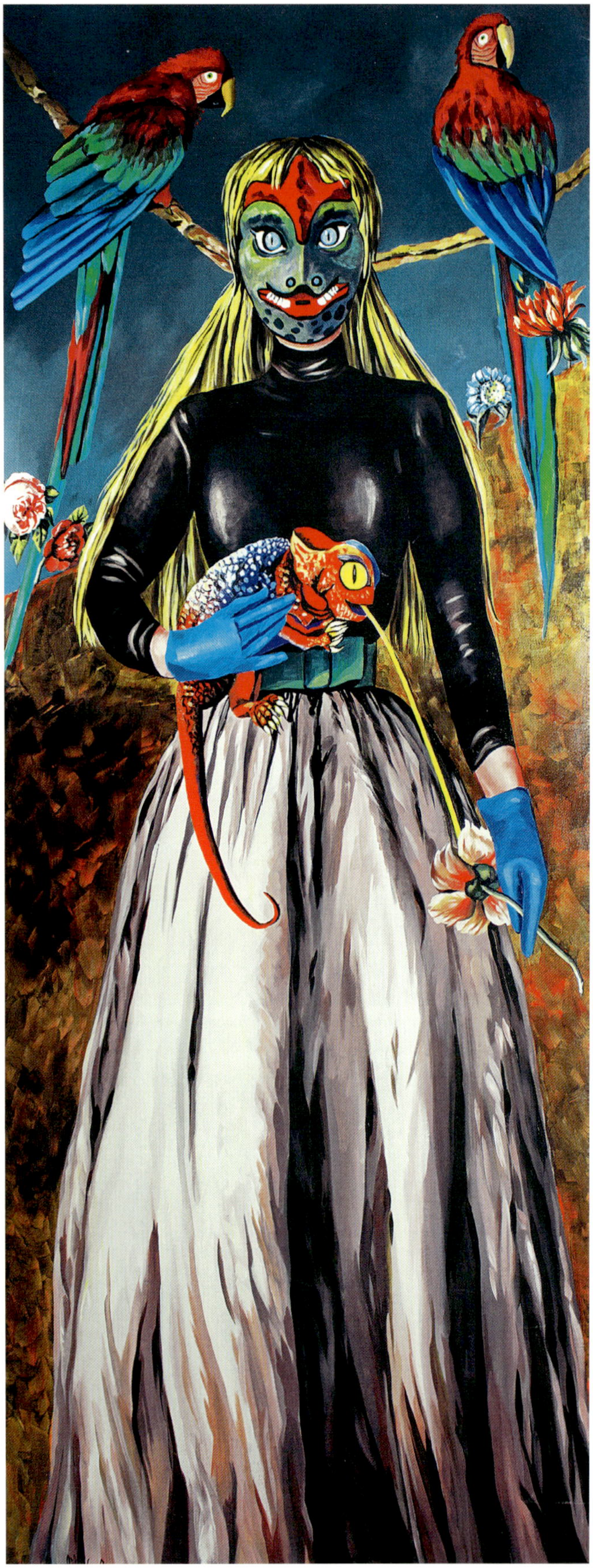

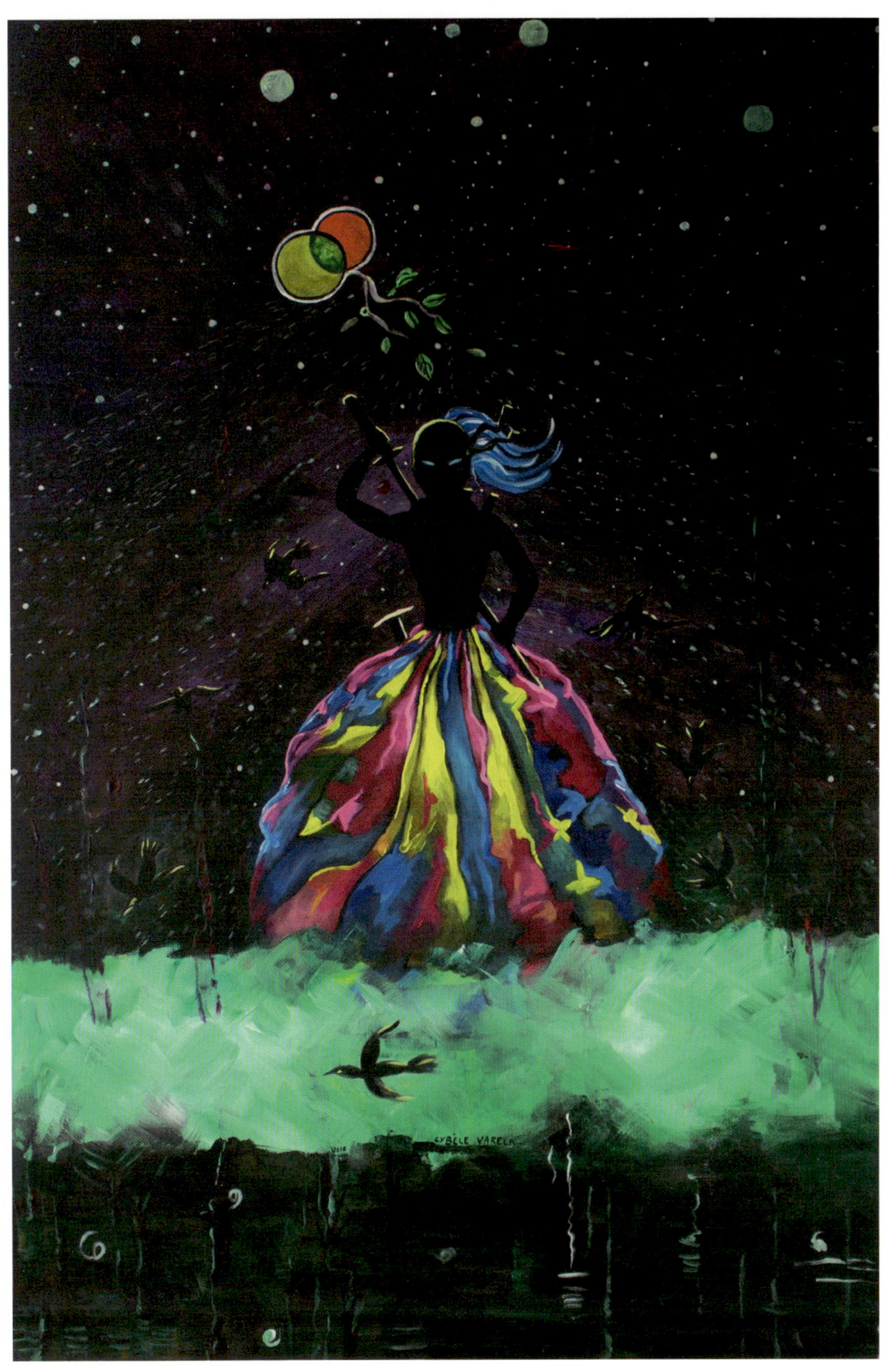

Printemps
2002

Automne
2002

O que é verdade é verdade
2010

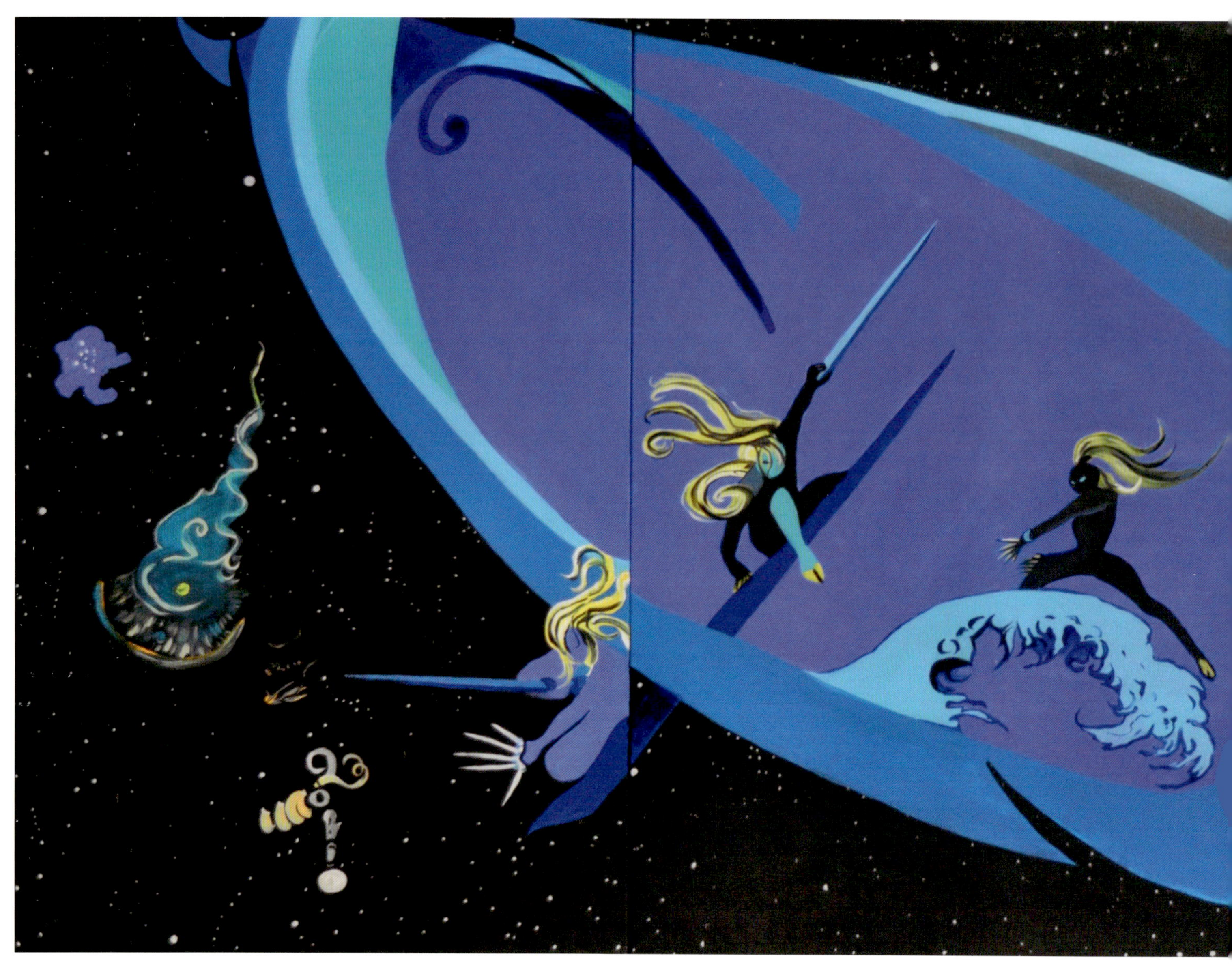

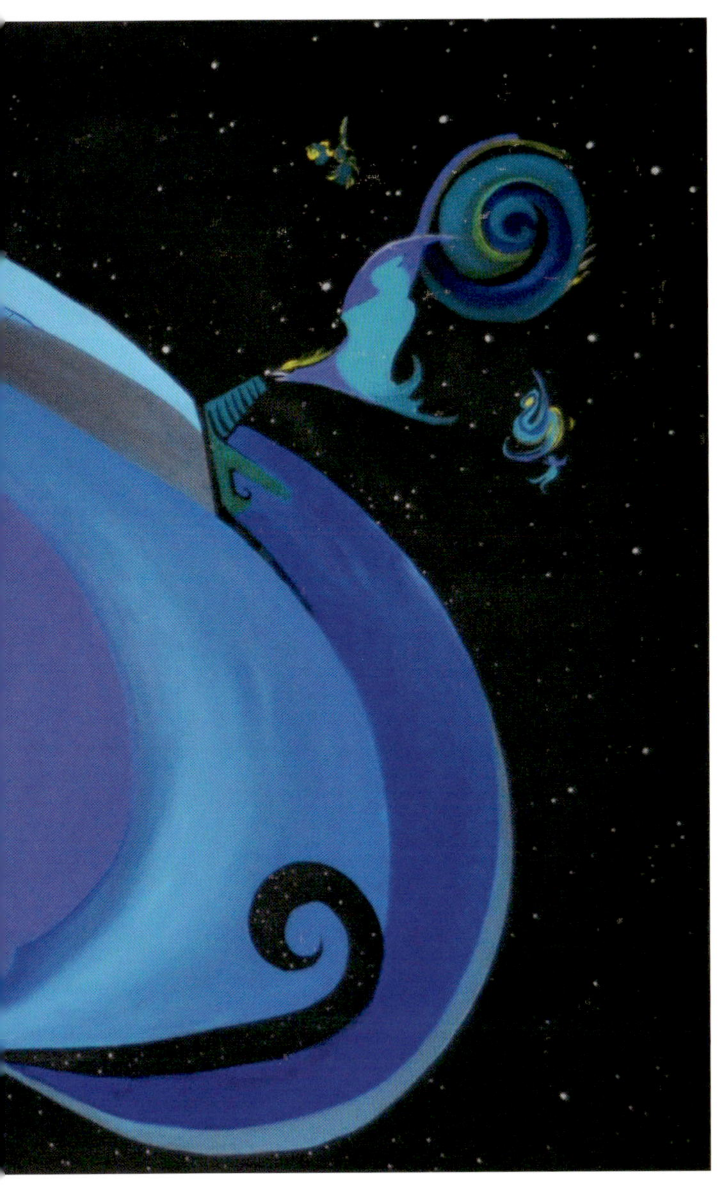

Danger
2012

Cybèle Varela started using a camera almost by chance. As she recounts: "At that time, it was the mid-1970s in Paris, I didn't have a camera and Alfred Pacquement, who later became the director of the Centre Pompidou, lent me a Super 8 so that I could produce my first short-film, *Image*." (fig. p. 85). The French museum later purchased her film for its permanent collection and showed it in 2009 on the occasion of the first edition of the exhibition *elles@centrepompidou*, organized to celebrate the work of women artists represented in the permanent collection. When Varela realized *Image*, she had just met the Argentinian kinetic artist Julio Le Parc. This encounter triggered her interest in questions related to rhythmic movement and Optic and Video Art. *Image* is turned in black and white, using a minimalistic approach and playing on the contrast of light and shadows to emphasise movement and forms – an approach which is also fundamental to Varela's other film *Image* (figs. p. 87), produced in Geneva, and to her series of paintings bearing the same title (figs. pp. 36–37, 64–69).

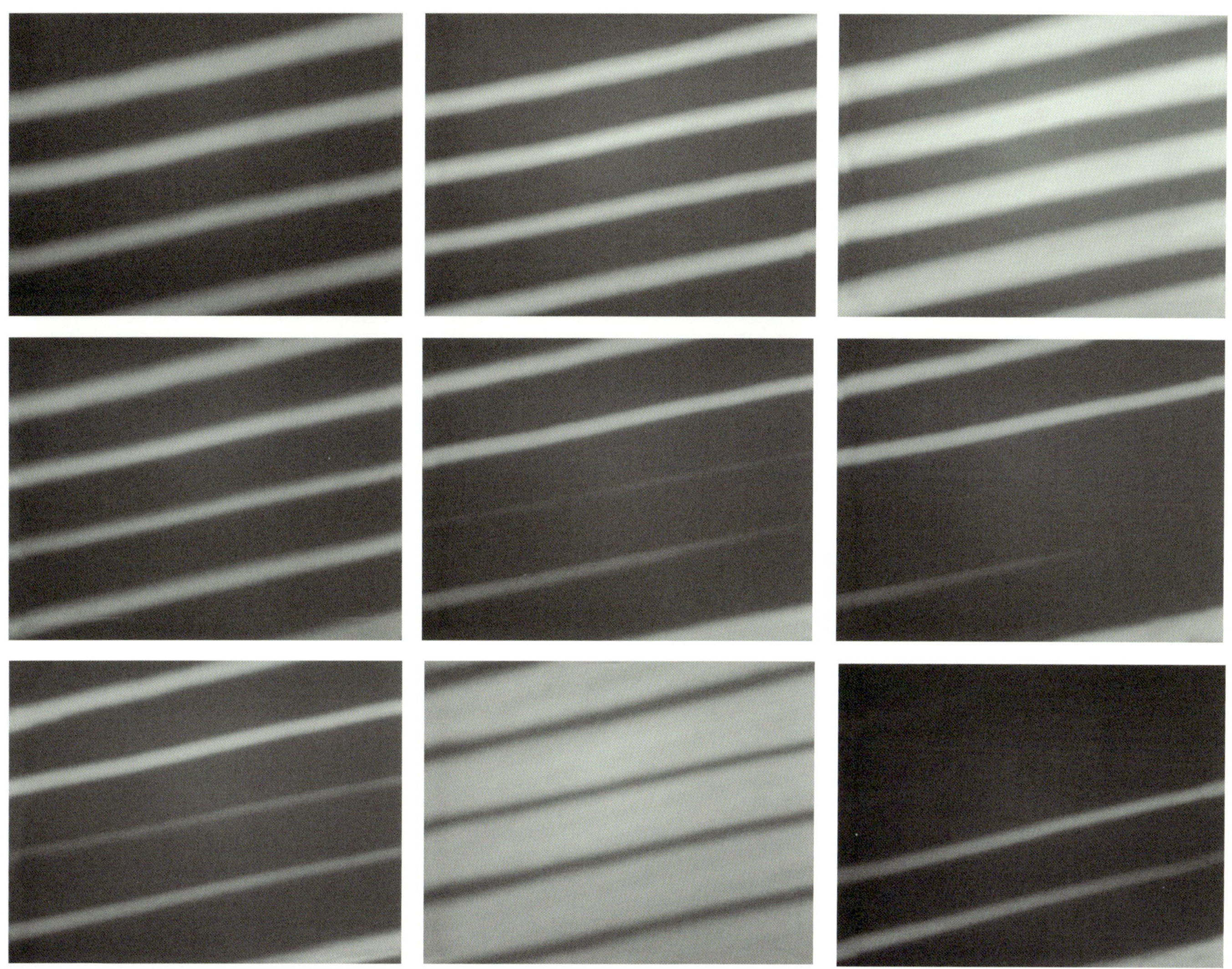

Image
1976

Amongst Varela's later video works, two more are shown in the present exhibition, both produced with a digital camera. In *Transfer* (figs. pp. 88–89) the artist chooses luxuriant colors and "tropicalist" warmth to pursue her investigation of the relation between form, light, sound and movement. A rainbow cloth is followed by the eye of the camera as it drifts away on a gentle rip current on the shoreline, provoking in the viewer a reflection on the transient character of life. The same spiritual and meditative component that is intrinsic to the sound of splashing water is also protagonist in *Fontana di Trevi* (figs. pp. 90–91). Here, what at first glance seems abstract reveals to be a sophisticated play of images taken from reality. The video poetically points to the contradictions of life nowadays in the Italian capital, where the grandeur of the Baroque past meets the triviality of human activities. VL

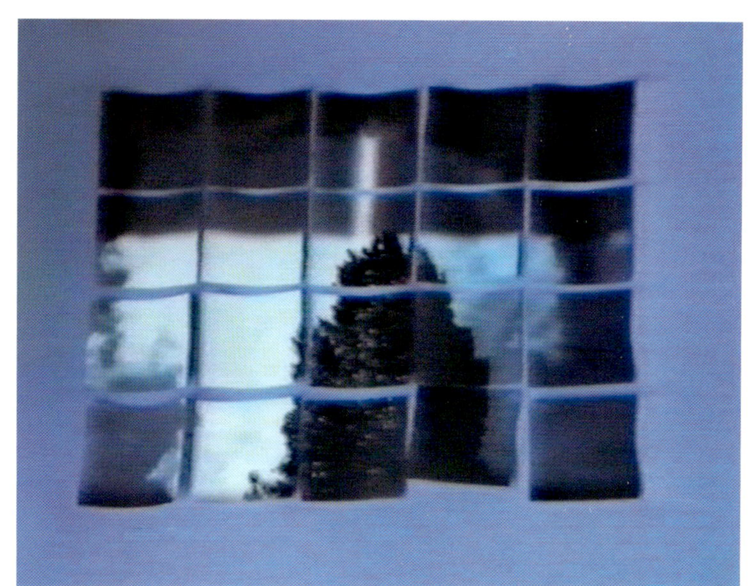

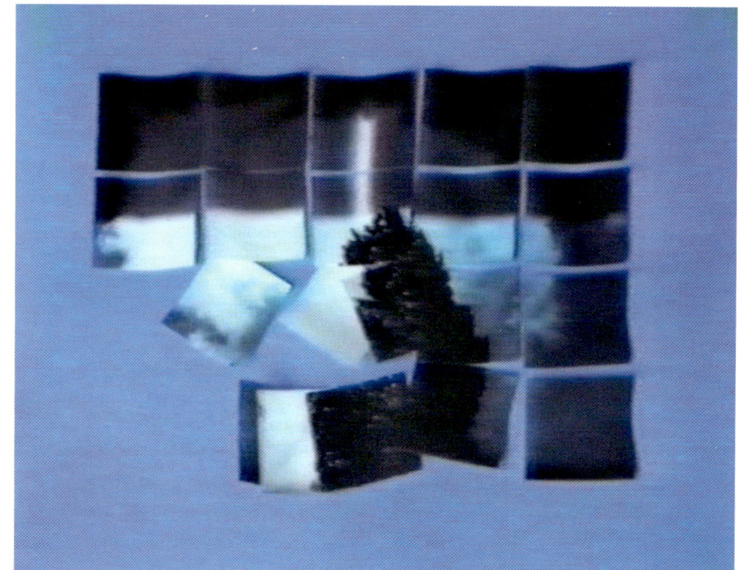

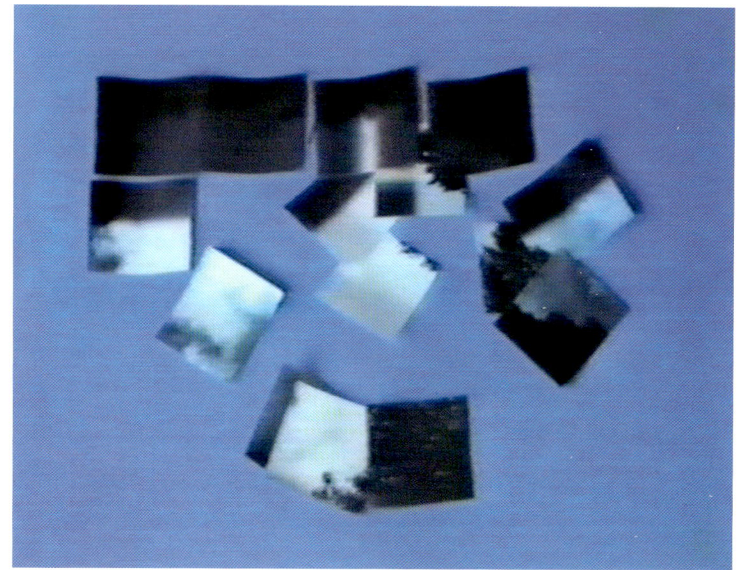

Image
1980

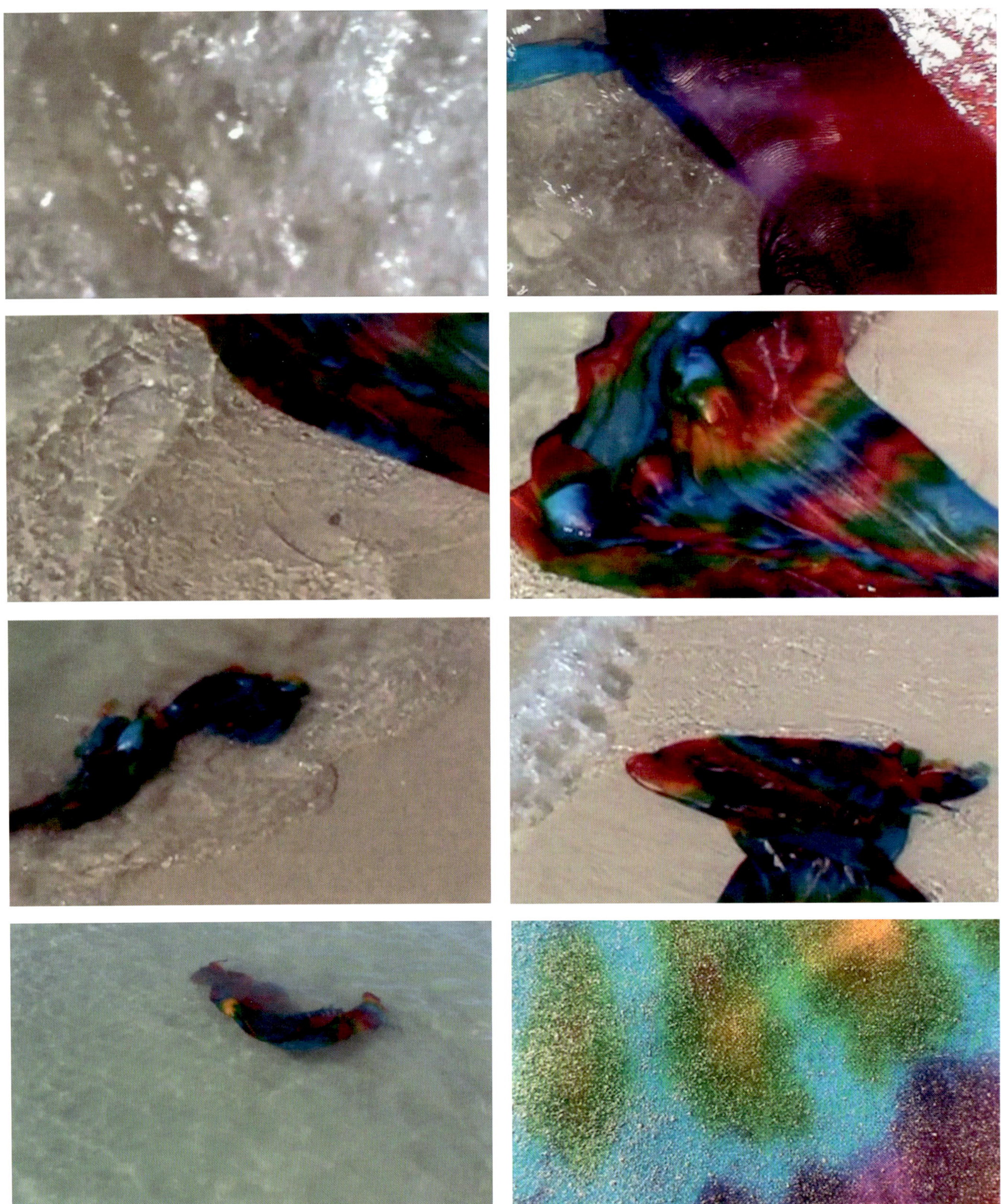

Transfer
2010

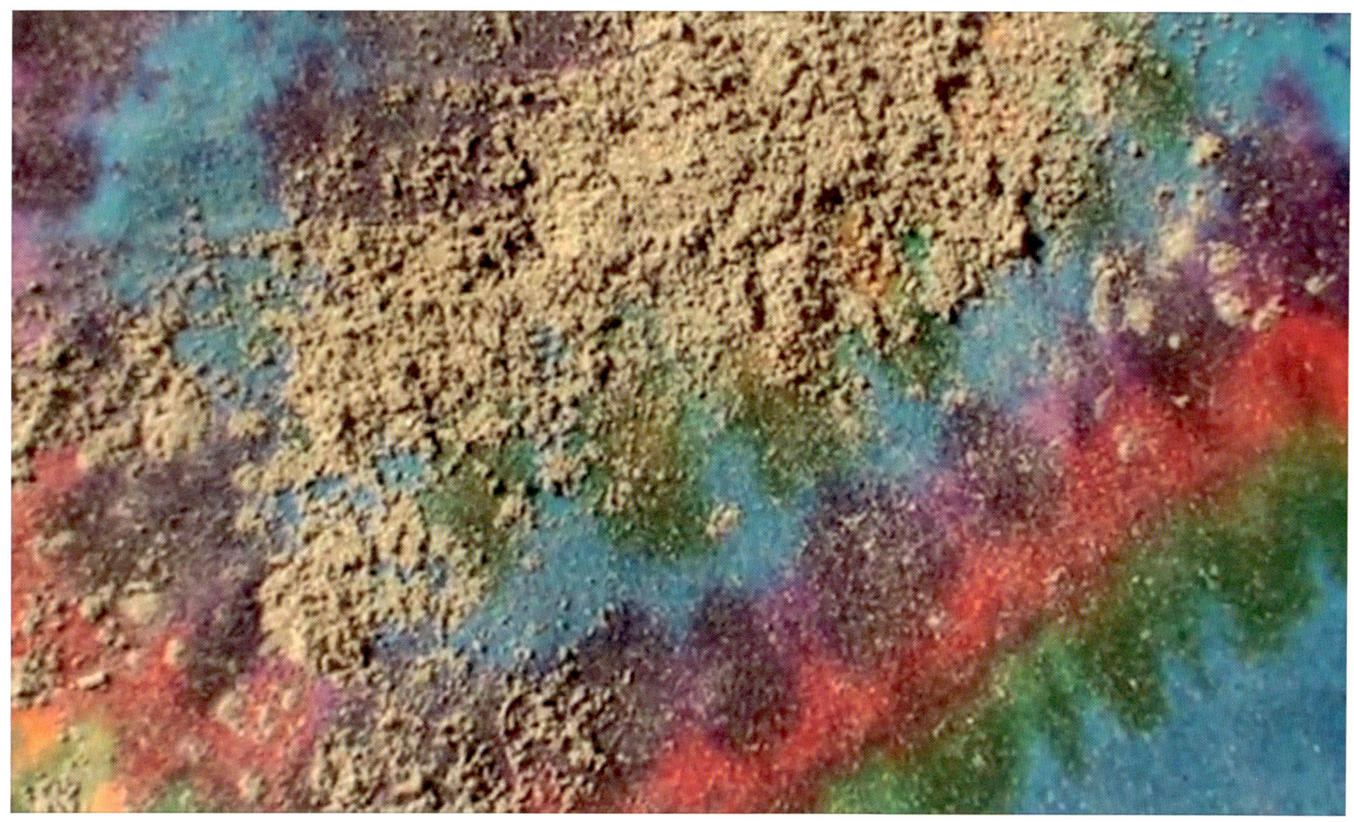

Cybèle Varela entdeckte die Fotokamera durch Zufall. So berichtet sie, dass sie, als sie sich Mitte der 1970er Jahre in Paris aufhielt, keine Fotokamera besass. Alfred Pacquement, der später zum Direktor des Centre Pompidou ernannt wurde, lieh ihr eine Super-8-Kamera, mit der sie ihren ersten Kurzfilm *Image* (Abb. S. 85) produzieren konnte.
Das französische Museum erwarb den Film später für seine permanente Sammlung und präsentierte diesen im Jahr 2009 anlässlich der ersten Ausgabe der Ausstellung *elles@centrepompidou*, die die Arbeiten der in der permanenten Sammlung vertretenen weiblichen Künstlerinnen zelebrierte.
Als Varela mit der Realisation von *Image* begann, war sie kurz vorher dem argentinischen kinetischen Künstler Julio Le Parc begegnet. Dieses Aufeinandertreffen weckte ihr Interesse für Fragestellungen bezüglich der rhythmischen Bewegung sowie der Op-Art und der Videokunst. *Image* ist in Schwarz und Weiss gehalten, wobei Varela einen minimalistischen Ansatz wählte und mit Licht- und Schattenkontrasten spielte, um Bewegungen und Formen hervorzuheben – ein Ansatz, der auch für Varelas zweiten *Image*-Film (Abb. S. 87), den sie in Genf produzierte, sowie ihre Bilderserie mit dem gleichen Titel (Abb. S. 36–37 und 64–69) relevant ist.
Zwei weitere aktuellere Videos Varelas, die beide mit einer Digitalkamera entstanden, werden in dieser Ausstellung vorgeführt. In *Transfer* (Abb. S. 88–89) wählt Varela üppige Farben und eine »tropikalistische« Wärme, um das Verhältnis von Form, Licht, Ton und Bewegung vertieft zu erkunden. Die Kamera verfolgt ein Stück Stoff in den Farben des Regenbogens, das von einem leichten Brandungsrückstrom entlang an der Küste davongetragen wird und dem Betrachter somit die Vergänglichkeit des Lebens in Erinnerung ruft.
Dieselbe spirituelle und meditative Komponente ist dem Geräusch von aufschlagendem Wasser inhärent, das zum Protagonisten in *Fontana di Trevi* (Abb. S. 90–91) wird. Was hier auf den ersten Blick abstrakt erscheint, offenbart sich als ein raffiniertes Zusammenspiel von Bildern, die der Realität entnommen wurden. Das Video verweist in poetischer Weise auf die Widersprüche, die sich im heutigen Lebensalltag in der italienischen Hauptstadt manifestieren, in der die Pracht der barocken Vergangenheit auf die Banalität der menschlichen Tätigkeiten trifft. VL

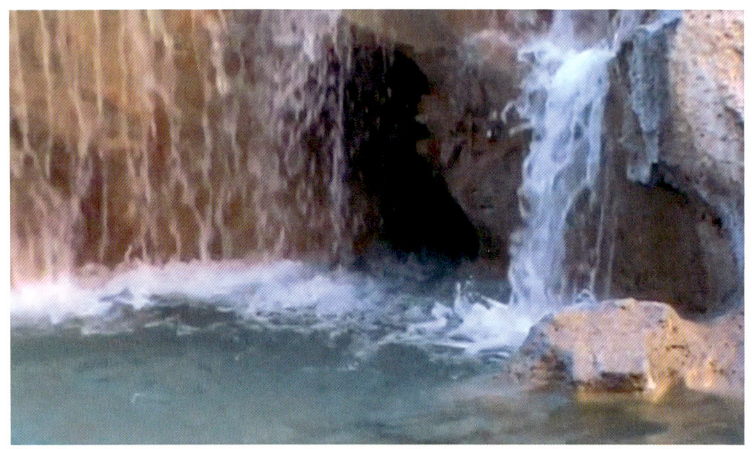

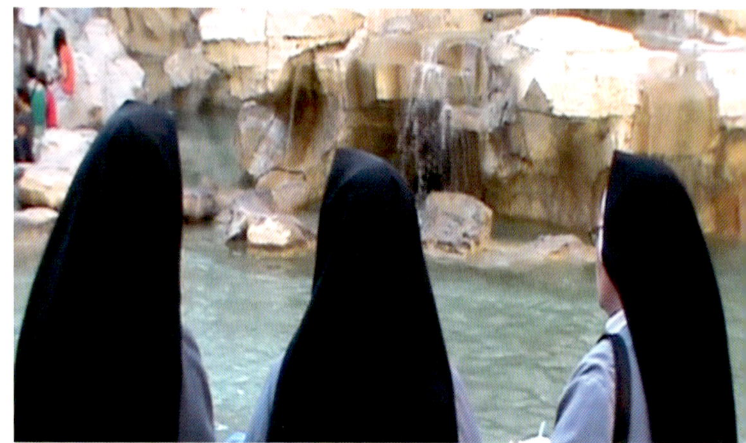

Fontana di Trevi
2014

Cybèle Varela começou a manusear uma câmera quase por acaso. Como ela mesma conta, "naquela época, estávamos na metade dos setenta, em Paris, eu não tinha câmera e Alfred Pacquement, quem mais tarde teria se tornado o diretor do Centre Pompidou, emprestou-me uma Super 8. Assim eu pude produzir minha primeira curta-metragem, *Image*." (il. p. 85). Mais tarde, o museu francês iria comprar o filme para inclui-lo em seu acervo permanente, e foi exibido em 2009, na ocasião da primeira edição da mostra *elles@centrepompidou*, organizada para celebrar a obra de mulheres artistas representadas na coleção permanente.

Quando Varela realizou *Image*, tinha acabado de encontrar o artista cinético argentino Julio Le Parc. O encontro é um marco fundamental para seu interesse nas questões relativas ao movimento rítmico, à Videoarte e à Op Art. *Image* é gravado em preto e branco, com uma abordagem minimalista, e lança mão do contraste entre luz e sombras para enfatizar movimento e formas – aspecto, este, fundamental, que reencontramos no outro filme *Image* de Varela (ils. p. 87), gravado em Genebra, e na série de pinturas que trazem o mesmo título (ils. pp. 36-37, 64-69). Entre as obras posteriores, em vídeo, de Varela, mais duas são exibidas nesta mostra, ambas produzidas com uma câmera digital. Em *Transfer* (ils. pp. 88-89) a artista escolhe as cores luxuriantes e o calor "tropicalista" para prosseguir sua investigação sobre relação entre forma, luz, som e movimento. O olho digital da câmera segue um pano multicolorido, parecendo um arco-íris que é levado suavemente pelo vaivém das ondas, à beira do mar, despertando no observador uma reflexão sobre o caráter transitório da vida. A mesma componente espiritual e meditativa, que é intrínseca ao som da queda d'agua, é protagonista também de *Fontana di Trevi* (ils. pp. 90-91). Aqui, aquilo que, a um primeiro olhar, parece abstrato, revela-se ser um sofisticado jogo de imagens tomadas da realidade. O vídeo poeticamente aponta para as contradições da vida de hoje na capital italiana, onde a grandeza passada do Barroco encontra a trivialidade das atividades humanas. VL

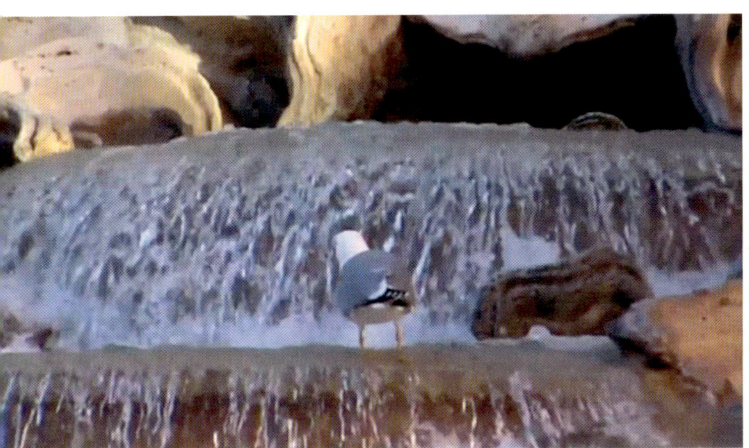

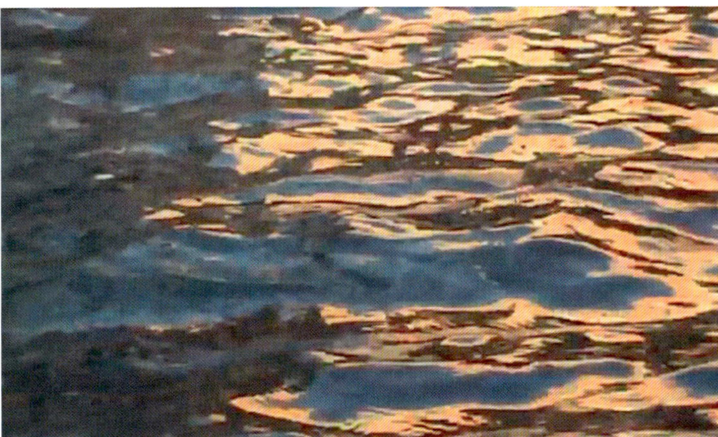

In this series, Cybèle Varela brings to the fore the Brazilian "cangaço" and its strong folkloristic imaginary. In the "Nordeste" (Brazil's Northeastern states) of the late 19th and early 20th centuries, the "cangaço" was a phenomenon in which groups of outlaws ("cangaceiros") united in search of justice and revenge. The most famous "cangaceiros" were Virgulino Lampião and his band, who became part of popular myth, as a mixture of heroes and bandits, whose exploits are praised by cordel literature ("literatura de cordel"), popular and inexpensive pamphlets containing poems, usually sold in street markets in the Northeast. Varela's first works related to the "cangaço" date back to the mid-1960s. In *Antonio das Mortes* (fig. p. 94) or *Corisco* (fig. p. 93), the childish comic strip reveal messages of social claims which echo Glauber Rocha's emblematic film *Deus e o diablo na Terra do Sol* (1964), a work that marked a milestone in Brazil's Cinema Novo movement, addressing the socio-political problems of the time.

Forty years later, Varela returned to the "cangaceiros" with her exhibition *Surroundings* at the Museu Nacional de Belas Artes in Rio de Janeiro (2003) and the Museu de Arte Contemporânea in São Paulo (2005). In paints, photographs and video, she deconstructed the narrative of the popular myth, portraying Lampião and his acolytes (figs. pp. 96–99) almost as epic heroes, close-up, insisting on the mystical religiosity of the "sertão" (backcountry) rustic

Catholicism and its superstitions. In *Maria Bonita* (fig. p. 95), Lampião's partner, the viewer is attracted by the magnetic look of Maria "the Beautiful", whose image appears wrapped in clear cellophane, trapped in a distant and parallel reality. Her emblematic figure has become a product of collective memory and cultural industry. AVB

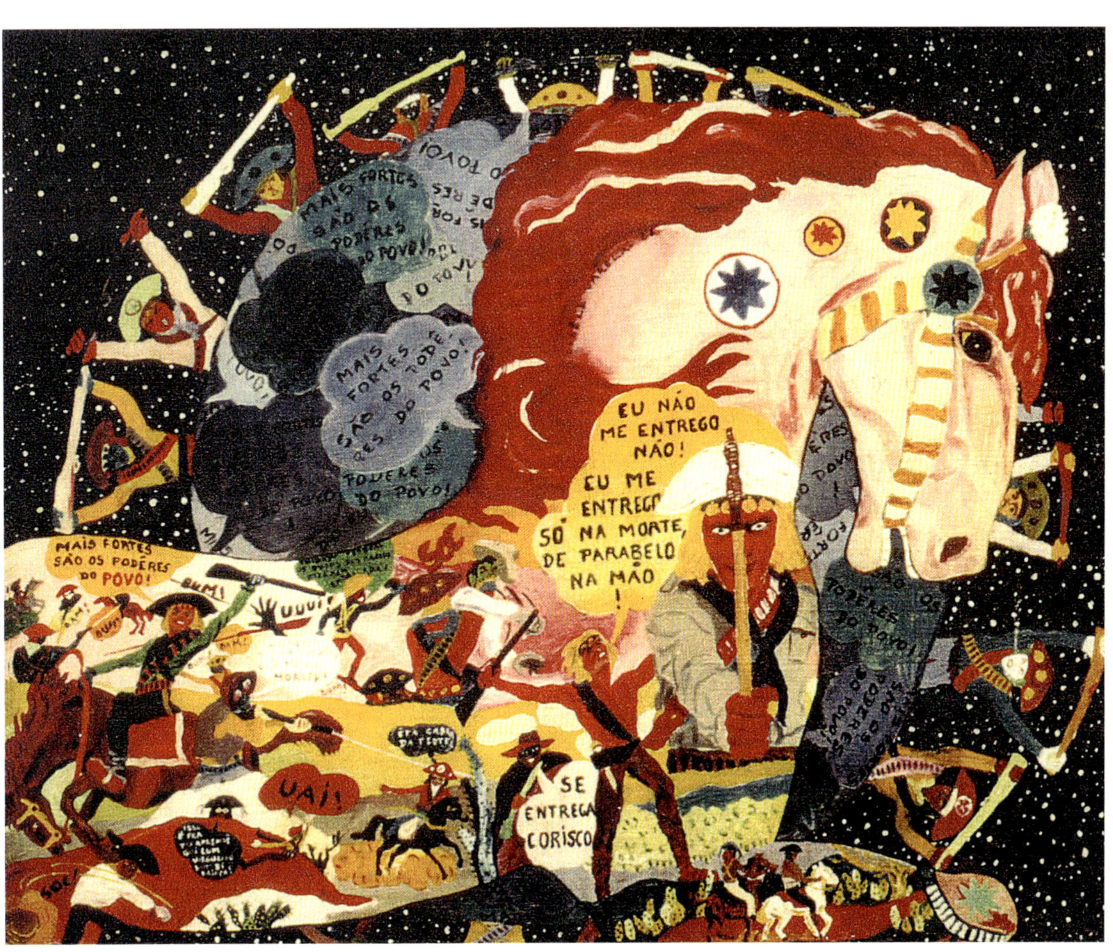

Corisco
1966

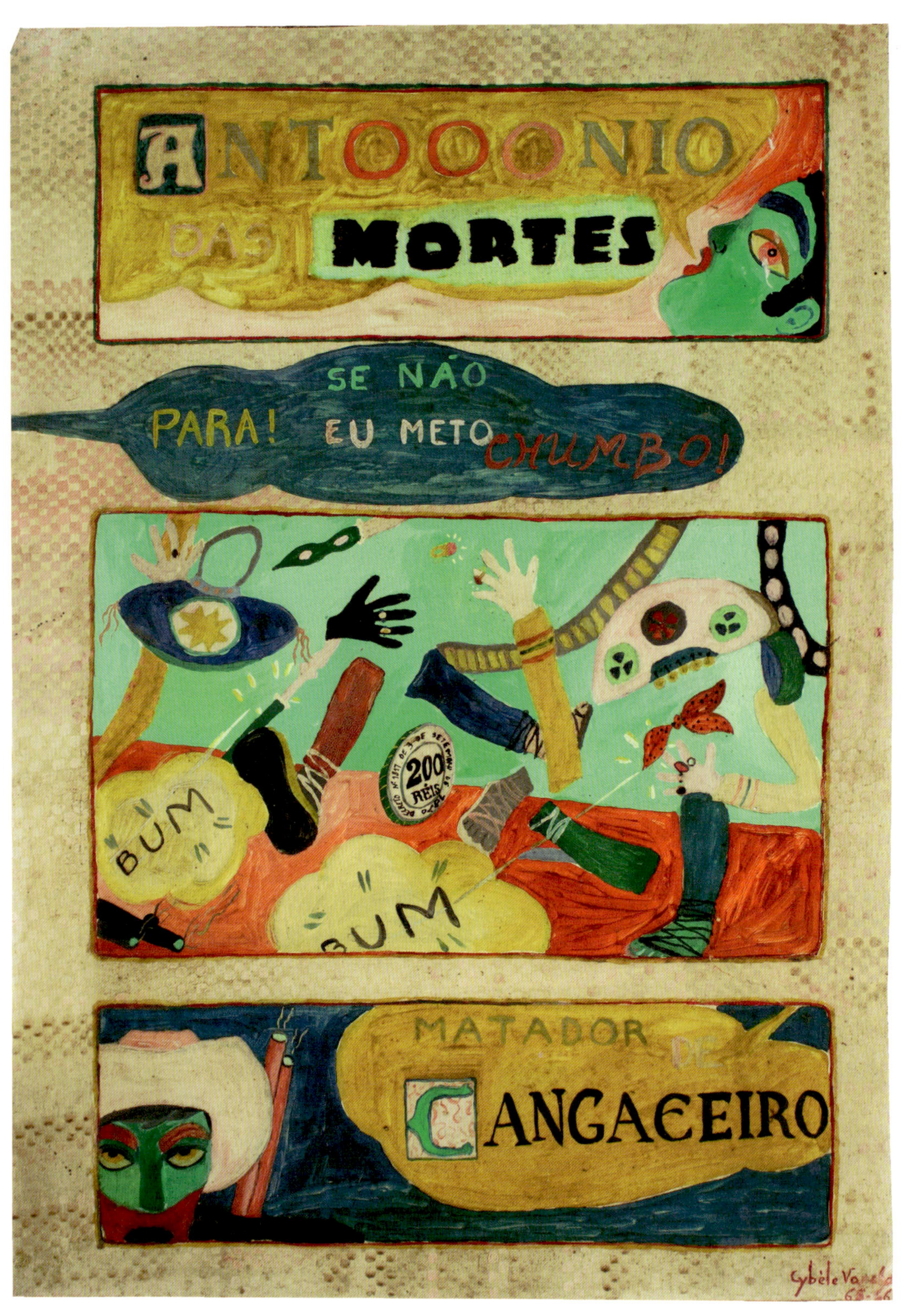

Antonio das Mortes
1965–1966

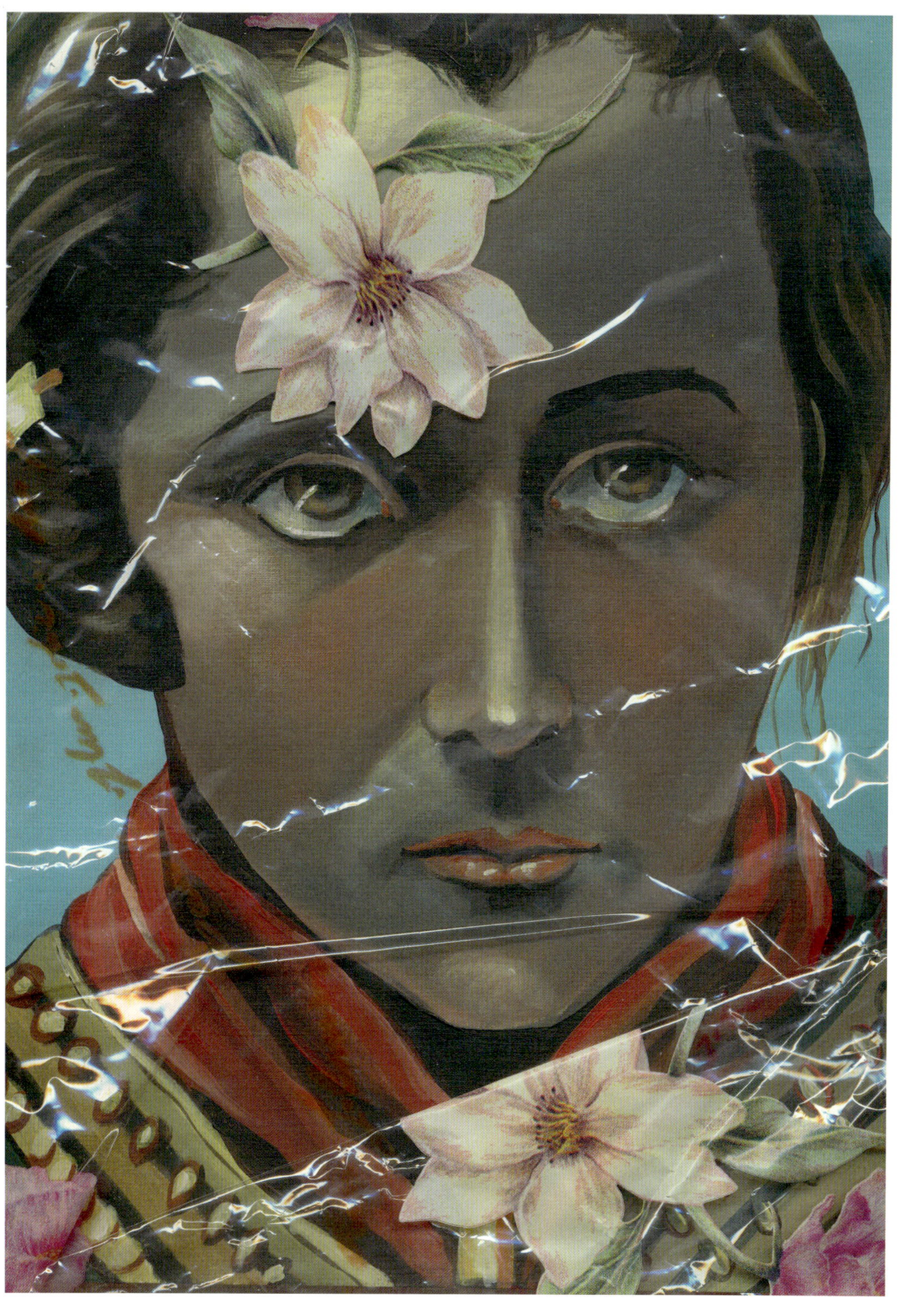

Maria Bonita
2003

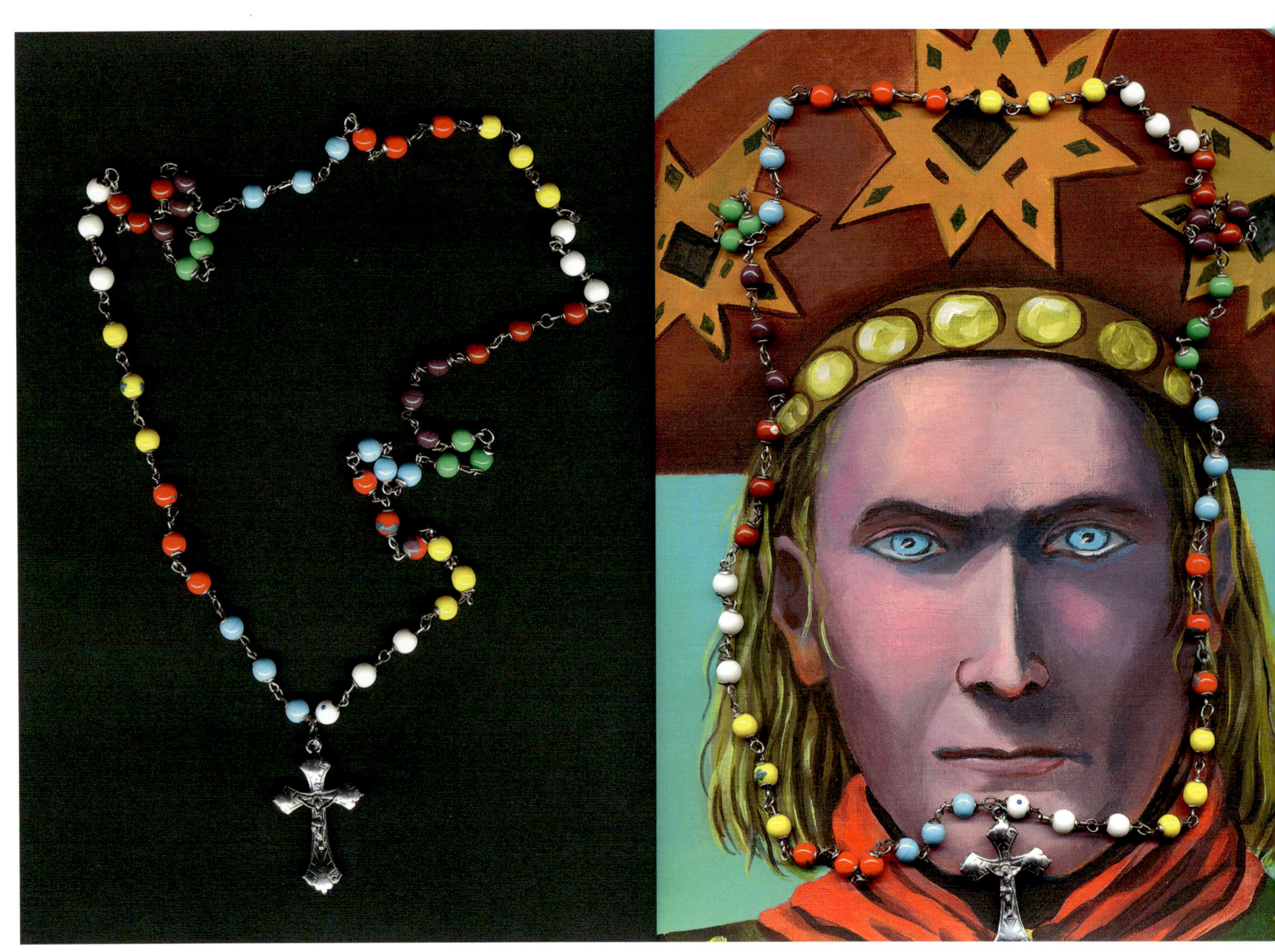

Corisco e os terços
2003

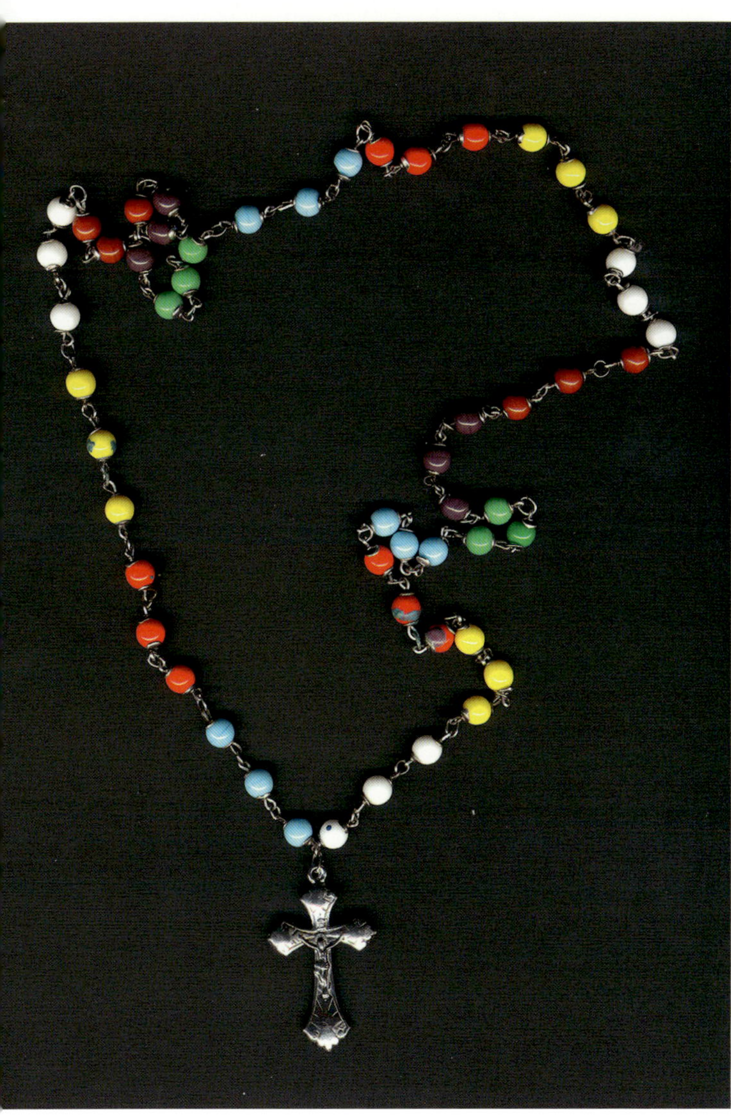

In dieser Serie stellt Cybèle Varela das brasilianische »Cangaço«-Banditentum und seine ausgeprägte folkloristische Vorstellungswelt in den Fokus. In den »Nordeste« (Nordostregion) trat im späten 19. und frühen 20. Jahrhundert das Phänomen des »Cangaço«-Banditentums auf. Es handelte sich hierbei um Banditen (»Cangaceiros«), die sich auf der Suche nach Gerechtigkeit und Rache zu Gruppen zusammenschlossen. Die berühmtesten »Cangaceiros« waren Virgulino Lampião und seine Ganovenbande, um die sich ein Volksmythos rankte. Sie galten als eine Mischung aus Helden und Banditen, deren Taten in der Literatura de Cordel und in günstigen, auf den Strassenmärkten in der Nordostregion angebotenen Gedichtheftchen gepriesen wurden. Varelas erste Arbeiten, die sich auf das »Cangaço«-Banditentum beziehen, gehen auf die Mitte der 1960er Jahre zurück. In *Antonio das Mortes* (Abb. S. 94) oder *Corisco* (Abb. S. 93) enthält der naiv anmutende Comicstrip Botschaften, die einen sozialen Anspruch vermitteln und auf Glauber Rochas emblematischen Film *Deus e o diablo na Terra do Sol* (1964) verweisen, eine Arbeit, die als Schlüsselwerk des brasilianischen »Cinema Novo« (Neuen Kino) gilt, das sich mit den damaligen gesellschaftspolitischen Problemen auseinandersetzte. Vierzig Jahre später kam Varela anlässlich ihrer Ausstellung *Surroundings* im Museu Nacional de Belas Artes in Rio de Janeiro (2003) und im Museu de Arte Contemporânea in São Paulo (2005) erneut auf die »Cangaceiros« zurück. In Bildern, Fotografien und Videos dekonstruierte sie das Narrativ des Volksmythos und porträtierte Lampião und seine Ganovenbande als quasi epische Helden in Close-up-Aufnahme (Abb. S. 96–99), wobei sie der mystischen Religiosität des für den »Sertão« (Hinterland) typischen ländlichen Katholizismus und seines Aberglaubens treu blieb. In *Maria Bonita* (Abb. S. 95), die Lampiãos Gefährtin war, wird der Betrachter vom Anblick Marias, »der Schönen«, in den Bann gezogen. Maria, die, eingewickelt in Zellophan, einer weit entfernten, parallelen Realität verhaftet zu sein scheint, wurde als emblematische Figur zu einem Produkt des kollektiven Gedächtnisses und der Kulturindustrie. AVB

Com esta série, Cybèle Varela traz em sua obra o fenômeno brasileiro do cangaço e seu forte imaginário folclórico. O cangaço caracterizou o período entre final do século XIX e início do século XX em todo o Nordeste brasileiro. Grupos de fora-da-lei, os cangaceiros, juntavam-se em busca de justiça e vingança. O mais famoso cangaceiro foi sem dúvida Virgulino Ferreira da Silva, o Lampião, que, com seu bando, tornou-se parte de um mito popular, que à figura do bandido sobrepõe os traços do herói, cujos feitos têm sua tradução artística na literatura de cordel e seus panfletos simples dedicados à publicação de poemas, geralmente vendidos nos mercados de rua do Nordeste brasileiro.
As primeiras obras de Varela ligadas ao cangaço são de meados da década de sessenta. Em *Antônio das Mortes* (il. p. 94) ou *Corisco* (il. p. 93), os quadrinhos infantis revelam mensagens de reinvindicações sociais que fazem eco ao emblemático filme de Glauber Rocha, *Deus e o diabo na Terra do Sol* (1964), uma obra que representa um marco no Cinema Novo do Brasil, abordando problemas sócio-políticos daquela época.
Quarenta anos mais tarde, Varela retoma o tema dos cangaceiros com sua mostra *Surroundings* no Museu Nacional de Belas-Artes do Rio de Janeiro (2003) e o Museu de Arte Contemporânea de São Paulo (2005). Com pinturas, fotos e vídeos, Cybèle desconstrói a narrativa do mito popular, oferecendo um retrato de Lampião e seus acólitos (ils. pp. 96-99) quase como se fossem heróis épicos, insistindo na religiosidade mística do sertão, suas superstições e seu Catolicismo rustico. Em *Maria Bonita* (il. p. 95), a companheira de Lampião, o observador é atraído pelo olhar magnético da bela Maria, cuja imagem é apresentada envolvida em celofane transparente, presa numa realidade paralela e distante. A sua emblemática figura tornou-se um produto do imaginário coletivo e da indústria cultural. AVB

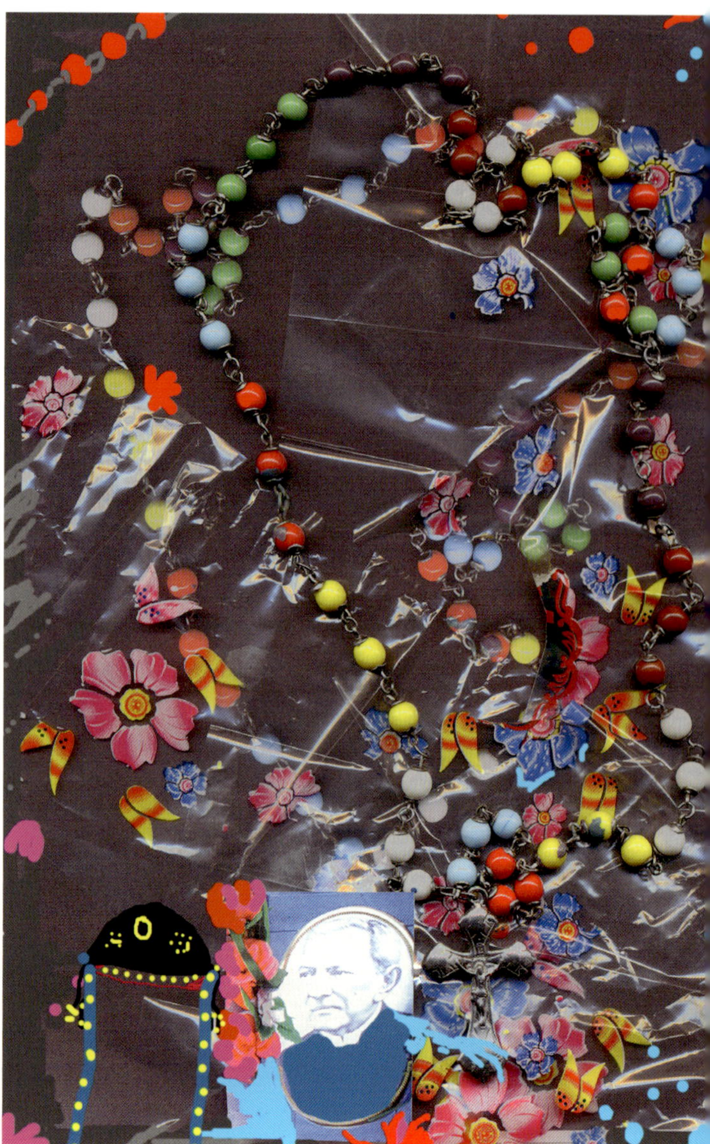

Jurití
2003

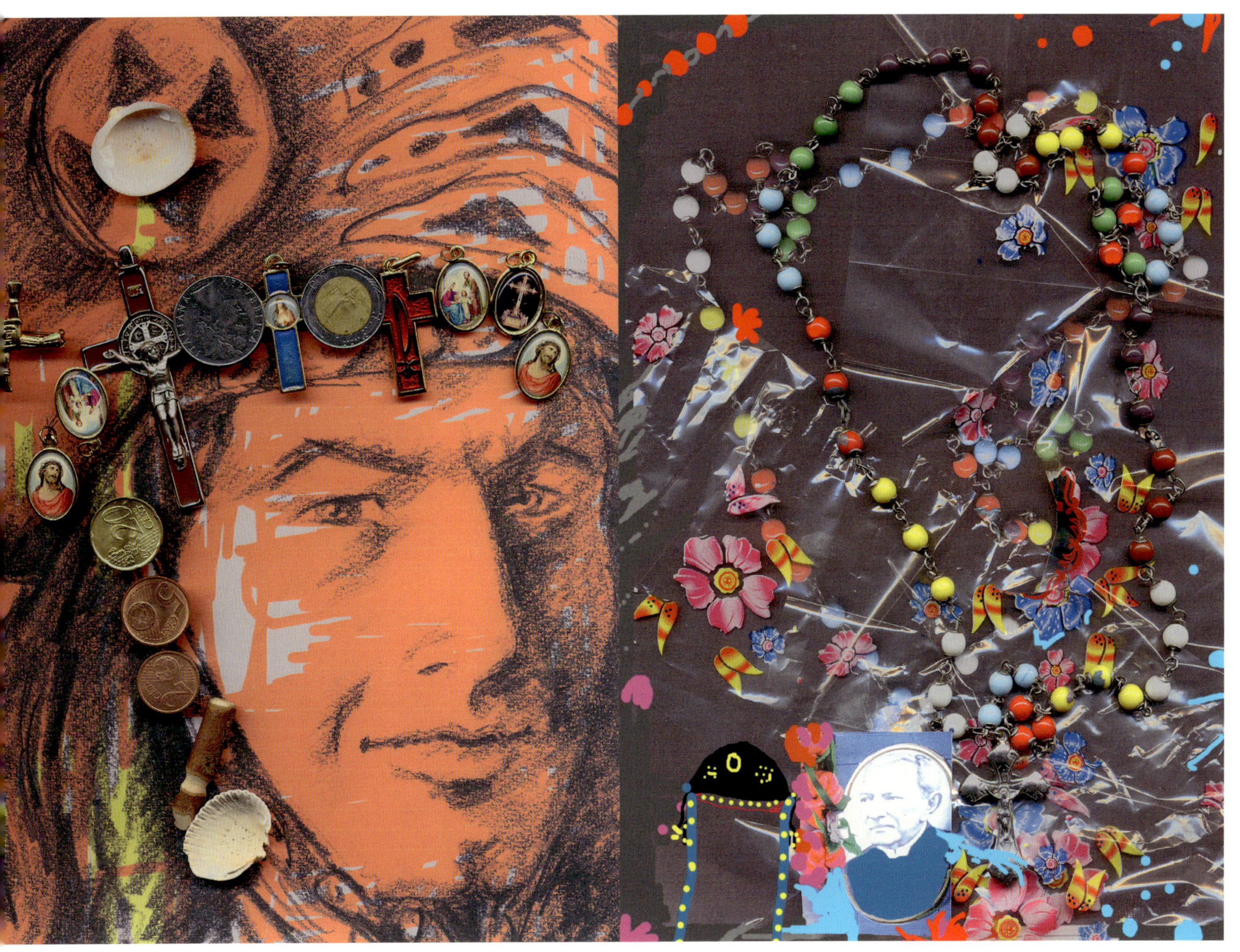

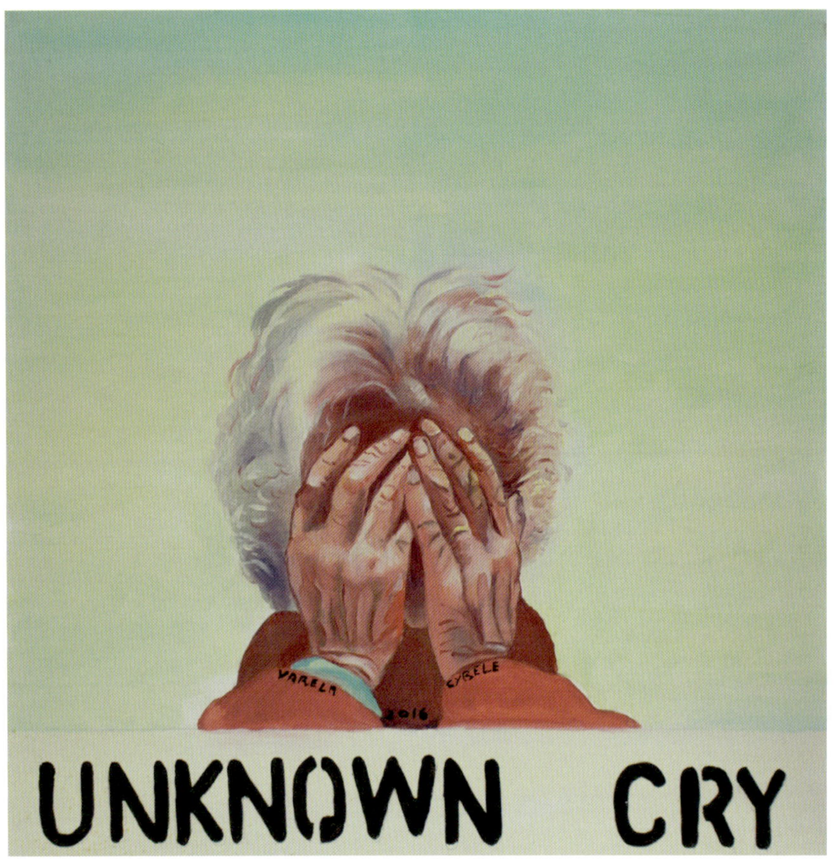

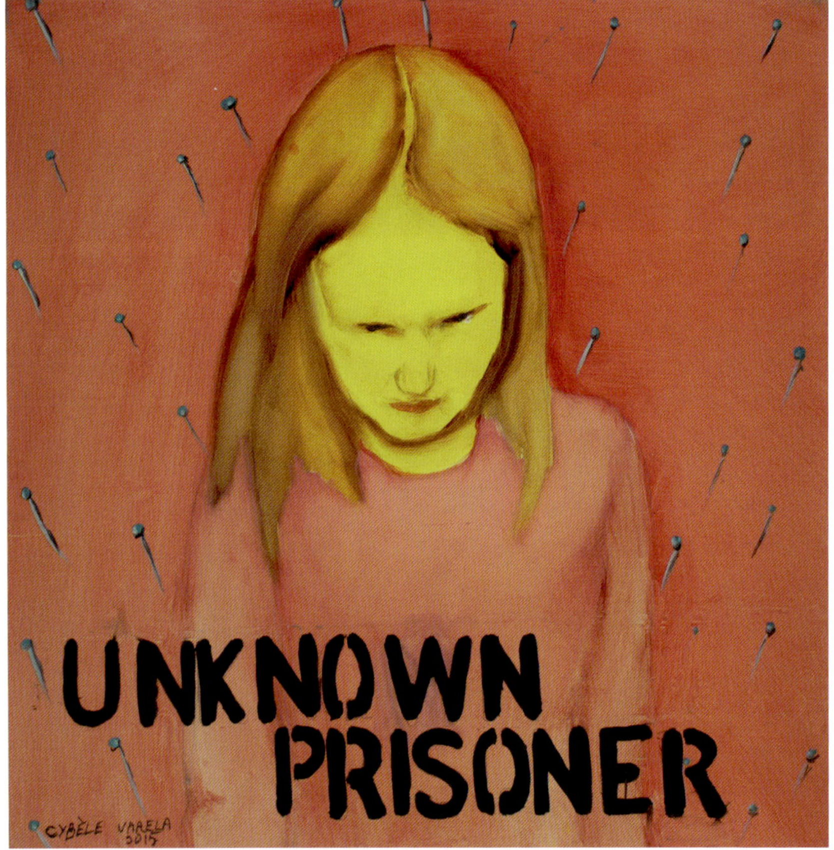

"...this series is about the forgotten ones, the cruelty of the indifference that absorbs the spectator, the indifference for human beings, animals and other elements of nature, which becomes abandonment and gratuitous elimination. Dealing with the changes and the migrations running through our history, *Unknown* is about everything that should have been considered but wasn't".

Cybèle Varela

Unknown Cry
2016

Unknown Prisoner
2015

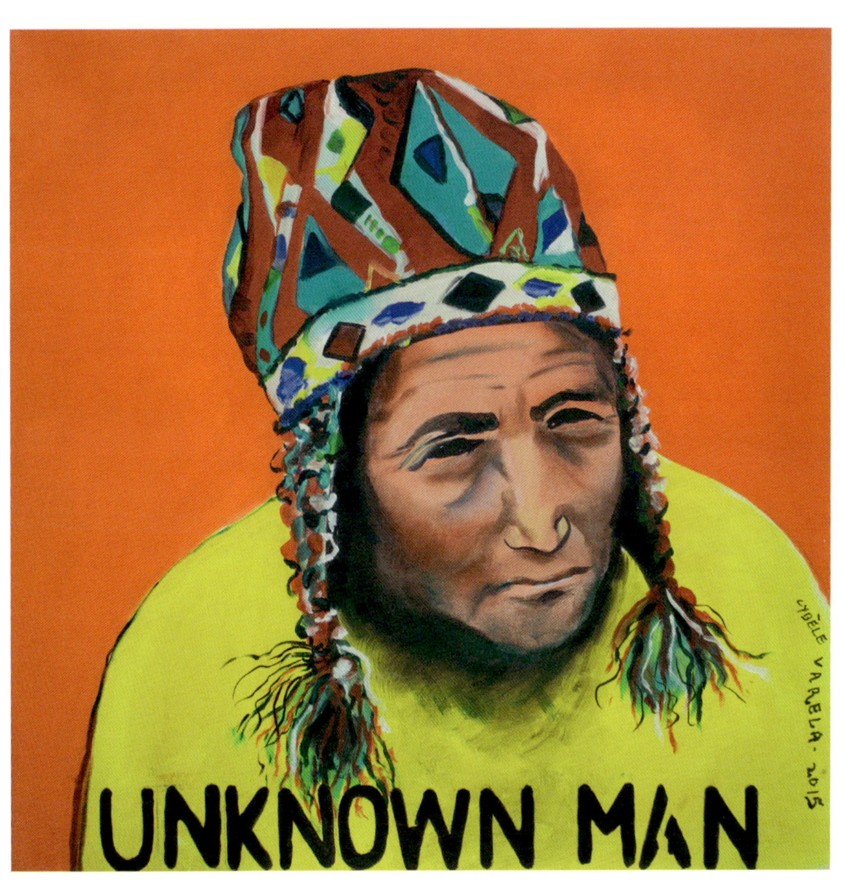

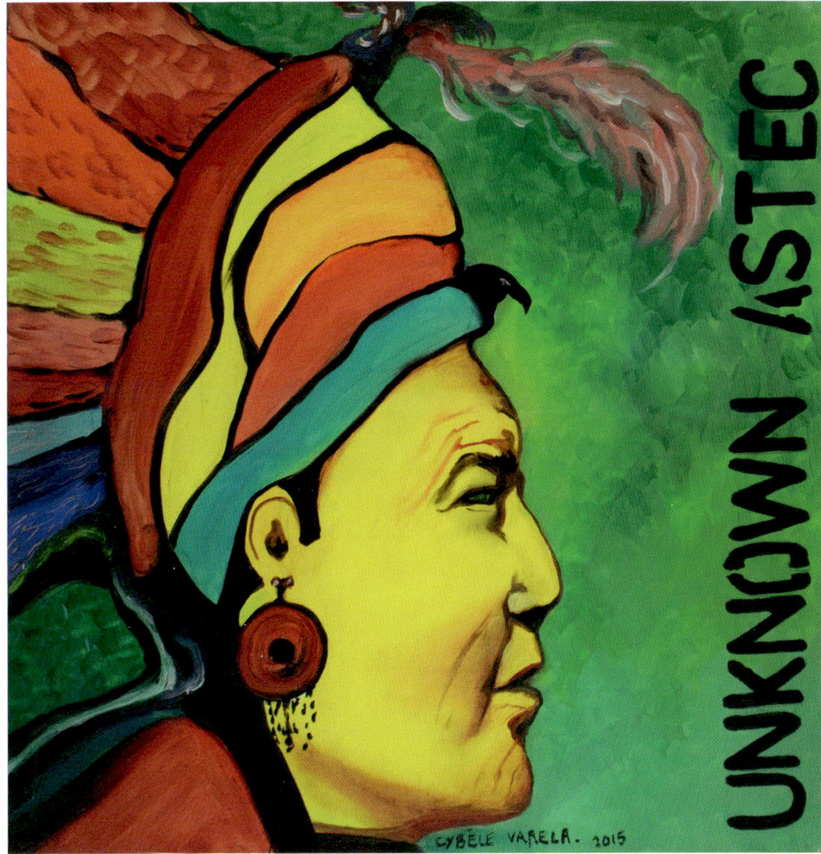

Unknown Man
2015

Unknown Aztec
2015

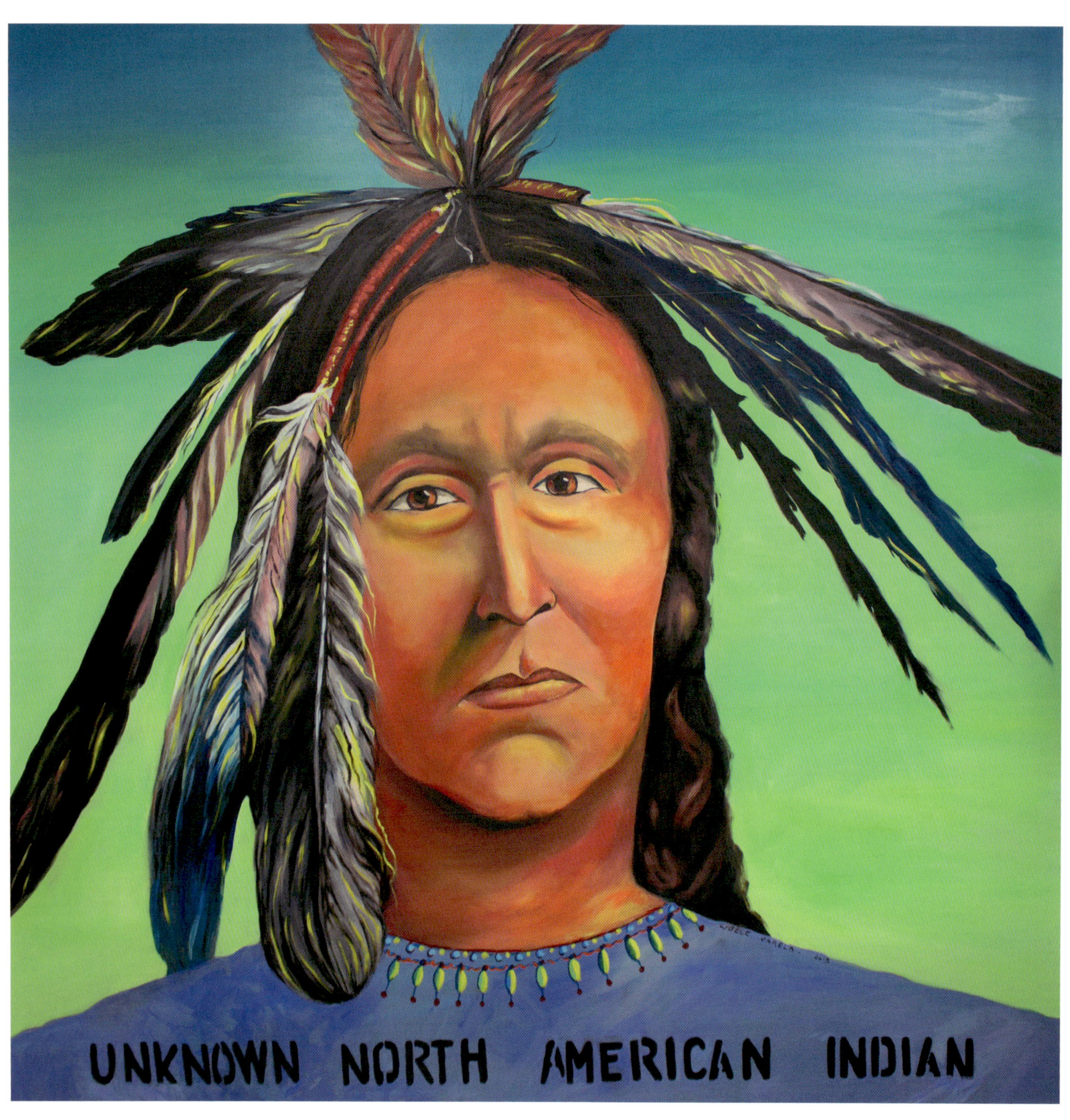

Unknown North
American Indian
2016

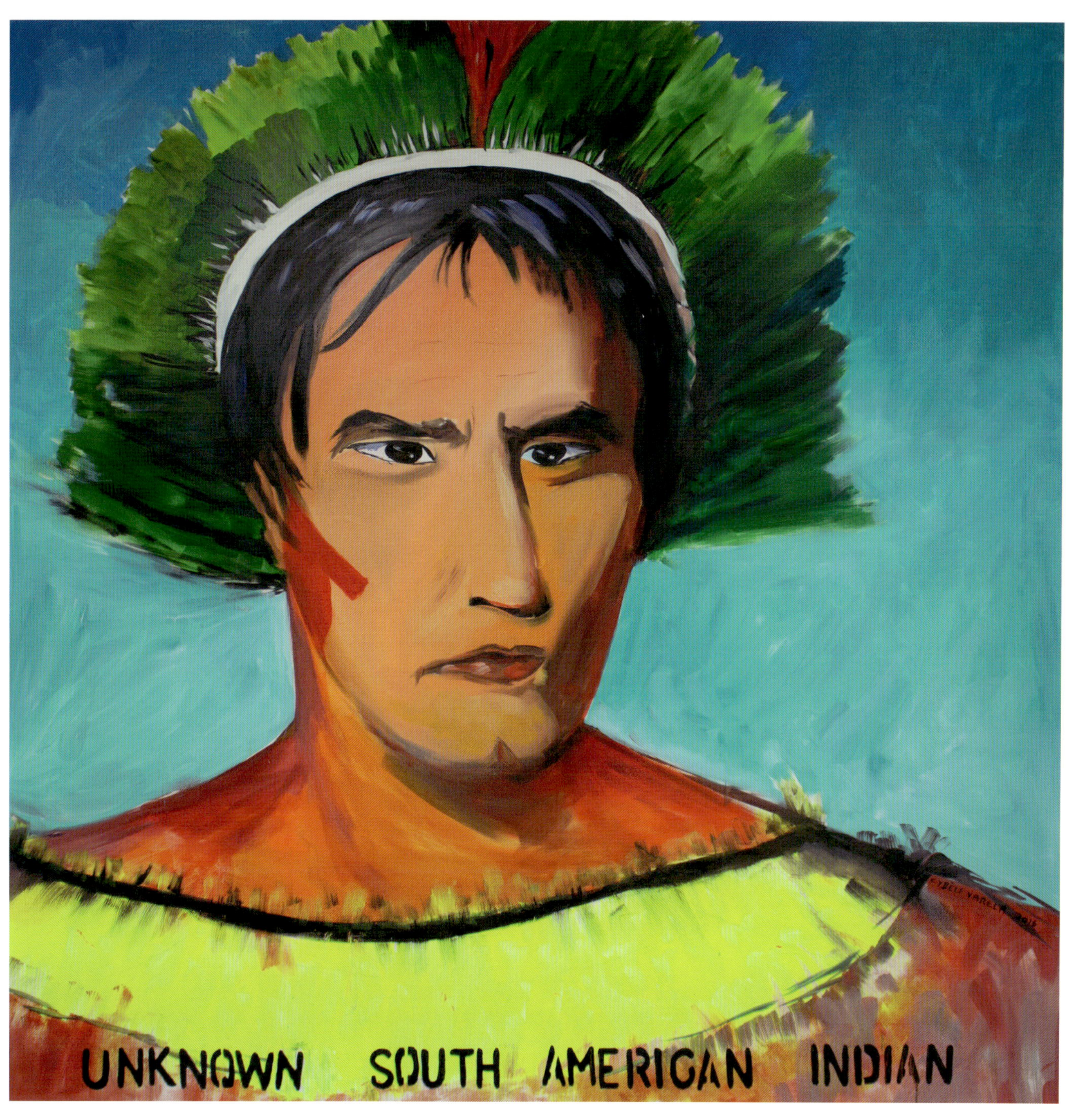

Unknown South
American Indian
2016

»… diese Serie handelt von den Vergessenen, der Grausamkeit der Gleichgültigkeit, die sich des Betrachters bemächtigt, die Gleichgültigkeit gegenüber menschlichen Wesen, Tieren und anderen Naturelementen, die zur Vernachlässigung und freiwilligen Beseitigung wird. Über die Veränderungen und die Wanderungen, die sich durch unsere Geschichte ziehen. *Unknown* handelt von all dem, was berücksichtigt hätte werden sollen und es doch nie wurde.«

Cybèle Varela

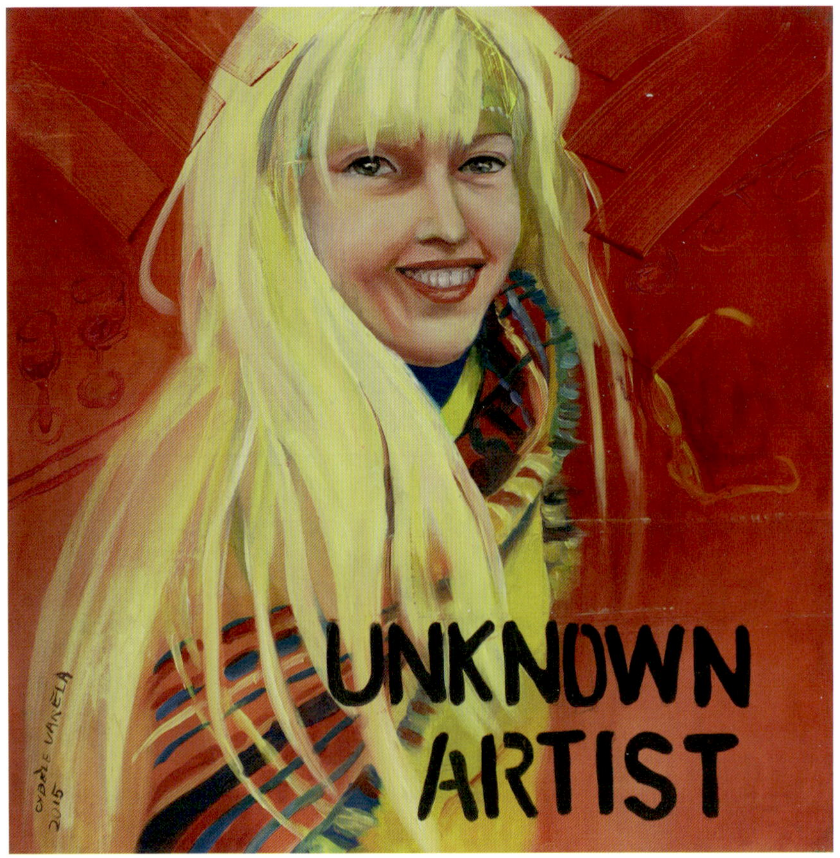

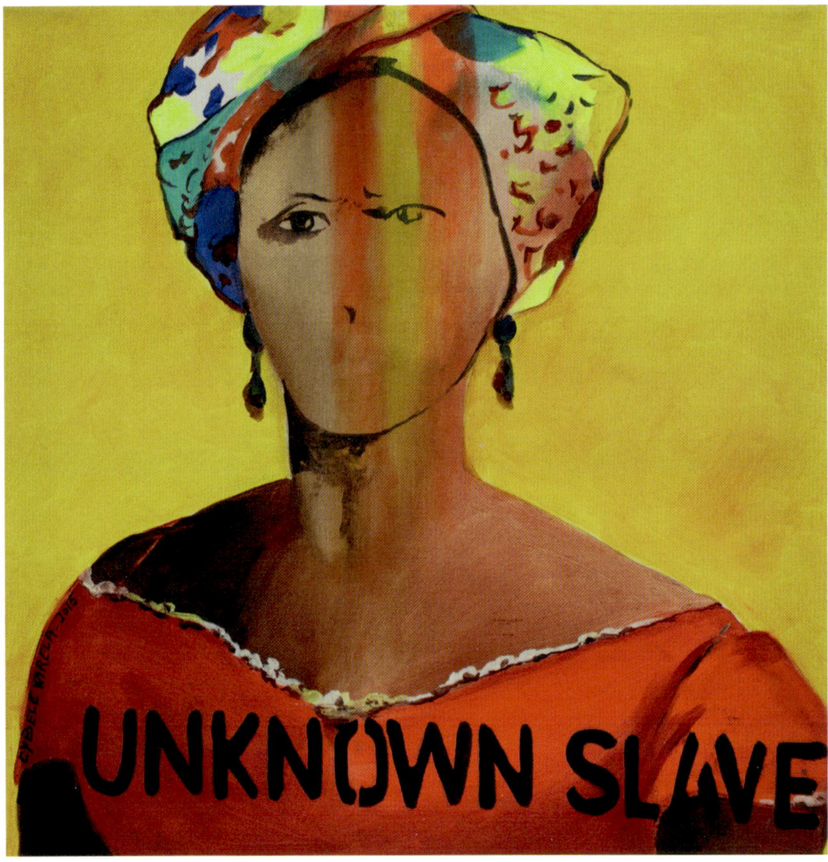

Unknown Artist
2015

Unknown Slave
2015

"... esta serie é sobre os esquecidos, a crueldade da indiferença que absorve o espectador, a indiferença pelos seres humanos, animais e outros elementos da Natureza, indiferença esta que se torna abandono e eliminação gratuita. Sobre as mudanças e as migrações que atravessam nossa história. *Unknown* é sobre tudo aquilo que deveria ter sido considerado e que não foi".

Cybèle Varela

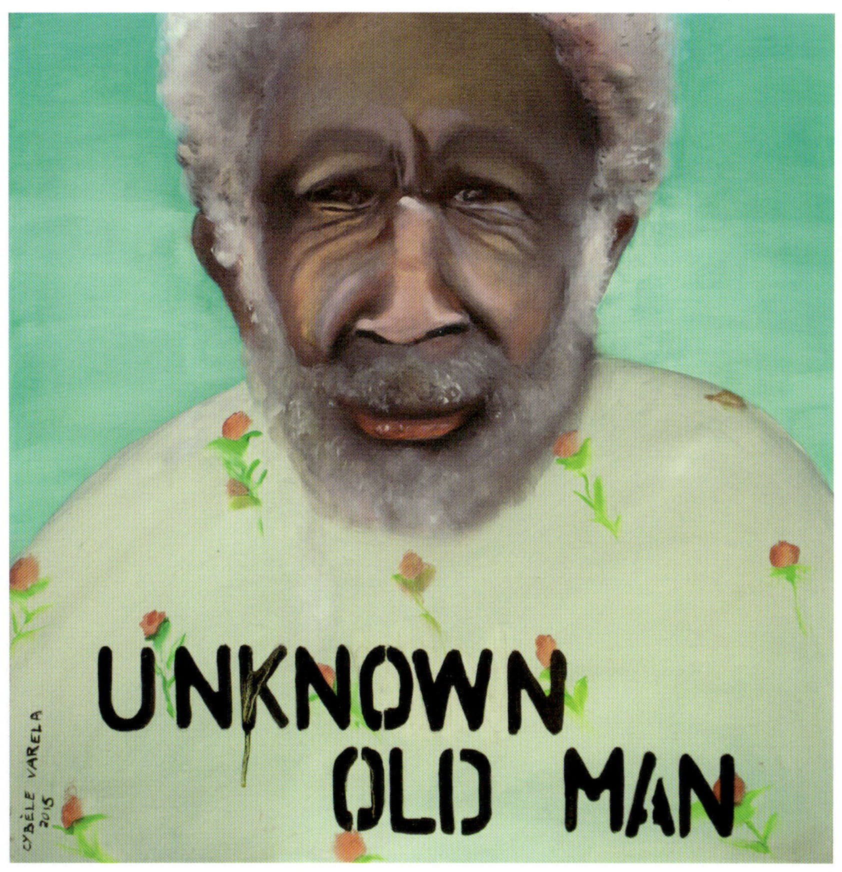

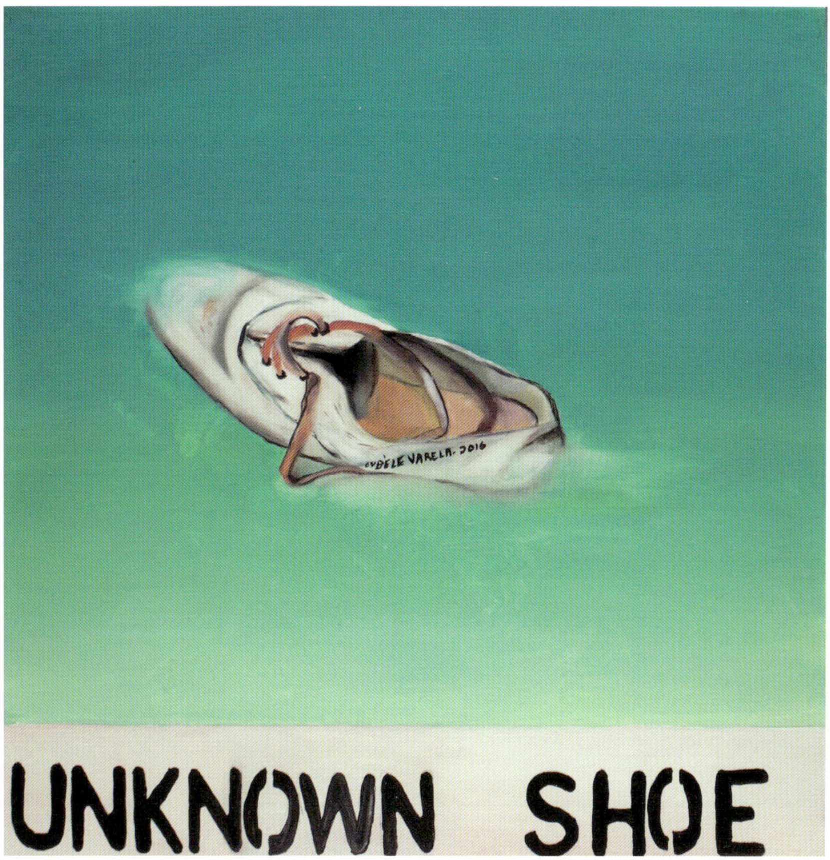

Unknown Old Man
2015

Unknown Shoe
2016

Appendix

Anhang
Apêndice

List of Exhibited Works
Liste der ausgestellten Werke
Lista das obras expostas

All works / Alle Werke / Todas as obras: Collection of the artist / Sammlung der Künstlerin / Coleção da artista, Madrid

Antonio das Mortes
1965–1966
Oil on wood fiber / Öl auf Holzfaser / Óleo sobre fibra de madeira, 81 × 65 cm
Fig. p. / Abb. S. / Il. p. 94

Telefone Real
1967
(Royal Telephone / Königliches Telefon)
Oil on wood / Öl auf Holz / Óleo sobre madeira, 17 × 27 × 20 cm
Fig. p. / Abb. S. / Il. p. 21

Maison du Brésil
1973
Industrial paint on wood / Industrielack auf Holz / Pintura industrial sobre madeira, 90 × 63 cm
Fig. p. / Abb. S. / Il. p. 32

O tucano
1973
Industrial paint on wood / Industrielack auf Holz / Pintura industrial sobre madeira, 90 × 63 cm
Fig. p. / Abb. S. / Il. p. 25

Pantanal
1973
Industrial paint on wood / Industrielack auf Holz / Pintura industrial sobre madeira, 90 × 63 cm
Fig. p. / Abb. S. / Il. p. 25

Image 1, 2, 3
1975
Acrylic on canvas / Acryl auf Leinwand / Acrílico sobre tela, 73 × 60 cm (triptych / Triptychon / tríptico)
Fig. p. / Abb. S. / Il. p. 64

Image
1976
Video (super 8 film), 22:32 min., b/w, sound / Video (Super-8-Film), 22:32 Min., s/w, Ton / Video (super 8 film), 22:32 min., p/b, som
Fig. p. / Abb. S. / Il. p. 85

Image
1977
Color print on photo paper / Farbabzug auf Fotopapier / Impressão a cores sobre papel fotografico, 10 × 15 cm
Fig. p. / Abb. S. / Il. p. 66

Image
1977
Color print on photo paper / Farbabzug auf Fotopapier / Impressão a cores sobre papel fotografico, 10 × 15 cm
Fig. p. / Abb. S. / Il. p. 66

Image
1980
Color print on photo paper / Farbabzug auf Fotopapier / Impressão a cores sobre papel fotografico, 10 × 15 cm
Fig. p. / Abb. S. / Il. p. 66

Image
1980
Color print on photo paper / Farbabzug auf Fotopapier / Impressão a cores sobre papel fotografico, 10 × 15 cm
Fig. p. / Abb. S. / Il. p. 66

Image
1980
Video (super 8 film), 31 min., color, sound / Video (Super-8-Film), 31 Min., in Farbe, Ton / Video (super 8 film), 31 min., cores, som
Fig. p. / Abb. S. / Il. p. 87

Image
1982
Acrylic on canvas / Acryl auf Leinwand / Acrílico sobre tela, 80 × 100 cm
Fig. p. / Abb. S. / Il. p. 68

Image
1982
Acrylic on canvas / Acryl auf Leinwand / Acrílico sobre tela, 80 × 100 cm
Fig. p. / Abb. S. / Il. p. 69

Once Upon a Time
1998
(Es war einmal / Era uma vez)
Print on paper and wood / Druck auf Papier und Holz / Impressão sobre papel e madeira, 12 × 17 × 4 cm
Fig. p. / Abb. S. / Il. p. 16

The Artist 2
1999
(Die Künstlerin 2 / A artista 2)
Acrylic and industrial paint on canvas / Acryl- und Industrielack auf Leinwand / Acrílico e pintura industrial sobre tela, 280 × 114 cm (5 panels / 5-teilig / 5 painéis)
Fig. p. / Abb. S. / Il. p. 71

Corisco e os terços
2003
(Corisco and the Chaplets / Corisco und die Rosenkränze)
Color print on photo paper / Farbabzug auf Fotopapier / Impressão a cores sobre papel fotografico, 63 × 29 cm
Fig. p. / Abb. S. / Il. p. 96

Jurití
2003
Color print on photo paper / Farbabzug auf Fotopapier / Impressão a cores sobre papel fotografico, 63 × 29 cm
Fig. p. / Abb. S. / Il. p. 98

Maria Bonita
2003
Color print on photo paper / Farbabzug auf Fotopapier / Impressão a cores sobre papel fotografico, 79 × 68 cm
Fig. p. / Abb. S. / Il. p. 95

O caminho
2005
(The Path / Der Weg)
Acrylic and wool on textile / Acryl und Wolle auf Textilien / Acrílico e lã sobre têxtil, 320 × 160 cm
Fig. p. / Abb. S. / Il. p. 77

Jeanne & Jeannette
2006
Acrylic and industrial paint on canvas / Acryl- und Industrielack auf Leinwand / Acrílico e pintura industrial sobre tela, 70 × 50 cm
Fig. p. / Abb. S. / Il. p. 79

T.C.G.H.
2006
Acrylic and industrial paint on canvas / Acryl- und Industrielack auf Leinwand / Acrílico e pintura industrial sobre tela, 70 × 50 cm
Fig. p. / Abb. S. / Il. p. 78

Tre amici
2006
(Three Friends / Drei Freunde / Três amigos)
Acrylic and industrial paint on canvas / Acryl- und Industrielack auf Leinwand / Acrílico e pintura industrial sobre tela, 70 × 50 cm
Fig. p. / Abb. S. / Il. p. 78

Transfer
2010
Single-channel video, 13:02 min., color, sound / Ein-Kanal-Video, 13:02 Min., Farbe, Ton / Mono-canal video, 13:02 min., cor, som
Edition of / Auflage von / Edição de 5
Fig. p. / Abb. S. / Il. p. 88

Fontana di Trevi
2014
Single-channel video, 3:02 min., color, sound / Ein-Kanal-Video, 3:02 Min., Farbe, Ton / Mono-canal video, 3:02 min., cor, som
Edition of / Auflage von / Edição de 5
Fig. p. / Abb. S. / Il. p. 90

Unknown Artist
2015
(Unbekannte Künstlerin / Artista desconhecida)
Oil on canvas / Öl auf Leinwand / Óleo sobre tela, 50 × 50 cm
Fig. p. / Abb. S. / Il. p. 104

Unknown Aztec
2015
(Unbekannter Azteke / Asteca desconhecido)
Oil on canvas / Öl auf Leinwand / Óleo sobre tela, 50 × 50 cm
Fig. p. / Abb. S. / Il. p. 101

Unknown Man
2015
(Unbekannter Mann / Homem desconhecido)
Oil on canvas / Öl auf Leinwand / Óleo sobre tela, 50 × 50 cm
Fig. p. / Abb. S. / Il. p. 101

Unknown Old Man
2015
(Unkebannter alter Mann / Homem velho desconhecido)
Oil on canvas / Öl auf Leinwand / Óleo sobre tela, 50 × 50 cm
Fig. p. / Abb. S. / Il. p. 105

Unknown Prisoner
2015
(Unbekannte Gefangene / Prisioneira desconhecida)
Oil on canvas / Öl auf Leinwand / Óleo sobre tela, 50 × 50 cm
Fig. p. / Abb. S. / Il. p. 100

Unknown Cry
2016
(Unbekannter Weinen / Chorro desconhecido)
Oil on canvas / Öl auf Leinwand / óleo sobre tela, 50 × 50 cm
Fig. p. / Abb. S. / Il. p. 100

Unknown North American Indian
2016
(Unbekannter nordamerikanischer Indianer / Indio norte americano desconhecido)
Oil on canvas / Öl auf Leinwand / Óleo sobre tela, 150 × 150 cm
Fig. p. / Abb. S. / Il. p. 102

Unknown Shoe
2016
(Unbekannter Schuh / Sapato desconhecido)
Oil on canvas / Öl auf Leinwand / Óleo sobre tela, 50 × 50 cm
Fig. p. / Abb. S. / Il. p. 105

Unknown Slave
2015
(Unbekannte Sklavin / Escrava desconhecida)
Oil on canvas / Öl auf Leinwand / óleo sobre tela, 50 × 50 cm
Fig. p. / Abb. S. / Il. p. 104

Unknown South American Indian
2016
(Unbekannter südamerikanischer Indianer / Indio sul americano desconhecido)
Oil on canvas / Öl auf Leinwand / Óleo sobre tela, 150 × 150 cm
Fig. p. / Abb. S. / Il. p. 103

Siga em frente
2016
(Go Ahead / Vorwärts)
Industrial paint on wood / Industrielack auf Holz / Pintura industrial sobre madeira, 92 × 92 × 5 cm
Fig. p. / Abb. S. / Il. p. 12

Souvenir de Rio 2
2016
Industrial paint on canvas / Industrielack auf Leinwand / Pintura industrial sobre tela, 100 × 240 cm (3 panels / 3-teilig / 3 painéis)
Fig. p. / Abb. S. / Il. p. 6

Uma rosa para Rosa
2016
(A Rose for Rose / Eine Rose für Rose)
Industrial paint on wood / Industrielack auf Holz / Pintura industrial sobre madeira, 92 × 92 × 5 cm
Fig. p. / Abb. S. / Il. p. 10

Not Exhibited Works

Nicht ausgestellte Werke
Obras não expostas

Unless specified otherwise, all works: / Wenn nicht anders angegeben, alle Werke / Se não mencionado, todas as obras: Collection of the artist / Sammlung der Künstlerin / Coleção da artista, Madrid

Corisco
1966
Oil on wood / Öl auf Holz / Óleo sobre madeira, 97 × 130 cm
Private collection / Privatsammlung / Coleção privada, Brasil
Fig. p. / Abb. S. / Il. p. 93

Cinco moças passeando
1967
(Fünf gehende Mädchen / Five girls walking)
Industrial paint on wood fiber / Industrielack auf Holzfaser / Pintura industrial sobre fibra de madeira, 90 x 110 cm
Museu de Arte Contemporânea do Paraná (PR), Brasil
Fig. p. / Abb. S. / Il. p. 30

Cybèle aos 5 anos
1967
(Cybèle, aged 5 / Cybèle im Alter von 5 Jahren)
Industrial paint on wood fiber / Industrielack auf Holzfaser / Pintura industrial sobre fibra de madeira, 100 × 84 cm
Fig. p. / Abb. S. / Il. p. 39

De tudo aquilo que poderia ter sido e que não foi
1967
(Of All That Could Have Been But Was Not / Von allem, was hätte sein können und nicht stattfand)
Industrial paint on wood / Industrielack auf Holz / Pintura industrial sobre madeira, 80 × 100 cm each / jeweils / cada
Museu de Arte Contemporânea de São Paulo (MAC-USP), Brasil
Fig. p. / Abb. S. / Il. p. 60

O Presente
1967
(The Gift / Das Geschenk)
Industrial paint on wood fiber / Industrielack auf Holzfaser / Pintura industrial sobre fibra de madeira, 100 × 100 × 20 cm (closed / geschlossen / fechado), 100 × 200 × 20 cm (open / offen / aberto)
No longer existing / Existiert nicht mehr / Não existe mais
Fig. p. / Abb. S. / Il. p. 22

Pedestres
1967
(Pedestrians / Fussgänger)
Industrial paint on wood / Industrielack auf Holz / Pintura industrial sobre madeira, 120 × 80 cm each / jeweils / cada
No longer existing / Existiert nicht mehr / Não existe mais
Fig. p. / Abb. S. / Il. p. 53

Cenas de rua
1968
(Street scenes / Strassenszenen)
Industrial paint on wood / Industrielack auf Holz / Pintura industrial sobre madeira, 150 × 150 cm each / jeweils / cada
Museu de Arte Contemporânea de São Paulo (MAC-USP), Brasil
Fig. p. / Abb. S. / Il. p. 59

Miss Brasil e o cisne
1968
(Miss Brazil and the Swan / Miss Brasilien und der Schwan)
Industrial paint on wood / Industrielack auf Holz / Pintura industrial sobre madeira, 80 × 100 cm
Museu de arte contemporânea (MAC) de Niterói, coleção João Sattamini, Brasil
Fig. p. / Abb. S. / Il. p. 62

O bolo
1969
(The Cake, Der Kuchen)
Industrial paint on wood / Industrielack auf Holz / Pintura industrial sobre madeira, 150 × 260 cm
Private collection / Privatsammlung / Coleção privada, Brasil
Fig. p. / Abb. S. / Il. p. 17

O encontro
1969
(The Encounter / Die Begegnung)
Industrial paint on wood / Industrielack auf Holz / Pintura industrial sobre madeira, 80 × 130 cm
Private collection / Privatsammlung / Coleção privada, Brasil
Fig. p. / Abb. S. / Il. p. 63

O papagaio
1969
(The Parrot / Der Papagei)
Industrial paint on wood / Industrielack auf Holz / Pintura industrial sobre madeira, 150 × 260 cm
Private collection / Privatsammlung / Coleção privada, Brasil
Fig. p. / Abb. S. / Il. p. 63

Um passeio feliz
1970
(A Happy Walk / Ein freudiger Spaziergang)
Industrial paint on wood / Industrielack auf Holz / Pintura industrial sobre madeira, 100 × 100 × 5 cm
Museu de Arte Moderna (MAM) de São Paulo, Brasil
Fig. p. / Abb. S. / Il. p. 23

Image
1980
Acrylic on canvas / Acryl auf Leinwand / Acrílico sobre tela, 65 × 81 cm
Musée cantonal des Beaux-Arts, Lausanne, Suisse
Fig. p. / Abb. S. / Il. p. 66

Image
1989
Oil on canvas / Öl auf Leinwand / Óleo sobre tela, 81 × 100 cm
Fig. p. / Abb. S. / Il. p. 37

1114 estrelas polares
1997
(1114 Polar Stars / 1114 Polarsterne)
Illustrated poem, ink and print on paper / Illustriertes Gedicht, Tinte und Druck auf Papier / poema ilustrado, tinta e impressão sobre papel, 25x19 cm
Fig. p. / Abb. S. / Il. p. 55

The Artist 1
1999
(Die Künstlerin 1 / A artista 1)
Acrylic and industrial paint on canvas / Acryl- und Industrielack auf Leinwand / Acrílico e pintura industrial sobre tela, 280 × 114 cm (in 2 parts / 2-teilig / em 2 partes)
Fig. p. / Abb. S. / Il. p. 74

L'ombrello 1, 2, 3
2000
(The Parasol / Der Sonnenschirm / O guardasol)
Acrylic on canvas / Acryl auf Leinwand / Acrílico sobre tela, 70x 60 cm, 60 × 70 cm, 70 × 60 cm
Fig. p. / Abb. S. / Il. p. 76

Automne
2002
(Autumn / Herbst / Outono)
Acrylic on canvas / Acryl auf Leinwand / Acrílico sobre tela, 180 × 80 cm
Fig. p. / Abb. S. / Il. p. 80

Printemps
2002
(Spring / Frühling / Primavera)
Acrylic on canvas / Acryl auf Leinwand / Acrílico sobre tela, 180 × 80 cm
Fig. p. / Abb. S. / Il. p. 80

O que é verdade é verdade
2010
(What Is True Is True / Was wahr ist, ist wahr)
Acrylic on canvas / Acryl auf Leinwand / Acrílico sobre tela, 120x80 cm
Fig. p. / Abb. S. / Il. p. 81

Danger
2012
(Danger / Gefahr / Perigo)
Acrylic and industrial paint on canvas / Acryl- und Industrielack auf Leinwand / Acrílico e pintura industrial sobre tela, 120 × 240 cm (in 3 parts / 3-teilig / em 3 partes)
Fig. p. / Abb. S. / Il. p. 83

Another Wonderful Summer
2013
(Ein weiterer wunderbarer Sommer / Um outro maravilhoso verão)
Acrylic on canvas / Acryl auf Leinwand / Acrílico sobre tela, 120 × 240 cm (in 3 parts / 3-teilig / em 3 partes)
Collection of the artist / Sammlung der Künstlerin / Coleção da artista, Brasil
Fig. p. / Abb. S. / Il. p. 26

Cybèle Varela. Biography
Biografie
Biografia

1943
Born in Petrópolis (RJ) /
Geboren in Petrópolis (RJ) /
Nasceu em Petrópolis (RJ).
Lives in / Lebt in / Vive em Madrid.

Education
Ausbildung
Formação

1962–1966
Attends the Course of Painting of the / Besucht den Malerei Kurs vom / Frequenta o Curso de Pintura, Museu de Arte Moderna (MAM), Rio de Janeiro.

1963–1965
Founds and directs the / Gründet und leitet die / Funda e dirige a Associação Paulista dos Amigos da Arte, Petrópolis (RJ).

1968–1969 / 1971–1972
Obtains two scholarships of the French government and studies at the / Erhält zwei Stipendien der französischen Regierung und studiert an der / Recebe duas bolsas de estudo do governo françês, estuda na École du Louvre, Paris.

1973–1974
Artist in Residence / Künstler-Residenz / Artista em residência, Cité Internationale des Arts, Paris.

1976–1978
Studies Social Anthropology at the / Studium der Sozialanthropologie an der / Estudos de Antropologia Social na École Pratique des Hautes Études-Sorbonne, Paris.

Awards
Auszeichnungen
Prêmios

1959
Associação dos Artistas Brasileiros, Rio de Janeiro (Menção Honrosa)

1962
Associação dos Artistas Brasileiros, Rio de Janeiro (Bronze Medal / Bronzemedaille / Medalha de Bronze)

1967
Prêmio Jovem Arte Contemporânea (JAC), Museu de Arte Contemporânea (MAC-USP), São Paulo; Prêmio Acquisição, XXIV Salão Paraná, Curitiba

1969
XIX Salão de Arte Moderna, São Paulo (Silver Medal / Silbermedaille / Medalha de Prata); Prêmio Aroldo Propaganda, Rio de Janeiro

1970
Prêmio Acquisição, Salão de Belo Horizonte

1971
Prêmio Banestado, Salão de Campinas, São Paulo

1972
Prix Bernheim de Villers, Société Internationale des Arts, Paris

Solo Exhibitions (Selection)
Einzelausstellungen (Auswahl)
Exposições Individuais (Seleção)

1962
Hall Santa Isabel, Petrópolis (RJ)

1966
Museu Imperial, Petrópolis (RJ)

1968
Galeria Goeldi, Rio de Janeiro

1970
ICBEU – Istituto Cultural Brasil-Estados Unidos, Belo Horizonte
Galeria Copacabana Palace, Rio de Janeiro

1971
Galeria Copacabana Palace, Rio de Janeiro

1972
Galerie Debret, Paris

1973
Cité Internationale des Arts, Paris

1974
Galerie Liliane François, Paris

1975
Galerie Camille Renault, Paris
Ibero-Amerikanisches Institut, Bonn
Galeria Bonino, Rio de Janeiro

1976
Canning House, London
Deutsch-Amerikanisches Institut, Frankfurt am Main

1977
Galerie Camille Renault, Paris
Galeria Arte Global, São Paulo
Galeria Ipanema, Rio de Janeiro

1980
Musée cantonal des Beaux-Arts, Lausanne
Museu de Arte Contemporânea (MAC-USP), São Paulo
Canon Photo Gallery, Genève

1981
FUNARTE – Galeria Sergio Millet, Rio de Janeiro

1982
Galerie Engelberts, Genève
CAYC – Centro de Arte y Communicacion, Buenos Aires

1983
Galerie Callart, Genève
Galleria Bonaparte, Milano

1984
Galeria Bonino, Rio de Janeiro

1985
Focus Gallery, Lausanne
Galeria Seta, São Paulo

1986
Galeria Bonino, Rio de Janeiro
Demenga's Gallery, Basel

1987
Museum of Modern Art of Latin America (Art Museum of the Americas), Washington D.C.
Wallace Wentworth Gallery, Chicago

1988
Galeria Bonino, Rio de Janeiro

1989
Demenga's Gallery, Riehen, Basel

1990
Demenga's Gallery, Basel
Clausen Art Gallery, Chicago
T.C. Downtown Gallery, Michigan

1991
Galerie Levy, Bourg-en-Bresse (France / Frankreich / França)

1992
Galeria Bonino, Rio de Janeiro
Galerie Zinzen, Bruxelles
Museu Imperial, Petrópolis (RJ)
Galeria Renato Magalhães Gouvêa, São Paulo

2001
Demenga's Gallery, Berlin
Demenga's Gallery, Basel

2003
Museu Nacional de Belas Artes (MNBA), Rio de Janeiro

2005
Museu de Arte Contemporânea (MAC-USP), São Paulo

2007
Palazzo Pamphilj, Roma

2008
Palazzo Reale, Biblioteca Nazionale, Napoli
Collegio Romano, Sala Crociera, Roma

2013–2014
Museu de Arte Contemporânea de Niterói (RJ)

Group Exhibitions (Selection)
Gruppenausstellungen (Auswahl)
Exposições Coletivas (Seleção)

1959
Salão dos Artistas Brasileiros, Museu Nacional de Belas Artes (MNBA), Rio de Janeiro

1960
Salão dos Artistas Brasileiros, Museu Nacional de Belas Artes (MNBA), Rio de Janeiro

1964
Museu de Arte Moderna (MAM), Rio de Janeiro

1966
I Bienal da Bahia, Salvador da Bahia

1967
IV Salão de Arte Moderna, Brasília
III Salão de Arte Contemporânea, Campinas, São Paulo
I Jovem Arte Contemporânea (JAC), Museu de Arte Contemporânea (MAC-USP), São Paulo
XIII Salão de Belo Horizonte
IX Bienal de São Paulo
Concurso de Caixas, Petite Galerie, Rio de Janeiro
XXIV Salão do Paraná, Curitiba

1968
Aspectos Contemporâneos da Pintura Brasileira, travelling exhibition / Wanderausstellung / exposição, South America / Südamerika / América do Sul
II Salão ESSO dos Jovens Artistas, Museu de Arte Moderna (MAM), Rio de Janeiro
XVII Salão National de Arte Museu de Arte Moderna (MAM), Rio de Janeiro
II Bienal da Bahia, Salvador da Bahia
XVII Salão de Arte Moderna, São Paulo
Iconografia de Massa, ESDI, Rio de Janeiro
XXV Salão do Paraná, Curitiba

1969
Salão da Bússola, Museu de Arte Moderna (MAM), Rio de Janeiro
Forum des Arts, ORTF – Office de radiodiffusion télévision française, Paris
X Bienal de São Paulo
V Salão de Arte Contemporânea, Campinas, São Paulo
XIX Salão de Arte Moderna, São Paulo

1970
II Panorama da Arte Atual, São Paulo
Bienal de Montevideo

1971
VII Salão de Arte Contemporânea, Campinas, São Paulo
Salão Luz e Movimento, Museu de Arte Moderna (MAM), Rio de Janeiro

1972
Salon Comparaisons, Paris
IV Panorama da Arte Atual, São Paulo
Salon Société Internationale des Beaux-Arts, Paris
Boursiers du Gouvernement Français, Vincennes (France / Frankreich / França)
Cité Internationale des Arts, Paris
Les chroniques de l'Œil de Bœuf 62-72, Galerie l'Œil de Bœuf, Paris

1974
Paysages, Galerie Rencontres, Paris
Salon de Mai, Paris
Salon Comparaisons, Paris

Festival du Marais, Paris
La Nouvelle Peinture Réaliste, Centre Culturel, Malakoff (France / Frankreich / França)
Les Hyperréalistes, Château de Vascoeuil (France / Frankreich / França)
Alma Brasileira, Galleria Internazionale d'Arte, Ascona (Switzerland / Schweiz / Suiça)
VII Festival de la Peinture, Cagnes-sur-Mer (France / Frankreich / França)

1975
Aspectos do Realismo Europeu, Galeria Gordillo, Lisboa
Salon Féminin, UNESCO, Paris
Salon La Nationale, Paris
Mai à la Défense, Grand Palais, Paris
Grands et jeunes d'aujourd'hui, Grand Palais, Paris
30 Créateurs – Selection 75, travelling exhibition / Wanderausstellung / exposição itinerante, France / Frankreich / França
Dhabiat Abdulla al Salem Gallery, Kuwait City
Salon Dialogues, Paris
Un discours d'intervention, Galerie Camille Renault, IX Biennale, Paris

1976
Grands et jeunes d'aujourd'hui, Grand Palais, Paris
Salon Comparaisons, Paris
Formes et Couleurs du Brésil, Crédit Commercial de France – Passy, Paris

1977
Artistes en Liberté dans la Perche, Bellême (France / Frankreich / França)
Prospectives pour un collectionneur, Galerie l'Estérel, Paris

1979
Artists from the World, travelling exhibition / Wanderausstellung / exposição itinerante, Japan / Japão

1980
Artistes de Genève – media mixtes, Musée Rath, Genève
Galleria Cenobio-Visualità, Milano

1981
XVI Bienal de São Paulo
Post Tenebra Lux, Geneva Video Circuit, Genève

1982
Mail Art, Nishinomya (Japan / Japão)

1984
Anos 60: Figuração e Objetos, Museu de Arte Contempôranea (MAC-USP), São Paulo
Galerie Kasper, Morges (Switzerland / Schweiz / Suíça)

1985
Pace e Libertà, Mail Art, Ragusa
Centre d'art visuel, Genève

1986
Síntese da Arte Brasileira no Acervo: 1920-1980, Museu de Arte Contemporânea (MAC-USP), São Paulo

1987
Art Basel, Basel
Art LA, Los Angeles
Galerie Editart, Genève

1988
Art LA, Los Angeles
Art Basel, Basel

1989
Arte Brasileira – Acervo, Muse de Arte Contemporânea (MAC-USP), São Paulo

1990
Espaço Banco BNDES, Rio de Janeiro

1991
Demenga's Gallery, Basel

1992
O que faz você agora Geração 60?: Jovem arte contemporânea dos anos 60, Muse de Arte Contemporânea (MAC-USP), São Paulo

1993
Galerie Zinzen, Bruxelles

1994
Europ'art, Genève
Gallerie Patrick Barrer, Genève

1996
Arte Brasileira: 50 anos de historia no acervo MAC, Museu de Arte Contemporânea (MAC-USP), São Paulo
Mulheres Artistas no acervo do MAC, Museu de Arte Contemporânea (MAC-USP), São Paulo

1997
A Cidade dos Artistas, Museu de Arte Contemporânea, São Paulo

1999
Das 20. Jahrhundert, Demenga's Gallery, Basel
A Cidade dos Artistas, Galeria Itaú Cultural, Brasília
O Brasil do Século das Artes, Museu de Arte Contemporânea (MAC-USP), São Paulo

2001
Art Affair, Zürich

2003
Arte Conhecimento: 70 Anos, Muse de Arte Contemporânea (MAC-USP), São Paulo

2004
Anos 60 na Coleção Sattamini, Museu de Arte Contemporânea, Niterói (RJ)

2006
Museu de Arte Assis Chateaubriand (MASP), São Paulo
Outros 60s, Museu de Arte Contemporânea do Paraná, Curitiba

2008
Arte Brasileira no acervo do MAC USP, Palácio das Artes, Salvador da Bahia

2009–2011
elles@centrepompidou, Centre George Pompidou, Paris

2010
Red Dot Art Fair, Miami
Entre Atos 1964/68, Museu de Arte Contemporânea, São Paulo

2011
Red Dot Art Fair, New York

2012
Mulheres, Museu de Arte Contemporânea, Niterói (RJ)
Salão Paranaense: uma retrospectiva – Desejo de Salão, Museu Oscar Niemeyer, Curitiba

2014
Anos 80: liberdade e figuração, Museu de Arte de Goiânia
Re-Existência da arte e política 1964–2014, Museu de Arte Contemporânea, Niterói (RJ)

2016
Visões da arte no acervo do MAC-USP, Muse de Arte Contemporânea (MAC-USP), São Paulo
Útero do Mundo, Museu de Arte Moderna (MAM), São Paulo
Ephemera: Diálogos entre vistas – coleção João Sattamini, Museu de Arte Contemporânea, Niterói (RJ)
Elas. Mulheres artistas no acervo do MAB, Museu de Arte Brasileira, São Paulo

Museums and public collections

Museen und öffentliche Sammlungen
Museus e coleções públicas

Centre Georges Pompidou, Paris
Centro Cultural de São Paulo
Ambassade du Brésil, Paris
Fonds de Décoration de la Ville de Genève
Fonds National d'Art Contemporain, Paris
Centro Cultural de Petrópolis
Museu de Arte Moderna (MAM), Rio de Janeiro
Museum of Modern Art of Latin America, Washington D.C.
Museu de Arte Moderna de Campinas, São Paulo
Museu Assis-Chateaubriand de São Paulo (MASP)
Museum of Contemporary Art of Curitiba, Paraná
Museu de Arte Moderna (MAM), São Paulo
Museu de Arte Moderna (MAC–USP), São Paulo
Museu de Arte Moderna de Belo Horizonte, Minas Gerais
Museu de Arte Contemporânea de Niterói, Rio de Janeiro
Museu Nacional de Belas Artes (MNBA), Rio de Janeiro
Musée cantonal des Beaux-Arts, Lausanne
Musée Voltaire, Genève
Observatorio do Rio de Janeiro
Palais des Nations – ONU, Genève
Temple de l'Humanité – Musée Auguste Comte, Paris
Touring Club do Brasil, Rio de Janeiro
Touring Club do Brasil, Petrópolis
Nestlé Art Collection, Vevey (Switzerland / Schweiz / Suíça)
WIPO (World Intellectual Property Organization), Genève

Selected Bibliography

Ausgewählte Bibliografie
Bibliografia selecionada*

Jean-Luc Chalumeau, *Initiation à la lecture de l'art contemporain* (Paris, 1976)

Cybèle Varela, exh. cat. / Ausst.-Kat. / cat. expo., Musée cantonal des Beaux-Arts de Lausanne (Lausanne, 1980)

Cybèle Varela: peintures, 1960-1984 (Genève, 1984)

Cybèle Varela, exh. cat. / Ausst.-Kat. / cat. expo., Museu Nacional de Belas Artes (MNBA) (Rio de Janeiro, 2003)

Cybèle Varela, exh. cat. / Ausst.-Kat. / cat. expo., Palazzo Pamphilj (Roma, 2007)

Cybèle Varela. Ad Sidera per Athanasius Kircher, exh. cat. / Ausst.-Kat. / cat. expo., Palazzo del Collegio Romano (Roma, 2008)

Cybèle Varela, Espaços Simultâneos: pinturas, fotos e vídeos 2009–2013, exh. cat. / Ausst.-Kat. / cat. expo., Museu de Arte Contemporânea de Niterói (Niterói, 2013)

elles@centrepompidou, artistes femmes dans la collection du Musée national d'art moderne, ed. by / hrsg. von / ed. por Camille Morineau, exh. cat. / Ausst.-Kat. / cat. expo., Centre Pompidou (Paris, 2009), p. / S. 222

Elles: Mulheres artistas na coleção do Centro Pompidou, ed. by / hrsg. von / ed. por Cécile Debray, Emma Lavigne, exh. cat. / Ausst.-Kat. / cat. expo., Centro Cultural do Banco do Brasil (Rio de Janeiro-Belo Horizonte, 2013), p. / S. 66

Giulia Lamoni, "Unfolding the 'Present': Some Notes on Brazilian 'Pop'", in *The World Goes Pop*, ed. by / hrsg. von / ed. por Jessica Morgan, Flavia Frigeri, exh. cat. / Ausst.-Kat. / cat. expo., Tate Modern (London, 2015), pp. / S. 70–71.

Les Hyperréalistes, ed. by / Hrsg. von / ed. por Pierre Restany, exh. cat. / Ausst.-Kat. / cat. expo., Centre Culturel International de Vascoeuil (Vascoeuil, 1974), p. / S. 44

* For a comprehensive bibliography see / Für eine umfassende Bibliografie siehe / Para uma bibliografia maia completa veja: www.cybelevarela.com

The Authors

Die Autoren

Os autores

Daniel Faust (b. 1975, Dieburg, Germany) is Director of the Brasilea Foundation. He studied Architecture at the universities of Darmstadt and Barcelona, attended the Mies van der Rohe Masterclass of Kazuyo Sejima in Barcelona and recently earned a Master in Cultural Management at the University of Basel. He has curated more than forty exhibitions and co-organized four art fairs in Basel (*bâlelatina*, 2006–09). In 2016 he was awarded the prestigious "Prêmio Itamaraty de Diplomacia Cultural" by the Brazilian Ministry of Foreign Affairs for his commitment to promoting cultural exchange between Brazil and Switzerland.

Daniel Faust (geb. 1975, Dieburg, Deutschland) ist Direktor der Stiftung Brasilea. Er studierte Architektur an den Universitäten von Darmstadt und Barcelona, besuchte die Mies van der Rohe Masterclass von Kazuyo Sejima in Barcelona und absolvierte den Master in Kulturmanagement an der Universität in Basel.
Er kuratierte mehr als vierzig Ausstellungen und war Mitorganisator von vier Kunstmessen in Basel (*bâlelatina*, 2006–09). 2016 bekam er für seine Kulturvermittlung zwischen Brasilien und der Schweiz den renommierten »Prêmio Itamaraty de Diplomacia Cultural« des brasilianischen Aussenministeriums verliehen.

Daniel Faust (n.1975, Dieburg, Alemanha) é Diretor da Fundação Brasilea. Estudou arquitetura nas universidades de Darmstadt e Barcelona, cursou o Mies van der Roher Masterclass de Kazuyo Sejima em Barcelona e obteve recentemente um Máster em gestão cultural pela Universidade de Basileia. Foi o curador de mais de quarenta exposições e co-organizou quatro feiras de arte em Basileia (*bâlelatina* 2006-2009). Em 2016 recebeu o prestigioso "Prêmio Itamaraty de Diplomacia Cultural" do Ministério de Relações Exteriores brasileiro pelo seu empenho na promoção no intercâmbio cultural entre o Brasil e a Suíça.

Giulia Lamoni (b. 1977, Turin, Italy) is FCT Researcher and Visiting Assistant Professor at the Institute of Art History at the Universidade Nova de Lisboa. Her investigation focuses on the relationship between contemporary art and feminism, contemporary artistic productions and migratory processes, and the history of contemporary art in and beyond Latin America through transnational perspectives. She published essays for the Tate Modern, Centre Pompidou and Centro de Arte Moderna da Fundação Calouste Gulbenkian, and in several periodicals. She co-curated the exhibition *Co-habitar* at the Casa da América Latina/ UCCLA in 2016–2017 and solo-curated *Eugénia Mussa: Meridiano Pacífico* at Quadrum Gallery in 2017, both in Lisbon.

Giulia Lamoni (geb. 1977, Turin, Italien) ist FCT Forscherin und Gastprofessorin am Kunsthistorischen Institut der Neuen Universität Lissabon. Schwerpunkte ihrer Forschung sind das Verhältnis von zeitgenössischer Kunst und Feminismus, von zeitgenössischer künstlerischer Produktion und Migrationsprozessen, als auch die Geschichte der zeitgenössischen Kunst in Lateinamerika und darüber hinaus aus transnationalen Perspektiven. Sie publizierte bereits Essays für Museen wie das Tate Modern, das Centre Pompidou und das Centro de Arte Moderna da Fundação Calouste Gulbenkian und in verschiedenen Periodika. In Lissabon war sie Mitkuratorin für die Ausstellungen *Co-habitar* in der Casa da América Latina / UCCLA (2016) und Kuratorin für die Ausstellung *Eugénia Mussa: Meridiano Pacífico* in der Quadrum Galerie (2017).

Giulia Lamoni (n. 1977, Turim, Itália) é pesquisadora FCT e Professora Auxiliar Convidada no Instituto de História da Arte da Universidade Nova de Lisboa. Seu trabalho de investigação foca-se nas relações entre arte contemporânea e feminismo, produção artística contemporânea e processos migratórios, bem como na história da arte contemporânea dentro e além das fronteiras da América Latina através da articulação de perspectivas transnacionais. Publicou textos para a Tate Modern e o Centro de Arte Moderna da Fundação Calouste Gulbenkian, assim como em varias revistas. Foi co-curadora da exposição *Co-habitar* na Casa da América Latina/ UCCLA em 2016-2017 e curadora de *Eugénia Mussa: Meridiano Pacífico* na Galeria Quadrum em 2017, ambas em Lisboa.

Valentina Locatelli (b. 1979, Bergamo, Italy) curated the following exhibitions for Kunstmuseum Bern: *Mexico Mirrored in its Art: Prints, Independence, and Revolution* (2013), *Open Sesame! Anker, Hodler, Segantini... Masterpieces from the Foundation for Art, Culture and History* (2014) and *Without Restraint: Works by Mexican Women Artists from the Daros Latinamerica Collection* (2016). She co-edited the catalogue *Kunstmuseum Bern: Masterpieces* (Munich, 2016) and implemented eight publication projects for Foundation Beyeler. She studied art history, literature and museum studies at the universities of Bergamo, Munich and Geneva. Her Ph.D. dissertation on the art connoisseur Giovanni Morelli was published in 2011.

Valentina Locatelli (geb. 1979, Bergamo, Italien) kuratierte am Kunstmuseum Bern die Ausstellungen *Mexiko im Spiegel seiner Kunst: Druckgrafik, Unabhängigkeit und Revolution* (2013), *Sesam öffne Dich! Anker, Hodler, Segantini... Meisterwerke aus der Stiftung für Kunst, Kultur und Geschichte* (2014) und *Without Restraint: Werke mexikanischer Künstlerinnen aus der Daros Latinamerica Collection* (2016). Sie ist Mitherausgeberin des Katalogs *Kunstmuseum Bern: Meisterwerke* (Hirmer, München 2016) und betreute redaktionell acht Publikationen für die Fondation Beyeler. Sie studierte Kunstgeschichte, Literatur und Museologie an den Universitäten Bergamo, München und Genf. Ihre Doktorarbeit zu dem Kunstkenner Giovanni Morelli wurde 2011 publiziert.

Valentina Locatelli (n. 1979, Bergamo, Itália) foi curadora das seguintes exposições para o Kunstmuseum Bern: *Mexico Mirrored in its Art: Prints, Independence, and Revolution* (2013), *Open Sesame! Anker, Hodler, Segantini... Masterpieces from the Foundation for Art, Culture and History* (2014) e *Without Restraint: Works by Mexican Women Artists from the Daros Latinamerica Collection* (2016). Coeditou o catalogo *Kunstmuseum Bern: Masterpieces* (Munich: 2016) e implementou oito projetos de publicações para a Foundation Beyeler. Estudou historia da arte, literatura e museologia nas universidades de Bergamo, Munique e Genebra. Sua tese de doutorado sobre o *connaisseur* de arte Giovanni Morelli foi publicada em 2011.

Ariane Varela Braga (b. 1978, Paris, France) is SNFS Research Assistant at the Institute of Art History at the University of Zurich. She participated in the organization of exhibitions in Brazil, Switzerland and Germany and co-edited volumes on decorative arts, Orientalism in architecture and artistic migration. She is the creator and co-founder of the Rome Art History Network, in the framework of which she coordinated several workshops, scientific meetings and conferences since 2010. She studied at the universities of Geneva and Neuchâtel. Her Ph.D. dissertation on Owen Jones' *Grammar of Ornament* was published in 2017.

Ariane Varela Braga (geb. 1978, Paris, Frankreich) ist wissenschaftliche Mitarbeiterin am Kunsthistorischen Institut der Universität in Zürich. Sie gehörte verschiedenen Organisationsteams von Ausstellungen in Brasilien, der Schweiz und Deutschland an und ist Mitherausgeberin diverser Bände zu den dekorativen Künsten, dem Orientalismus in der Architektur und zu künstlerischer Migration. Sie konzipierte und mitbegründete das Rome Art History Network, in dessen Rahmen sie zahlreiche Workshops, wissenschaftliche Tagungen und Konferenzen seit 2010 koordiniert. Sie studierte an den Universitäten von Genf und Neuchâtel. Ihre Doktorarbeit zu Owen Jones' *Grammar of Ornament* wurde 2017 publiziert.

Ariane Varela Braga (n. 1978, Paris, França) é assistente científico no Instituto de Historia da Arte na Universidade de Zurique. Participou da organização de exposições no Brasil, na Suíça e na Alemanha e coeditou volumes sobre as artes decorativas, o orientalismo na arquitetura e a migração artística. É a criadora e co-fundadora do Rome Art History Network, no âmbito do qual vem coordenando várias oficinas, encontros científicos e conferências desde 2010. Estudou nas universidades de Genebra e Neuchâtel. Sua tese de doutorado sobre a *Grammar of Ornament* de Owen Jones foi publicada em 2017.

Exhibition / Ausstellung / Exposição

Cybèle Varela: Tropicalismo Remixed
Brasilea Stiftung
18.01.2018 – 31.05.2018

Brasilea Stiftung
Westquaistrasse 39
CH – 4019 Basel
T +41 61 262 39 39
www.brasilea.com

Director / Direktor / Diretor
Daniel Faust

Assistant to the Director / Direktionsassistentin / Assistente do Diretor
Leonie Wienandts

Guest Curators / Gast-Kuratorinnen / Curadoras-convidadas
Valentina Locatelli, Ariane Varela Braga

Communication / Kommunikation / Comunicação
Pia Küchenmüller

Sponsoring, Fundraising
Valentina Locatelli, Ariane Varela Braga

Acknowledgements/ Dank/ Agradecimentos
The Brasilea Foundation would like to thank for the generous support / Die Brasilea Stiftung dankt für die grosszügige Unterstützung / A Fundação Brasilea gostaria de agradecer pelo apoio generoso:

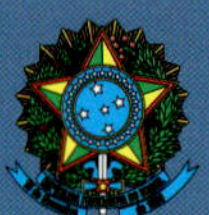

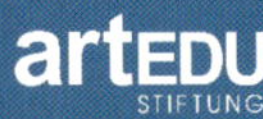

The Brasilea Foundation would like to thank the following persons for their support in all matters / Die Brasilea Stiftung dankt den folgenden Personen für ihre Unterstützung in allen Belangen / A Fundação Brasilea gostaria de agradecer as seguintes pessoas pelo apoio: José Borges dos Santos Junior, Thomas Bürgi, Christopher Duckett, Ana de Fátima Ribeiro Bezerra, Dorit Faust, Kurt Haldimann, Rubens Lopes Braga, Gottlieb Prack, Enrico Tarelli, Stefanie Thierstein, Raffaello Tondolo, Jean-Marc Wallach, Felix Wüthrich, Simone Züger

Catalogue / Katalog / Catálogo

This book is published in conjunction with the exhibition / Diese Publikation erscheint anlässlich der Ausstellung / Este livro é publicado em conjunto com a exposição

Cybèle Varela: Tropicalismo Remixed
Brasilea Stiftung
18.01.2018 – 31.05.2018

Editors / Herausgeber / Editores
Valentina Locatelli, Ariane Varela Braga, for the / für die / para a Stiftung Brasilea

Managing Editors / Redaktion / Redação
Valentina Locatelli, Ariane Varela Braga

Photo Credits / Fotonachweis / Créditos fotográficos
Courtesy of the artist
Romulo Fialdini, Courtesy of Museu de Arte Contemporânea de São Paulo (MAC-USP): pp. / S. 2, 60–61
Romulo Fialdini, Courtesy of Museu de Arte Moderna de São Paulo (MAM): p. / S. 23

Paper / Papier / Papel
matt coated paper 170 gsm; Sirio Limone 115 gsm

Cover Illustration / Umschlagabbildung / Capa
Cybèle Varela, *Souvenir de Rio 2*, 2016 (detail / Detail / detalhe)

Frontispice Image / Frotispize / Folha de rosto
p. / S. 2 (detail / Detail / detalhe)
Cybèle Varela, *De tudo aquilo que poderia ter sido e que não foi*, 1967

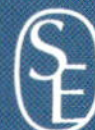

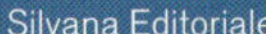

Silvana Editoriale

Direction / Verlagsleiter / Direção
Dario Cimorelli

Art Director
Giacomo Merli

Editorial Coordinator / Redaktionskoordinator / Coordenador de redação
Sergio Di Stefano

Copy Editor / Lektor / Revisores
Lorena Ansani, Ondina Granato

Translators / Übersetzer / Traduções
Contextus srl, Pavia (Stefania Buonamassa, Kathrin Fuchs, Johannes Reiss, Calum Short)

Layout / Layout und Textsatz / Layout
Mirco Ameglio

Production Coordinator / Produktionskoordinator / Coordenador de produção
Antonio Micelli

Editorial Assistant / Redaktionassistentin / Assistente editorial
Ondina Granato

Photo Editors
Alessandra Olivari, Silvia Sala

Press Office / Pressestelle / Assessoria de imprensa
Lidia Masolini, press@silvanaeditoriale.it

ISBN 9788836637362

Silvana Editoriale S.p.A.
via dei Lavoratori, 78
20092 Cinisello Balsamo, Milano
tel. 02 453 951 01
fax 02 453 951 51
www.silvanaeditoriale.it

Reproductions, printing and binding in Italy
Reproduktionen, Druck und Einbindung wurden in Italien ausgeführt
Reprodução, impressão e encadernação realizadas na Itália
Printed December 2017
Fertig gedruckt im Dezember 2017
Impresso em Dezembro 2017

Available through ARTBOOK | D.A.P.
155 Sixth Avenue, 2nd Floor, New York, N.Y. 10013
Tel: (212) 627-1999 Fax: (212) 627-9484